Villains of All Nations

Also by Marcus Rediker

*Between the Devil and the Deep Blue Sea: Merchant Seamen,
Pirates, and the Anglo-American Maritime World, 1700–1750*

*The Many-Headed Hydra: Sailors, Slaves, Commoners,
and the Hidden History of the Revolutionary Atlantic*
(with Peter Linebaugh)

To learn more about Marcus Rediker and his work,
please visit http://www.MarcusRediker.com.

Villains of All Nations

ATLANTIC PIRATES IN THE GOLDEN AGE

MARCUS REDIKER

Beacon Press

BOSTON

Beacon Press
25 Beacon Street
Boston, Massachusetts 02108-2892
www.beacon.org

Beacon Press books
are published under the auspices of
the Unitarian Universalist Association of Congregations.

07 06 05 04 8 7 6 5 4 3 2 1

This book is printed on acid-free paper that meets the uncoated paper
ANSI/NISO specifications for permanence as revised in 1992.

The diagram entitled "Connections among pirate
crews, 1714–1727" was drawn by Hyla Willis.

Text design by Isaac Tobin
Composition by Wilsted & Taylor Publishing Services

Library of Congress Cataloging-in-Publication Data

Rediker, Marcus.
    Villains of all nations : Atlantic pirates in the golden age / Marcus
Rediker.
        p. cm.
    Includes bibliographical references and index.
        ISBN 0-8070-5024-5 (alk. paper)
    1. Pirates—Atlantic Coast (U.S.)—History—18th century. 2. Pirates—
Atlantic Coast (U.S.)—Biography. 3. Pirates—Caribbean Area History
—18th century. 4. Atlantic Coast (U.S.)—History, Naval—18th century.
5. Caribbean Area—History, Naval—18th century.
I. Title.

F106.R42 2004
910.4'5—dc22   2003021508

In memory of
Michael Jiménez (1948–2001)
and
Steve Sapolsky (1948–2001)

CONTENTS

Chapter One

A TALE OF TWO TERRORS

IN THE EARLY AFTERNOON of July 12, 1726, William Fly ascended Boston's gallows to be hanged for piracy. His body was nimble in manner, like a sailor going aloft; his rope-roughened hands carried a nosegay of flowers; his weather-beaten face had "a Smiling Aspect." He showed no guilt, no shame, and no contrition. Indeed, as attending minister Cotton Mather noted, he "look'd about him unconcerned." But once he stood on the gallows, he *became* concerned, although not in the way anyone might have expected. His demeanor quickened, and he immediately took charge of the stage of death. He threw the hanging rope over the beam, made it fast, and carefully inspected the noose that would go around his neck. He soon turned to the hangman in disappointment and reproached him "for not understanding his Trade." But Fly, a sailor who knew the art of tying knots, took mercy on the novice. He offered to teach him how to tie a proper noose. Then Fly, "with his own Hands[,] rectified Matters, to render all things more Convenient and Effectual," retying the knot himself as the multitude who had gathered around the gallows looked on in astonishment. He informed the hangman and the crowd that "he was not afraid to die," that "he had wrong'd no Man." Mather explained that he was determined to die "*a brave fellow.*"[1]

When the time came for last words on that awful occasion, Mather wanted Fly and his fellow pirates to act as preachers—that is, he wanted them to provide examples and warnings to those who were assembled to watch the execution.[2] They all complied. Samuel Cole, Henry Greenville, and George Condick, perhaps hoping for a last-minute pardon, stood penitently before the crowd and warned all to obey their parents and superiors and not to curse, drink, whore, or profane the Lord's day. These three pirates acknowledged the justice of the proceedings against them, and they thanked the ministers for their assistance. Fly, however, did not ask for forgiveness, did not praise the authorities, and did not affirm the values of Christianity, as he was supposed to do, but he did issue a warning. Addressing the port-city crowd thick with ship captains and sailors, he proclaimed his final, fondest wish: that "all Masters of Vessels might take Warning by the Fate of the Captain (meaning Captain *Green*) that he had murder'd, and to pay Sailors their Wages when due, and to treat them better; saying, that their Barbarity to them made so many turn Pyrates."[3] Fly thus used his last breath to protest the conditions of work at sea, what he called "*Bad Usage*." He would be launched into eternity with the brash threat of mutiny on his lips. Mather took pleasure in detecting what he thought was a slight tremor in the malefactor's hands and knees, but Fly nonetheless died on his own terms, defiantly and courageously. The ministers and magistrates of Boston, however, had reserved for themselves the last lines of the drama. If Fly would not warn people in the ways they deemed proper, they would do it themselves, and in so doing they would answer his threat. After the execution, they hanged Fly's body in chains at the entrance of Boston Harbor "as a Spectacle for the Warning of others, especially Sea faring Men."[4]

High drama had surrounded Fly and his crew from the moment they were brought into port as captives on June 28, 1726. Fly was a twenty-seven-year-old boatswain, a poor man "of very obscure Parents," who had signed on in Jamaica in April 1726 to sail with Captain John Green to West Africa on the *Elizabeth*, a snow (two-masted vessel) based in Bristol. Green and Fly soon clashed, and the boatswain began to organize a mutiny against Green's command. Fly and another sailor, Alexander Mitchell, roused Green from his sleep late one night, forced him on deck, beat him, and attempted to throw him over the side of the ship.

Figure 1. The hanging of pirate captain Stede Bonnet, Charleston, November 1718; Captain Charles Johnson, *A General History of the Robberies and Murders of the Most Notorious Pyrates* (London, 1724).

When Green caught hold of the mainsheet, one of the sailors picked up the cooper's broad ax and chopped off the captain's hand at the wrist. Poor Green "was swallowed up by the Sea." The mutineers then turned the ax on Thomas Jenkins, the first mate, and threw him, still alive, overboard after the captain. They debated whether their messmate, the ship's doctor, should follow them into the blue, but a majority of the crew decided he might prove useful and confined him in irons instead.[5]

Having taken possession of the ship, the mutineers prepared

a bowl of punch and ceremoniously installed a new shipboard order of things. These sailors, who routinely sewed canvas sails and were therefore expert with needle and thread, stitched a skull and crossbones onto a black flag, creating the Jolly Roger, the pirates' traditional symbol and instrument of terror. They renamed their vessel the *Fames' Revenge* and sailed away in search of prizes. They captured five vessels. After taking the *John and Hannah* off the coast of North Carolina, Fly punished its captain, John Fulker, by tying him to the geers and lashing him before sinking his ship. Fly's piratical adventures came to an end when a group of men he had forced aboard the pirate ship from prize vessels rose up and captured him. Fly and his crew were brought into Boston Harbor to stand trial for murder and piracy.[6]

Awaiting them in Boston was the Reverend Doctor Cotton Mather, the pompous, vain, and overbearing sixty-three-year-old minister of Old North Church who was probably the most famous cleric, maybe even the most famous person, in the American colonies at the time.[7] Mather took a personal interest in the case, vowing to bring Fly to salvation. He met with the former bosun, exhorted him to reform and repent, and commanded him to go to church. Benjamin Colman, another leading minister, joined the struggle to save Fly's soul, but it was all to no avail. Boston's most eminent men of the cloth failed miserably with their prisoner, who defied them, mocked them, and raged against them. Colman wrote that Fly "fell at times into the most desperate *ragings* ... cursing the very heavens & in effect the God that judged him."[8] Mather concluded that Fly was "a most uncommon and amazing Instance of Impenitency and Stupidity, and What *Spectacles of Obduration* the Wicked will be." At one of these meetings Fly had exploded in anger, *"I can't Charge myself,—I shan't own myself Guilty of any Murder,—Our Captain and his Mate used us Barbarously. We poor Men can't have Justice done us. There is nothing said to our Commanders, let them never so much abuse us, and use us like Dogs. But the poor sailors—"* At this point Mather apparently interrupted; he could bear to hear no more. Two discourses, one Christian and providential and the other maritime and social, came together in a cosmic clash.[9]

The hanging of the "poor man" William Fly was a moment of terror. Indeed, it might be said that the occasion represented a clash of two different kinds of terror. One was practiced by the likes of Cotton Mather—namely, ministers, royal officials, wealthy men; in short, rulers—as they sought to eliminate piracy as a crime against mercantile property. They consciously used terror to accomplish their aims: to protect property, to punish those who resisted its law, to take vengeance against those they considered their enemies, and to instill fear in sailors who might wish to become pirates. This they did in the name of the social order, as suggested by Colman, whose execution sermon (which Fly refused to attend) was a meditation on terror, on God as "*the king of terrors*" and hence the source of all social discipline. In truth, the keepers of the state in this era were themselves terrorists of a sort, decades before the word *terrorist* would acquire its modern meaning (as it would do in the Reign of Terror during the French Revolution). And yet we do not think of them in this way. They have become, over the years, cultural heroes, even founding fathers of sorts. Theirs was a terror of the strong against the weak.[10]

The other kind of terror was practiced by common seamen like William Fly who sailed beneath the Jolly Roger, the flag designed to terrify the captains of merchant ships and persuade them to surrender their cargo. Pirates consciously used terror to accomplish their aims—to obtain money, to punish those who resisted them, to take vengeance against those they considered their enemies, and to instill fear in sailors, captains, merchants, and officials who might wish to attack or resist pirates. This they did in the name of a different social order, as we will see in the chapters that follow. In truth, pirates were terrorists of a sort. And yet we do not think of them in this way. They have become, over the years, cultural heroes, perhaps antiheroes, and at the very least romantic and powerful figures in an American and increasingly global popular culture. Theirs was a terror of the weak against the strong. It formed one essential part of a dialectic of terror, which was summarized in the decision of the authorities to raise the Jolly Roger above the gallows when hanging pirates: one terror trumped the other.[11]

The dramas involving pirates—William Fly and the dozens of others we will meet in the pages that follow—concerned the fundamental issues of the age. As we will see, poor seamen who turned pirate dramatized concerns of class. Formerly enslaved Africans or African Americans who turned pirate posed questions of race. Women who turned pirate called attention to the conventions of gender. And all people who turned pirate and sailed under "their own dark flag," the Jolly Roger, enacted a highly political play about the nation. These events had their own theater, in both senses of the word—a specific geography and a particular dramatic form. They took place around the Atlantic, on the hastily constructed scaffolds of port-city gallows as in Boston, and on the heaving decks of deep-sea ships, as on the *Fames' Revenge*. The stages were transient, in motion, and simultaneously local and global, as were the subjects who acted on them.[12]

In the national drama, the pirate took the stage as a fierce and forbidding villain, described by ruling groups as a blood-lusting monster bent on destroying the social order. Beneath the rhetoric of demonization, which we explore in chapter 7, lay an actual history of national challenge and consequence. Some seafaring contemporaries of William Fly had worked during the War of Spanish Succession as privateers—that is, they labored in private men-of-war, with commissions from the King, to attack, capture, and plunder enemies in wartime. Leaders of European nations used privateers to supplement naval power, to disrupt supply lines and commercial circuits, and to accumulate wealth at the expense of their rivals. But when the war ended, they found that they could not control the privateers they had once employed. In 1716 a gang of pirates, for example, announced, boldly and self-importantly, that "they never consented to the Articles of Peace with the French and Spaniards" and would therefore continue to attack their ships. This very crew, captained by Benjamin Hornigold, added that "they meddle not with the English or Dutch."

Governor Alexander Spotswood of Virginia had heard such claims by and about pirates, but he did not believe them. In July 1716 he wrote to the Council of Trade and Plantations that the pirates who had recently congregated in the Bahama Islands had announced that they would not be "disturbing the English, and that they will only content themselves with making Prize of all French and Spanish they meet with." He continued: "yet there is so little trust to be given to such People, that it is not to be doubted they will use all Nations alike whenever they have an advantage." He was right. The logic of privateering would not hold for long. An astonished Hornigold would soon discover this for himself: his own, mostly English crew ousted him for refusing to take and plunder English vessels, which were, after all, the most plentiful and lucrative ships to be found in the seas they sailed.[13]

In a world increasingly dominated by the nation-state system, it became an issue of first importance that pirates "had not any Commission from any Prince or Potentate." After a bloody engagement in which HMS *Swallow*, a man-of-war, captured the crew of Bartholomew Roberts off the coast of West Africa in 1722, a judge sternly lectured the pirates in the emergency court set up in Cape Coast Castle, a slave-trading fortress; they had, he explained, "made this Fight and insolent Resistance Against the King's Ship, without any Pretence of Authority more than that of your own private depraved Wills, but did it also under a Black Flag, flagrantly by that denoting Your selves as common Robbers, Opposers, and Violators of all Laws humane and divine."

Pirates did not consider themselves "common Robbers,

Opposers, and Violators of all Laws humane and divine," but they did think of themselves as people without a nation. When pirates stitched together their black flag, the antinational symbol of a gang of proletarian outlaws, they "declared War against all the World." When hailed by another ship, pirates, who were multinational in origin, usually answered that they came "from the seas," not from any particular country. Some pirates explained to captives that they had "sold their nation" for booty. They made the point with brutal clarity after the declaration of war against Spain (the brief War of the Quadruple Alliance) in March 1719, when the British admiralty and royal officials throughout the Americas desperately hoped that pirates would come in, accept the King's commissions, and go back to sea as privateers. Many pirates did come in, did accept commissions, and did go back out as privateers—in the employ of Spain, to attack British ships! Historian Peter Earle writes that Spanish "privateers were said to be manned mainly by the subjects of Great Britain and France, another instance of the extreme disloyalty of the pirates of this period." The leaders of the nation would conclude that such people had to be exterminated.[14]

The pirates of the 1710s and 1720s were among the greatest ever in the long history of robbery by sea. They stood at the very pinnacle of what is called the golden age of piracy, which spanned the period from roughly 1650 to 1730. This era featured three distinct generations of pirates: the buccaneers of 1650–80, the mostly Protestant sea dogs of England, northern France, and the Netherlands, exemplified by the Jamaica raider Henry Morgan, who hunted wild game on deserted islands and attacked the ships of Catholic Spain; the pirates of the 1690s, the generation of Henry Avery and William Kidd, who moved into the Indian Ocean and built a pirate base on the island of Madagascar; and finally the subjects of this book, the pirates of the years 1716–26, who were the most numerous and successful of the three. They were epitomized by Edward Teach and Bartholomew Roberts, who attacked the ships of all nations and created a crisis in the lucrative Atlantic system of trade. They also generated most of the images of pirates that live on in modern popular culture, from swashbuckling figures such as Blackbeard, to the unnamed, unlimbed pirate who was the likely model for Robert Louis Stevenson's Long John Silver in *Treasure Island*, to the dreaded black flag with skull and bones, the Jolly Roger.

The multiethnic freebooters of 1716–26 numbered around four thousand over the decade. They wreaked havoc in the Atlantic system by capturing hundreds of merchant ships, many of which they burned or sank, and all of which they plundered of valuable cargo. They disrupted trade in strategic zones of capital accumulation—the West Indies, North America, and West Africa—at a time when the recently stabilized and expanding Atlantic economy was the source of enormous profits and re-newed imperial power. Usually sailors joined pirate ships after working on merchant and naval ships, where they suffered cramped quarters, poor victuals, brutal discipline, low wages, devastating diseases, disabling accidents, and premature death. Piracy, as we will see, offered the prospect of plunder and "ready money," abundant food and drink, the election of officers, the equal distribution of resources, care for the injured, and joyous camaraderie, all as expressions of an ethic of justice.

Piracy may have held out hope for a good life, but it was not to be a long one. The typical man sailed under the black flag for a year or two, and many if not most pirates lost their lives for it. Unusual was the man who served—or lasted—longer. The royal officials who prosecuted the crew of Roberts at Cape Coast Castle referred to the first group to be hanged, William Magnes, David Sympson, Thomas Sutton, Valentine Ashplant, and Richard Hardy, as "old Standers and notorious Offenders" even though each had been "upon the account" for only three to four years. Yet the danger of death was no deterrent for many, and in-deed the choice was summed up by Captain Roberts himself, who remarked that in the merchant service "there is thin Commons, low Wages, and hard Labour; in this, Plenty and Satiety, Pleasure and ease, Liberty and Power; and who would not ballance Creditor on this Side, when all the Hazard that is run for it, at worst, is only a sower Look or two at choaking. No, *a merry Life and a short one*, shall be my motto."[15]

The nation-state, as terrorist, was more than happy to oblige in making pirate lives short, and indeed the 1726 confrontation between William Fly and Cotton Mather in Boston was only one scene in a ten-year drama. The Atlantic empires, led by Britain, organized an international campaign of terror to eradicate piracy, using the gallows in highly public displays of power. Between 1716 and 1726 rulers hanged pirates in London; Edinburgh; Saint Michael's, the Azores; Cape Coast Castle, Africa; Salvador, Brazil; Curaçao; Antigua; Saint Kitts; Martinique; Kingston and Port Royal, Jamaica; the Bahama Islands; Bermuda; Charleston, South Carolina; Williamsburg, Virginia; New York; Providence, Rhode Island; and even Boston itself, where several pirates had already been executed in recent years. In all of these places authorities staged spectacular executions of those who had committed banditry by sea. Fly's hanging was one of the last of these grisly scenes.

Almost every hanging of pirates around the Atlantic had some of the drama created by Fly, his fellow pirates, and Mather. The penitents, like Cole, Greenville, and Condick, usually hoping for pardons, said what the authorities wanted them to say, and perhaps they meant it: do not use oaths; do not curse; do not take the Lord's name in vain; do not sing bawdy songs; do not gamble; do not visit the house of the harlot; do not profane the Sabbath; do not give in to uncleanness and lust; do not be greedy. Instead, obey all authorities; respect your parents; "pay the just Deference to the Rulers"; "Stay in your Place & Station Contentedly." A very few pirates did win pardons, but most, even the obedient and remorseful ones, did not.[16]

But what stands out about these hangings—what certainly stood out to the authorities at the time—was the amount of disorder and resistance they created. In 1717 an unruly mob in Kingston, Jamaica, rescued one pirate from the gallows. Royal authorities all around the Atlantic feared the same event on other occasions and beefed up their military guard as protection against it. Many pirates, like Fly, refused their prescribed roles and used the occasion for one last act of subversion. An endless train of pirates walked defiantly to the gallows and taunted the higher powers when they got there. Facing the steps and the rope in the Bahamas in 1718, pirate Thomas Morris expressed a simple wish: to have been "a greater Plague to these Islands." John Gow, who was a very strong man, broke the gallows rope at his hanging in 1726. He went to "ascend the ladder a second time, which he did with very little concern, dying with the same brutal ferocity which animated all his actions while alive."[17]

When Woodes Rogers, governor, captain general, and vice-admiralty judge of the Bahama Islands, prepared for a mass hanging of pirates in Providence in December 1718, he arranged to fly the infamous freebooter flag above the gallows, so that its grinning skull would look down on the place of execution. Fearful of a riot by the assembled crowd—many of whom had been pirates themselves—and, worse, of a rescue of the malefactors, Rogers deployed one hundred soldiers to escort Daniel Macarty and seven others to the gallows. They would be hanged for "Mutiny, Felony, Piracy." One after another, the pirates made defiant speeches, "crying up a Pyrate's Life to be the only Life for a Man of any Spirit." Macarty spoke of "the time when there was many brave fellows on the Island that would not suffer him to dye like a dog." But he acknowledged to the crowd that presently there was "too much power over their heads" for anyone to "attempt any Thing in his Favour." After drinks, toasts, uncomplimentary reflections on the government, and one reprieve, the order was given to haul away the butts holding up the gallows, whereupon "the stage fell and the Eight swang off."[18]

In 1720, when eight members of the crew of Bartholomew

Roberts were captured and tried in Virginia, they were rowdy and outrageous; they "behaved themselves with the greatest impudence at the Bar." As soon as their trial was over, "they vented their imprecations on their Judges and all concerned in their prosecution, and vow'd if they were again at Liberty they would spare none alive that should fall into their hands." They went to their deaths bidding defiance to mercy. As one observer explained, "They died as they lived, not showing any Sign of Repentance." Indeed, "When they came to the Place of Execution one of them called for a Bottle of Wine, and taking a glass of it, he drank Damnation to the Governour and Confusion to the Colony, which the rest pledged." The governor, Alexander Spotswood, was not amused by either the courtroom bluster or the gallows toast. He wrote, matter-of-factly, to another royal official: "I thought it necessary for the greater Terrour to hang up four of them in chains."[19]

The drama played out again and again. When the fifty-two members of Roberts's crew were hanged at Cape Coast Castle in 1722 before a concourse of Europeans and Africans, a group of pirates explained: "They were poor rogues, and so must be hanged while others, no less guilty in another Way, escaped." They referred to the wealthy rogues who bilked sailors of their rightful wages and proper food and thereby turned many of them toward piracy. When it came time to execute the "old" pirates Magnes, Sympson, Sutton, Ashplant, and Hardy, "none of them, it was observed, appeared the least dejected." Like Fly, they cursed the court and "walk'd to the Gallows without a Tear." Hardy paused to complain that "he had seen many a Man hang'd, but this Way of the Hands being ty'd behind them, he was a Stranger to, and never saw before in his Life." He had the temerity—or the humor—to suggest that the authorities did not even know how to carry out a proper execution![20] Here, as in other settings, the authorities displayed the Jolly Roger at the place of execution. Sail under it, they said, and you will die under it. And even the killing was not terror enough: the corpses of the pirates, like that of William Fly, were turned into a *"Profitable* and *Serviceable* Spectacle." In this case they were distributed up and down the African coast to disseminate the message as broadly as possible.[21]

Terror bred counterterror—tit for tat. In 1717, after Boston's rulers hanged eight members of Black Sam Bellamy's crew, pirates who were still at sea vowed to "kill every body they took belonging to New England." Edward Teach, also known as Blackbeard, and his crew burned a captured ship "because she belonged to *Boston* alledging the People of Boston had hanged some of the pirates."[22] When Bartholomew Roberts and his men learned that the governor and council of Nevis had executed some pirates in 1720, they were so outraged that they sailed into Basseterre's harbor, set several vessels on fire, and offered a big bounty to anyone who would deliver the responsible officials to their clutches so that justice could be served. They made the same threat to avenge the pirates who had taunted Governor Spotswood at their hanging in Virginia. They made good on such bluster when they happened to take a French vessel carrying the governor of Martinique, who had also hanged some members of "the brotherhood." Roberts took revenge by hanging the poor governor from his own yardarm. Thus did the pirates practice terror against the state terrorists. It was a war of nerves—one hanging for another—and constituted a cycle of violence.[23]

But in truth pirates had practiced terror from the beginning, before the authorities had hanged any of them. They had their own reasons, and their own methods. Piracy was predicated on terror, as all contemporaries of freebooting well understood. Captain Charles Johnson, who knew this generation of pirates (some of them individually) and chronicled their exploits in vivid detail, called them "the Terror of the trading Part of the World." Cotton Mather called them *"Sea-Monsters* who have been the *Terror* of *them that haunt the sea."* Pirates practiced terror against those who organized the trade, and against those who carried it out. It all began when a pirate ship approached a prospective prize and raised the primary instrument of terror, the Jolly Roger, whose message was unmistakable: surrender or die.[24]

Pirates used terror for several reasons: to avoid fighting; to force disclosure of information about where booty was hidden; and to punish ship captains. The first point to be emphasized is that pirates did not want to fight, no matter how bloodthirsty their image was in their own day and in ours. As Stanley Richards has written, "It was their ambition to acquire plunder and live to enjoy the pleasures that it brought them. A battle might deprive them of that ease of life. Hence on the chance occasion when they had to go into action against another ship, it was looked upon by them as almost a repulsive necessity. They were after booty, not blood."[25]

They would nonetheless use the threat of violence to get the booty. The primary idea was to intimidate the crew of the ship under attack so that they would not defend their vessel. The tactic worked, as numerous merchant ship captains explained: "up goe the Pirate Colours, at sight whereof our men will defend their ship no longer," wrote one. The raising of Jolly Roger "so much terrifyed" the crew of the *Eagle* that "the men not only refused to fight themselves but also hindered the officers" as they tried to do their "Duty of Defending" the ship. The frightened crew finally "ran into the hold" to hide. When Edward Low and his men sailed into Saint Michael's, Azores, "He threaten'd all with present Death who resisted, which struck such a Terror to them, that they yielded themselves up a Prey to the Villains, without firing a Gun." Why did crews refuse to defend their ships? They knew that if they did resist and were then overpowered, the pirates would probably torture them, to teach them—and other sailors—a lesson. Harsh treatment of those who resist, announced the *Boston News-Letter* in June 1718, "so intimidates our Sailors that they refuse to fight when the Pirates attack them." After all, the pirates would ask: why are you risking your life to protect the property of merchants and ship captains who treat you so poorly?[26]

Pirates also used violence to force prisoners, especially ship captains, to disclose the whereabouts of loot, to "confess what money was on board." Pirates told one captain that they would "throw him over board with a double headed Shot about his neck" if he concealed any money. They told another, if we catch you in "one Lye, we'll Damn you and your Vessel also." Some tried to hide valuables and got caught. Roberts and his crew brought the chief mate of a captured vessel "to the Gear, and whipt him within an Inch of his Life, by reason he had conceal'd two Gold Rings in his Pocket." In this practice of violence, pirates were no different from naval or privateering ships, who used the same methods. Indeed, a portion of pirate terror was the standard issue of war making, which pirates undertook without the approval of any nation-state.[27]

Pirates also practiced violence against the prize ship's cargo, destroying massive amounts of property in the most furious and wanton ways, as once-captured ship captains never grew tired of recounting. They descended into the holds of ships like "a Parcel of Furies," slashing boxes and bales of goods with their cutlasses, throwing valuable goods overboard, and laughing uproariously as they did so. They also destroyed a large number of ships, cutting away their masts, setting them afire, and sinking them, partly because they did not want news of their presence to spread from ship to ship to shore, but also because they wanted to destroy the property of merchants and ship captains they considered their enemies. They practiced indirect terror against the owners of mercantile property.[28]

The pirates' penchant for terror even seems to have had an intimidating effect on the officers and sailors of the British Royal Navy. From 1717 onward colonial officials and merchants voiced a chorus of complaints that His Majesty's Ships seemed none too eager to engage the freebooters who were so dramatically disrupting trade. Merchants especially grumbled that naval vessels would rather trade than fight pirates. In Jamaica, "the Captains of the Men of War station[ed] there [were] unwilling to hazard the King's Ships against such desperate Fellows, as the Pirates are reported to be." Governor Woodes Rogers of the Bahamas and Governor Archibald Hamilton and the assembly of Antigua complained that Captain Whitney of HMS *Rose* was told to go after Roberts and his consorts but refused to do so. Captain Cornwall of HMS *Sheerness* was accused of "neglecting or refusing to go in quest of other pirates." Captain Upton of HMS *London* was sent to the Indian Ocean to fight pirates, but once he encountered Edward England, he chose to sail away. Captain Thomas Matthews of HMS *Lion* apparently preferred illegal trading to the more dangerous duty of fighting. He was accused of collaborating and exchanging goods with pirates at Madagascar. Pirate Captain Edward Taylor saw the pattern and mocked the Royal Navy in a short speech to his crew in 1723: "Damne my Blood God forgive me for swearing here's a Squadron of Men of War sent to look after us but they don't much care for the seeing of us they are more upon the trading account but however lets stand by one another and take Care of ourselves."[29]

How did this dialectic of violence between pirates and the nation-state develop? What were its causes? How did piracy itself erupt in 1716? And how did it decline after 1726? Why did pirates express such rage—and seek such vengeance—against ship captains and royal officials? And why did they "cry up a Pyrate's Life to be the only Life for a Man of any Spirit"?

These fundamental questions are addressed in the pages that follow as we explore the social and cultural history of early-eighteenth-century pirates, those outlaws who made the last great moment in the golden age of piracy. We will see that the early-eighteenth-century pirate ship was a world turned upside down, made so by the articles of agreement that established the rules and customs of the pirates' alternative social order. Pirates "distributed justice," elected their officers, divided their loot equally, and established a different discipline. They limited the authority of the captain, resisted many of the practices of capitalist merchant shipping industry, and maintained a multicultural, multiracial, and multinational social order. They demonstrated quite clearly—and subversively—that ships did not have to be run in the brutal and oppressive ways of the merchant service and the Royal Navy.

For, as it happened, there were not merely two kinds of terror, the terror of the gallows and the terror of the Jolly Roger, but three. To understand William Fly and his dispute with the ministers of Boston, to understand the gallows drama repeated in one Atlantic port after another, and, most important, to understand the very explosion of piracy in the eighteenth century, we must attend to what Fly said of "*Bad Usage,*" of how his captain and mate used and abused him and his brother tars, treating them "barbarously," as if they were "dogs." He was talking about the violent disciplinary regime of the eighteenth-century deep-sea sailing ship, the ordinary and pervasive violence of labor discipline as practiced by the ship captain as he moved the commodities that were the lifeblood of the capitalist world economy. Even though there is no surviving evidence to show exactly what Captain Green did to Fly and the other sailors aboard the *Elizabeth* to produce the rage, the mutiny, the murder, and the decision to turn pirate, it is not hard to imagine. The High Court of Admiralty records for this period are replete with bloody accounts of lashings, tortures, and killings.[30] Fly was talking about the ship captain as terrorist.

The 1726 encounter between Fly and Mather in Boston was unusually combative, but it was not uncommon. Indeed, in this era Fly and others like him were the "Villains of all Nations." Made up of all nations, and attacking the commerce of the world without respect for nation or property, pirates produced a strange and fascinating drama, an eighteenth-century morality play full of overlarge characters, complicated plots, twists and turns, and even unexpected outcomes. One such outcome occurred when Fly won his argument with Mather. As it happened, the "stupid" and "impenitent" pirate was able to convince the self-righteous minister of at least one primary cause of piracy. During his execution sermon, Mather made it a point to address the ship captains in the crowd, telling them in no uncertain terms that they must hereafter avoid being "too like the *Devil* in their *Barbarous Usage* of the *Men* that are under them and lay them under *Temptations* to do *Desperate Things*."[31]

Chapter Two

THE POLITICAL ARITHMETIC OF PIRACY

THE OUTBURST OF PIRACY following the War of Spanish Succession (1702–13) took no one by surprise. A group of Virginia merchants, for instance, wrote to the Admiralty as early as 1713, setting forth "the apprehensions they have of Pyrates molesting their trade in the time of Peace." Edmund Dummer, a merchant responsible for the mail packet trade to the West Indies, believed that the "cursed trade" of privateering would in times of peace "breed so many pirates that ... we shall be in more danger from them than we are now from the enemy," France and Spain. What were the circumstances that made such an outburst not only likely but also predictable? More specifically, how did these circumstances—the organization and growth of the Atlantic economy—appear to the sailor who did its labor and who might or might not make the fateful decision to "go upon the account"? What would an experienced deep-sea sailor have known of the world in 1716, the moment when piracy would erupt on a massive scale? And once it erupted, would it indeed cause more danger to English shipping than had France and Spain in wartime? To answer these questions we will survey what someone in the early eighteenth century might have called the political arithmetic of economic life—the global realities of empire, commerce, war, and peace, all of which depended in some important measure on the ebbs and flows of the maritime labor market and the work of sailors in the deep-sea trades. Out of this complex array of forces would climb the pirate, with a dagger between his teeth.[1]

{ 19 }

The sailor knew that most of the lands surrounding the Atlantic, and most of the port cities to which he sailed, belonged to five nations that had become imperial powers—Spain, Portugal, the Netherlands, France, and England. The Spanish and the Portuguese had claimed large parts of the New World in the fifteenth and sixteenth centuries, and these lands were now home to two-thirds of the roughly 1.3 million Europeans and 1 million people of African descent who in 1700 lived alongside uncounted millions of Native Americans. The Dutch, who had few people but many ships, had become masters of the seas in the seventeenth century. The new challengers for global economic power were the French and the English, both of whom came relatively late to imperial adventure but prospered. In Spain colonial commerce and things maritime were handled by the House of Trade and the Council of the Indies; in Portugal, by the Overseas Council; in the Netherlands, by the Dutch West India Company; in France, by the Ministry of Marine Affairs; and in England, by the Privy Council, the Board of Trade, and the Council of Trade and Plantations. Operating from the great port cities of Seville, Lisbon, Amsterdam, and London, and linking the peoples, cultures, and economies of Europe and Africa to the Americas, all managed "factories-at-a-distance" through seafaring means. The sailor's labor was essential to the task.[2]

The sailor knew, by personal experience, that these Atlantic powers waged what seemed to be incessant war against each other. The typical working sailor in 1716 was a man in his late twenties who had known war for much of his life. Indeed, unless he had been "bred to the sea" as a young boy (that is, served an apprenticeship), his entire working life would have been spent within whiff of the cannon smoke of national and imperial hostility. The great Anglo-French rivalry that would dominate the eighteenth-century Atlantic had begun in 1689 with the opening shots of the War of the League of Augsburg, which would last until 1697. After five pirate-plagued years of peace, the War of Spanish

Succession broke out in 1702 between Spain and France on one side and Britain on the other, lasting until 1713. Twenty of the sailors' first twenty-five years were passed in an Atlantic world at war.[3]

The sailor knew that these wars were fought, for the most part, over wealth, a substantial portion of which was based on the key commodities of the Atlantic trades in which he worked—gold, silver, fish, furs, servants and slaves, sugar, tobacco, and manufactures. Earlier clashes among the great powers had centered on land and the acquisition of new territories, and all had been suffused with religious fervor as Protestant and Catholic nations waged bloody, self-righteous war. But by the early eighteenth century, the realms of the various empires were largely fixed (and would remain so for half a century) and religious war had given way to trade war. The Atlantic empires competed fiercely with each other, pursuing policies that would enhance their own power over and against their rivals, all certain that control of the seas was a key to increased trade, larger profits, far-reaching markets, economic growth, and national power. England in particular went through a "commercial revolution" between 1660 and 1700, when its trade tripled and it became a major player in the rapidly expanding Atlantic economy. New, independent traders surged to the fore to replace the old chartered companies of merchants. The Royal African Company, for example, lost its monopoly on the slave trade in stages, beginning in 1698 and ending in 1712, as the government unleashed hungry free traders on "black gold." Commercial and naval power expanded together as the Atlantic empires regarded long-distance trade, in the words of J. H. Parry, as "a mild form of war." The truth of this claim was evident in the well-armed merchantmen who plied the seas and in the fleets of half-commercial, half-military privateers (private men-of-war), which were mobilized by kings and queens to attack and plunder the trading vessels of wartime enemies, especially in the West Indies, where the imperial powers lived at close quarters in the "cockpit of war." Whether by moving commodities or waging war by sea, the sailor provided the labor power of transatlantic endeavor.[4]

The sailor knew that thousands of people were moving and laboring around the Atlantic, some willingly, some unwillingly, with many of them, like himself, subjected to violence. By 1716 a worldwide process of expropriation, called primitive accumulation, had already torn millions of people from their ancestral lands in Europe, Africa, and the Americas. Hundreds of thousands of Native Americans had already died in the genocidal assault on the New World, killed by warfare and the fatal spread of European diseases against which they had no immunities. Thousands of others relocated to the interiors of the Americas to escape the European settlers who hugged the coasts of North and South America. By 1716 2.5 million Africans had been ripped from their villages by warriors and raiders and sold to European merchants for shipment to Europe and the Americas. The enclosure movement and other mechanisms of dispossession had set thousands in motion on the roads and ways of England in particular and Europe in general. Masses of people flocked to the cities, where they found work, frequently as waged laborers, in manufacturing and especially in armies and navies, as war required vast amounts of labor. Hundreds of thousands more would embark for colonial plantations as laborers, whether free or unfree. Expropriation had "freed" millions of workers for redeployment to the far-flung edges of empire, often as indentured servants or slaves, on plantations that would produce what may have been the largest planned accumulation of wealth the world had yet seen. It was said that sugar, the leading and most lucrative Atlantic commodity of the eighteenth century, was made with blood. By 1716 big planters drove armies of servants and slaves as they expanded their power from their own lands to colonial and finally national legislatures. Atlantic empires mobilized labor power on a new and unprecedented scale, largely through the strategic use of violence—the violence of land seizure, of expropriating agrarian workers, of the Middle Passage, of exploitation through labor discipline, and of punishment (often in the form of death) against those who dared to resist the colonial order of things. By all accounts, by 1713 the Atlantic economy had reached a new stage of maturity, stability, and profitability. The growing riches of the few depended on the growing misery of the many.[5]

The sailor knew that trade was the unifying process of the world economy, that the oceangoing ship was the machine that made it possible, and that his own labor made the ship go. But he also knew that 1716 was a tough time for seafaring workers like himself. The end of the War of Spanish Succession had resulted in an extensive demobilization of the navies of Britain, France, and Spain. The British Royal Navy in particular plunged from 49,860 men in 1712 to 13,475 just two years later, and only by 1740 would the number of men increase to as many as 30,000 again. At the same time, privateering commissions (bills of marque) expired, adding to the number of sailors who were loose and looking for work in the port cities of the world. In England, wrote Captain Charles Johnson, multitudes of unemployed seamen were "straggling, and begging all over the Kingdom." Yet conditions for seamen did not worsen immediately, as historian Ralph Davis explained: "the years 1713–1715 saw—as did immediate post-war years throughout the eighteenth century—the shifting of heaped-up surpluses of colonial goods, the movement of great quantities of English goods to colonial and other markets, and a general filling in of stocks of imported goods which had been allowed to run down." This small-scale boom gave employment to some of the seamen who had been dropped from naval and privateering rolls. But by late 1715, a slump in trade had begun, lasting into the 1730s. The huge surplus of maritime labor produced jarring social effects. Wages contracted sharply, and merchant seamen who made 45–55s. per month in 1707 made only half that amount a few years later. Sailors were forced to compete for scarce jobs, and those lucky enough to find berths discovered that their customary arrangements aboard ship now included poorer-quality food and harsher discipline, which intensified over the course of the eighteenth century. War years, despite their deadly dangers, provided tangible benefits. The working seaman of 1716 knew that conditions had once been different, and for many they were decisively better.[6]

The sailor knew that the rulers of the Atlantic empires had taken a harsh new view of pirates as the enemies of imperial designs rather than as allies who might help to accomplish them. For much of the seventeenth century, pirates had been indirectly employed by the Netherlands, France, and England to harass Portugal and especially Spain in the New World, as well as to capture a portion of their glittering wealth. Operating largely from Caribbean islands, especially Jamaica, the sea rovers sacked Spanish American ports such as Veracruz and Panama City, repeatedly trashing Catholic churches and in many instances toting back to their ships as much silver plate as they could carry. But by the 1680s ruling-class attitudes had changed. Jamaica's bigwigs could make more money, more *predictable* money, by cultivating sugar, and members of Parliament in England sought a more stable and reliable system of international trade. Pirates, who disrupted both projects, began to be hanged in significant numbers in the 1690s. According to historian Max Savelle, the Treaty of Utrecht in 1713 "was thought of, both in Europe and in America, as a settlement that would establish a lasting peace in America, based on the principle of the balance of colonial power." Britain in particular hoped so because its traders, at home and in the colonies (especially Jamaica), had won the *Asiento*, an agreement with the Spanish government that allowed them officially to import 4,800 slaves per year and to smuggle a huge number more. The "Returns of the Assiento and private Slave-Trade" proved a more dependable way to exploit Spanish wealth. Pirates now stood squarely in the way of the hoped-for stability and profits.[7]

The sailor knew that whatever the attitude from on high, the Atlantic was a big place, that the empires were overextended and could not easily police the seas on which they depended, and that these cir-

cumstances created openings from below. The Atlantic powers, especially Spain and increasingly France and England, possessed
large masses of far-flung lands, but they could not easily control
the sea-lanes on which their commerce to and from them depended. As the Dutch legal scholar Cornelius van Bynkershoek
wrote in 1702, "The power of the land properly ends where the
force of arms ends." The sea, in his view, "can be considered subject as far as the range of cannon extends," which was the original formulation of the three-mile limit of national sovereignty
over coastal waters. But his most important conclusion was, "The
vast ocean cannot be possessed." It was a commons, a place to be
used by many, including the sailor who dared to turn pirate.[8]

*The sailor who embraced the Jolly Roger after 1716 came from a po-
tent experience of life and labor in a wooden world.* The sailor's
workplace, the deep-sea sailing ship, was something of a factory
in those days, a place where "hands"—those who owned no property and who therefore sold their labor for a money wage—
cooperated to make the machine go. Sailing these small, brittle
wooden vessels over the forbidding oceans of the globe, the seaman took part in a profoundly collective work experience, one
that required carefully synchronized cooperation with other
maritime workers for the sake of survival. Facing a ship captain
of almost unlimited disciplinary power and an ever readiness to
use the cat-o'-nine-tails, the sailor developed an array of resis-
tances against such concentrated authority that featured desertion, work stoppages, mutinies, and strikes. Indeed, the sailor
would *invent* the strike during a wage dispute in London in
1768 when he and his mates went from ship to ship, striking—
lowering—the sails in an effort to make merchants grant their
demands. Facing such natural and man-made dangers, which included a chronic scarcity of food and drink and a galling system
of hierarchy and privilege, the sailor learned the importance of
equality: his painfully acquired experience told him that a fair
distribution of risks would improve everyone's chances for survival. Separated from loved ones and the rest of society for ex-

tended periods, the sailor developed a distinctive work culture with its own language, songs, rituals, and sense of brotherhood. Its core values were collectivism, anti-authoritarianism, and egalitarianism, all of which were summarized in the sentence frequently uttered by rebellious sailors: "they were one & all resolved to stand by one another." All of these cultural traits flowed from the work experience, and all would influence both the decision to turn pirate and how pirates would conduct themselves thereafter, as we will see in subsequent chapters.[9]

If the sailor of 1716 had a set of experiences that would condition his attitude to piracy in the early eighteenth century, so did his class counterparts, the shipowner, merchant, and ruler of the Atlantic empires. As dominant groups their attitudes were embodied in legislation and had the force of law. When piracy broke out after the War of Spanish Succession, the governing law in effect in the English Atlantic was "An Act for the more effectual Suppression of Piracy" (11 and 12 Wm III, c. 7), originally drafted in 1698 and 1699 and made perpetual in 1700, in response to the last major peacetime explosion of piracy, in the 1690s. This act incorporated elements from earlier legislation (28 Hen VIII, c. 15, 1536), which had been modernized in the early seventeenth century by Sir Edward Coke, who added the implication of petit treason and imported the phrase *hostes humani generis* (common enemies of mankind) from Roman law to describe pirates. In *Rex v. Dawson*, a trial involving members of Henry Avery's pirate crew in 1696, the Admiralty judge Sir Charles Hedges had rather grandly ruled that English courts and English judges such as he had jurisdiction over all people—anywhere on earth—who interfered with English commerce. The act of 1700 expanded the definition of the pirate beyond the person who committed robbery by sea to include the mutineer who ran away with the ship and the sailor who interfered with the defense of his vessel when pirates attacked. It also provided pensions for those wounded in defending the ship; in the event of death the money would go to the sailor's wife and children. Merchant seamen who deserted their ships—they were believed to be prime recruits for pirate ships—would be stripped of their wages.[10]

The law was renewed in 1715 and again in 1719, but between those dates, in 1717 and again in 1718, the King offered pardons to try to rid the sea of robbers. Since the graces specified that only crimes committed at certain times and in particular regions would be forgiven, many pirates saw enormous latitude for official trickery and refused to surrender. Others accepted the amnesty and then simply resumed their piracies, as Governor Robert Johnson of South Carolina explained to the Council of Trade and Plantations in 1718: "I don't perceive H.M. gracious proclamacon of pardon works any good efect upon them, some few indead surrender and take a certificate of there so doing and then severall of them return to the sport again." Governor Walter Hamilton of Antigua agreed, writing to the same body: "your Lords-ships may now plainly perceive how little Acts of Grace and Mercy work on these vermine," many of whom, it seemed, took the pardon, went back to plundering, then took it again. In any case, for most men, accepting and abiding by the rules of the pardon would have meant a return to the dismal conditions from which they had escaped.[11]

Their tactic failing, English imperial rulers toughened the law of piracy in 1721 (8 Geo I, c. 24, 1721), promising death to anyone who cooperated with pirates and the loss of wages and six months' imprisonment to those who refused to defend their ship. They also decreed that naval ships were not to trade but to chase and fight pirates, which they had shown considerable disinclination to do, much to the dismay of both merchants and royal officials. Seamen injured in battle against pirates "shall be provided for as if they were actually in the service of the Crown," explained the *Boston News-Letter*. Parliament also left no doubt about the transoceanic reach of the new act of 1721: it "shall extend to all his Majesty's Dominions in *Asia, Africa,* and *America*."

According to Alfred P. Rubin, the leading scholar of the international law of piracy, the main impulse behind these laws was to protect "private property crossing national boundaries."[12]

From antiquity onward, piracy always depended on a particular set of material circumstances to emerge and flourish. The most essential precondition through the ages has been the existence of trade, in which valuable commodities are transported by sea through remote, poorly defended regions populated by poor people. These poor people in turn had to have access to seagoing craft, which were usually smaller, lighter, faster, and more maneuverable than the heavy-laden vessels they chased and sought to capture. Pirates had to have the skills to handle their craft exceptionally well, underlining the old adage that "the pick of all seamen were pirates." They had expert local knowledge of winds and waters, shoals and coastlines, sea-lanes and shipping patterns. They had places to lurk and hide near the main routes of trade and communities of people to support them. They also had fences and markets to and in which they could sell or trade the goods they captured.[13]

All of these conditions obtained in the 1710s and 1720s. Trade, as we have seen, was a dynamic engine of global economic development, a source of gleaming wealth, and yet the imperial nations of the day did not have the military capacity to project their sovereignty over all of the world's seas and oceans. Captain Charles Johnson emphasized the "great Commerce" of Spain, France, the Netherlands, and England in and around the West Indies, where great sums of money, provisions, clothing, and naval stores might be had. Poor people, especially highly skilled, unemployed, and desperate sailors, thronged almost every port city. It was not difficult for them to get possession, by theft or mutiny, of what was perhaps the world's most sophisticated and economically valuable piece of technology of the day, the deep-sea sailing ship, especially small, fast, and well-armed craft such as sloops. The West Indies were a classical setting and "a natural Security" for such people and ships, as its small inlets, lagoons, and shallow waters made it difficult for larger vessels such as men-of-war to pursue the bandits by sea. Admiral Edward Vernon once remarked that dispatching a large naval vessel after a pirate ship was like sending "a Cow after a Hare." The only way the big, slow creature would ever catch one was by accident. These small islands also abounded with provisions—water and food, turtle, seafowl, shellfish and fish. And there were, at least early in the period under consideration, always people who were willing to support pirates, merchants willing to buy and sell their booty. Pirates "continually found Favours and Encouragers," even in Jamaica after the sugar planters consolidated their ruthless power. The coexistence of these conditions is the major reason the explosion of piracy was not only likely but predictable after the War of Spanish Succession.[14]

Contemporary estimates of the pirate population during the period under consideration placed the number between 1,000 and 2,000 at any one time. In 1717 Philadelphia merchant James Logan estimated that 1,500 pirates were active, 800 of them based at Providence, their Bahamas rendezvous. Three different commentators, from the Bahamas, South Carolina, and Bermuda, put the number at or near 2,000 between 1718 and 1720. The *American Weekly Mercury* (published in Philadelphia) claimed that 32 pirate ships—which would have carried about 2,400 men—were prowling the Caribbean in late 1720. In the only estimate we have from the other side of the law, by a band of pirates in 1716, "30 Company of them," again roughly 2,400 men, plied the oceans of the globe.[15]

These figures seem broadly accurate.[16] From records that describe the activities of pirate ships and from reports or projections of crew sizes, it appears that 1,500 to 2,000 pirates sailed the sea between 1716 and 1718, 1,800 to 2,400 between 1719 and 1722, and

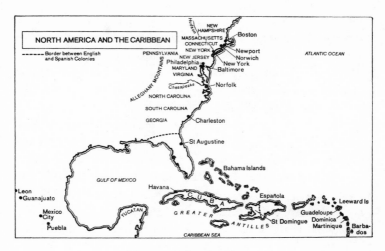

Figure 2. The Caribbean.

1,000 in 1723, declining rapidly to 500 in 1724, to fewer than 200 by 1725 and 1726. In all, some 4,000 went, as they called it, "upon the account." The pirates' chief military enemy, the British Royal Navy, employed an average of only 13,000 hands in any given year between 1716 and 1726. Pirates sailed in well-armed vessels and represented a formidable military force, especially during the years 1718–22, when they were at their peak.[17]

Like all earlier pirates, these sea robbers followed a lucrative trade and sought bases for their depredations in places distant from the seats of imperial power, choosing especially the Caribbean Sea and the Indian Ocean. The Bahama Islands, undefended and ungoverned by the Crown, began, in 1716, to attract pirates by the hundreds. Governor Alexander Spotswood noted that pirates used the Bahamas as a "General Rendezvous & seem to look upon those Islands as their own." Since no government existed in the Bahamas, every man there was, according to a disturbed observer, "doing onely what's right in his own eyes." These pirates called themselves the Flying Gang. By 1718 a torrent of complaints moved George I to commission Woodes

Rogers to lead an expedition to bring the islands under control. Rogers's efforts largely succeeded, and pirates scattered in all directions; some sailed north to the unpopulated inlets of the Carolinas, some set their compasses west or south for smaller Caribbean islands, and others headed eastward across the Atlantic to Africa.[18]

Pirates had begun to settle in Madagascar as early as 1691; their presence had long caused "a great Deal of uneasiness and Fear in the Several Nations trading to the Indies." They intermixed with the indigenous population, forming "a dark Mulatto Race," which, over time, became a new ethnicity. By 1718 Madagascar served as a pirate settlement, an entrepôt for booty, and, for the maritime powers of Europe, a nightmarish model of a place they could not control. Pirates played with the fears of Atlantic rulers by threatening to turn the Bahamas into "a second Madagascar" or to take Bermuda "and make a new Madagascar of it." At the mouth of the Sierra Leone River on Africa's western coast, pirates stopped off for "whoring and drinking" and to unload goods. Some authorities feared that pirates might "set up a sort of Commonwealth"—and they were precisely correct in their designation—in these distant regions, since "no Power in those Parts of the World could have been able to dispute it with them."[19] Theaters of operation among pirates shifted, however, according to season, shipping schedules, the availability of prizes, and naval policing designs. But generally, as one pirate noted, these rovers were "dispers't into several parts of the World." Sea robbers sought and usually found bases near major trade routes that were as distant as possible from the powers of the state.[20]

Did pirates cause a crisis in trade? Captain Charles Johnson believed that pirates were deeply "destructive to the Navigation of the Trading World," and of course merchants and royal officials in both the colonies and the metropolises warmly agreed, though

their comments must be seen as those of self-interested men trying to move the government to protect their own economic en-
terprises. Governor Spotswood of Virginia was one of the first to
sound an alarm that would be repeated again and again over the
next ten years; pirates were swarming everywhere, he warned in
July 1716, and "the whole Trade of the Continent may be endan-
gered if timely measures be not taken to suppress this growing
evil." The royal pardons did not work, and the community of pirates continued to expand. By April 1717 Virginia merchants
were writing, "our Coast is now infested with Pyrates. God
knows what damage they'l do to Trade. Ships are dailey going
out & coming [back] in." Sam Bellamy and the pirates of the
Whydah had effectively shut down the commerce of the Chesapeake Bay, and shippers' fears multiplied; nervous captains now
assumed that every sail on the horizon was a pirate.[21]

Other regions were affected according to the ebbs and flows
of pirate expeditions and the patrols of the small number of naval
warships based in the Americas. When Blackbeard and his crew
blockaded Charleston in April 1717 to procure medicines with
which to treat their sick and wounded, a South Carolinian wrote,
"The Trade of this Place was totally interrupted," and the whole
province was in "a great Terror." Bartholomew Roberts and his
convoy paralyzed trade in the West Indies in late 1721. Shortly
thereafter, in July 1722, Philadelphia felt the shock when its entire trade halted for a week. The cries of merchants and officials
continued to make their way across the Atlantic to the seat of empire in London: "except [unless] effectual measures are taken the
whole trade of America must soon be ruin'd." If the depredations
continued unchecked, "all the *English Plantations* in *America* will
be totally ruin'd in a very short time." Governor Hamilton of
Antigua expressed the anguish of the planters on the small islands of the West Indies. "What," he wondered, "have we that
lyes not at the mercy of these villains?" The problem was so severe as to force imperial rivals to cooperate; in 1721 the British
and French governments in the Lesser Antilles agreed to com-

mon military protection against pirates. One imperial observer claimed that piracy was damaging not only transatlantic and intercolonial trade but also industry in England. The American and African trades, which carried manufactures in their outward passages, seemed especially hard hit.[22]

One of the greatest claims for the crisis was made by Captain Johnson, who stated that between 1716 and 1726 pirates captured more vessels and did greater damage to trade than had been done by the combined naval and privateering campaigns that Spain and France undertook during the War of Spanish Succession. This is an extraordinary statement. Could a few thousand ragged outlaws be more powerful than the combined naval and privateering forces of two of the world's greatest nations? Historian Ralph Davis has estimated that England lost about two thousand vessels during the war but added that its own maritime predations captured roughly an equal, if not slightly larger, number of vessels. By this equation, there can be no doubt that Johnson was right. Let us look at the matter more closely.[23]

The impact of piracy on trade can be estimated in two complementary ways. First, by looking at contemporaneous comments (some of them provided by pirates themselves), we can suggest roughly how many merchant vessels pirates captured and plundered. The crew of Bartholomew Roberts alone took more than 400 craft between 1719 and 1722. Edward Low and his gang took approximately 140 vessels, Blackbeard perhaps fewer. Sam Bellamy and his fellow pirates captured more than 50 before they were fatally shipwrecked in a storm. Others who took sizable numbers included Edward England and Charles Vane (at least 50 each), Charles Harris (45), Francis Spriggs (40), James Phillips (34), George Lowther (33), and Richard Holland (25). If we estimate that the remaining seventy or so pirate captains took an average of 20 vessels each (roughly the average after we remove the highest figures, to produce a conservative estimate), we would get a total of more than 2,400 vessels captured and plundered.[24]

Most of these captures were not total losses, and indeed a few of them resulted in the loss of little or no cargo at all. In a letter to his employing shipowner in 1719, Captain William Snelgrave provided a list of ships recently captured by pirates around the Sierra Leone River in West Africa, a few of them with the notation "Plundered but little." If the vessel was small, or if the captain proved to have "a good character," pirates often returned the prize to its crew after modest takings. In some cases all they wanted was food and drink, and in others they had no use for the cargo, not least because they had lost many of their connections to merchants who might at an earlier point have fenced the goods for them. In most instances, big shipments of sugar, tobacco, or slaves were out of the question for pirates; they simply had no way to sell them and hence no use for them.[25]

But if these circumstances diminish in one direction the significance of the total number of prizes taken by pirates, two other circumstances expand it in the other. First, there were very few compensatory captures, by Britain or anyone else, to balance these losses, as only a few pirate ships were taken, and fewer still were flush with treasure. Perhaps even more important, a significant portion of the vessels that pirates took as prizes were completely destroyed, evidence of which we have glimpsed earlier. Unlike navies and privateers, pirates routinely sunk or burned their prizes, which increased the short- and long-term economic losses to shipping and commerce and prompted numerous complaints by royal officials. General Peter Heywood, commander in chief of Jamaica, wrote to the Council of Trade and Plantations in 1716 that pirates were taking half the vessels bound to and from English, French, and Spanish Caribbean settlements, "and very often burn their vessels and others they disable just leaving them sufficient to bring them down." It would appear that Captain Johnson knew whereof he spoke and may in the end have underestimated the damage freebooters did to commerce. Historians, unlike merchants and officials of the early eighteenth century, may have not noticed, but pirates did create something approaching a crisis in trade, which helps to account for the hugely indicative fact that there was zero growth in English shipping from 1715 to 1728, a prolonged period of stagnation between two phases of extensive growth.[26]

{ 35 }

The second way of exploring the impact of piracy on trade is through a sizable (though not random or comprehensive) sample of 545 vessels taken by pirates between 1716 and 1726. The peak years for capture were, as the aforementioned merchants and officials seem to suggest, 1717, 1718, 1720, and 1722. The sample also suggests a dramatic expansion of captures in 1717 and a fairly rapid decline after 1724, a pattern consistent with evidence presented in other chapters about the temporal rise and decline of piracy in the late golden age. It may also be of correlative significance that the years in which the greatest number of pirates were hanged were 1718 (110) and 1722 (148). Pirates disrupted some of the most lucrative zones of international trade, especially the West Indies, North America, and West Africa, where almost all (95 percent) of their prizes were taken. In the sample, roughly 11 percent of the vessels captured were known to be severely damaged or destroyed. If applied to the larger projection of 2,400 craft captured, this suggests that pirates ruined more than 250 ships. The conclusion must be that the merchants and officials knew whereof they spoke when they complained about the "infestation" of pirates and the tremendous damage they did to trade.[27]

To complete the overview, and to provide a temporal map to guide the reader in the following chapters, I note that the piracies of 1716–26 passed through three discernible stages. The first of these, as I have indicated, began soon after the Peace of Utrecht ended the War of Spanish Succession in 1713 and became a matter of international significance in 1716. Many of the early pirates had been privateers who preyed on the commercial vessels of Spain and France and whose external circumstances—

and hence legal definition—changed with the ending of the war. Pirates with captains such as Benjamin Hornigold, John Jennings, and Philip Cockram continued to attack their traditional enemies. They even announced to one captured ship captain that "they meddle not with English or Dutch, but that they never consented to the Articles of Peace with the French and Spaniards." As we will see in the next chapter, they drew self-consciously on the traditions of the buccaneers and established themselves as a community based in the Bahama Islands. They carried out almost all of their piracies in the West Indies, but altogether they captured only about 8 percent of the prizes taken during the ten-year span.[28]

A division soon developed among these pirates, opening the second—and most dramatic—stage in the history of piracy in the early eighteenth century. This stage began in 1717 when a multiethnic but mostly English crew of pirates overthrew Hornigold as commander because "he refused to take and plunder English vessels," which were, after all, the most numerous and often the richest vessels to be found in the Caribbean and the adjoining Atlantic. This stage, which lasted until 1722, was the greatest period of the golden age, the time when more than 70 percent of all prizes were captured, and indeed the time that produced the most enduring images of pirates. This was the heyday of Blackbeard and Bartholomew Roberts, the "great pirate" whose successes at sea dwarfed all others. Another critical development in this phase was the reestablishment of royal authority in the Bahama Islands by Woodes Rogers in 1718, thereby destroying the pirate rendezvous. In the resulting scatter, the pirates vastly expanded their theater of operation, moving up the coast of North America, across the Atlantic to West Africa, and around the Cape of Good Hope to Madagascar and the Indian Ocean as their forebears had done in the 1690s. The years 1718–22 represented the moment when common men of the deep gained control of the enterprise of piracy and used it for their own purposes, independent of the economic projects of the upper classes of the day. By 1720 the main purpose was no longer booty. It was, rather, the perpetuation of a "life of liberty."[29]

The third stage began in roughly 1722, with the naval defeat of Roberts and his two big ships and three hundred men off the coast of West Africa, and lasted until 1726, when Atlantic piracy effectively came to an end. In this phase the struggle turned murderous. Hundreds of pirates were killed in military actions or on the gallows as merchants and governmental officials set about exterminating robbery by sea and the alternative way of life it represented. Those pirates who remained at sea, in response, became more desperate and more violent and killed more of their captives, as they knew that they faced almost certain death for their actions. The years 1722–26 were a time when pirates fought less for booty than for their very survival. Their determination was more than matched by national governments, led by Great Britain. The result would be a bloodbath.[30]

The seaman who stood on the brink of piracy in 1716 knew that the world was divided into vast geopolitical empires, that wealth coursed through the trading veins of the Atlantic, that deep-sea ships were its carriers, and that seamanship was a key to it all. He knew that times were hard and that the overextended empires offered opportunities to those willing to risk their necks by becoming pirates. He did not know, however, that the next ten years would be a "golden age" of piracy. He did not know that thousands of people would go "upon the account." He did not know that those who did would capture hundreds, or indeed thousands, of ships, destroy many, and disrupt the Atlantic trading system. Finally, he did not know how many would die during an unprecedented wave of violent repression. Let us explore more closely the people who, out of ignorance, desperation, and hope, chose this fate.

Chapter Three

WHO WILL GO "A PYRATING"?

WALTER KENNEDY WAS BORN at Pelican Stairs, Wapping, the sailor town of London, in 1695, the year in which Henry Avery, "the maritime Robin Hood," led a mutiny, turned pirate, and captured a treasure ship in the Indian Ocean. Kennedy's family, like his community, lived by the sea. His father was an anchor smith "who gave his son Walter the best education he was able." The times were hard, and so was young Kennedy—he was poor, illiterate, known to have "a too aspiring temper," and often on the wrong side of the law. It was said that in his childhood he was "bred a Pick-Pocket" and that he later became a housebreaker. Meanwhile he served an apprenticeship to his father, but this came to an abrupt end when the old man died. Kennedy promptly gave his father's effects to his mother and brothers and "followed his own roving inclinations and went to sea." He served a long stint on a man-of-war in the War of Spanish Succession. There he heard the stories told on the lower deck about "the exploits of the pirates, both in the East and West Indies, and of their having got several islands into their possession, wherein they settled, and in which they exercised a sovereign power." Kennedy "became more than ordinarily attentive whenever stories of that sort were told, and sought every opportunity of putting his fellow sailors upon such relations." He learned of the adventures of Morgan, Avery, and other "maritime desperadoes," committing to memory their "principal expeditions." These tales "had [a] wonderful effect on Walter's disposition," creating in him "a secret ambition of making a figure in the same way." The yarns set him on his life's course.[1]

Kennedy was part of the naval force sent with Woodes Rogers

in an expedition to the Bahamas, to "recover that island by reducing the pirates, who then had it in their possession" and had "fortified themselves in several places." Kennedy's personal purpose, it seems, was not to assist in suppressing the pirates but rather to *find and join* them. Once he got to Providence, he shipped himself as a merchant seaman with several "reformed pirates" on the *Buck* sloop, in which he and five others (including Howell Davis and Thomas Anstis, both destined to be pirate captains) "conspired together to go off Pyrating with the Vessel." This core of conspirators would evolve into the most successful gang of pirates in the entire golden age.[2]

Kennedy would make a reputation for himself among the pirates as "a bold and daring Fellow, but very wicked and profligate." With the elected captain Howell Davis, he took part in several daring attacks against slave-trading fortresses in West Africa. The crew first assaulted the Portuguese at Saint Jago, then undertook a bigger, bolder action against Gambia Castle, where they captured "about two thousand Pounds Sterling in Bar Gold" and ended by "dismounting the Guns, and demolishing the Fortifications" of the castle. The next target was the fort at Sierra Leone, which was likewise taken and plundered. When Davis was subsequently killed by Portuguese soldiers at yet another slave-trading fortress, on the Princes Islands, Kennedy led a contingent of thirty pirates on a mission to avenge their fallen comrade. He conducted the company up a steep hill, "directly up under the fire of their Ship Guns" and into the slave factory, where the very sight of them caused the Portuguese guards to quit their posts and take flight. Kennedy and his gang "march'd in without Opposition, set Fire to the Fort, and threw all the Guns off the Hill into the Sea, which after they had done, they retreated quietly to their Ship."[3]

Kennedy was a man full of rage, or so it appeared in encounters with two ship captains off the coast of Africa in 1719. He decided to take as booty the wig of the captured captain William Snelgrave, who in turn tried to prevent him, and for his resistance got a stern and angry lecture: "I give you this Caution; never to dispute the Will of a Pirate: For, supposing I had cleft your Scull asunder for your impudence, what would you have got by it but destruction? Indeed you may flatter your self, I should have been put to death for killing a Prisoner in cold Blood; but assure your self my Friends would have brought me off on such an Occasion." Kennedy thus taunted his prisoner with the leveling force of death, contempt for the English legal system, and faith in his comrades, all of which gushed out of a tussle over a symbol of class privilege, the wig.[4] When the pirates later took Captain Thomas Grant, Kennedy declared, "Damn you I know you and will sacrifice you & then with his fist struck the informant with great Violence upon his Mouth which occasioned his Nose & Mouth to Bleed." Kennedy wanted to kill Grant for some unstated previous offense but was prevented from doing so by his shipmates. The matter was finally resolved by the common council in debate, wherein it was decided that Grant should live but his ship should be sunk, as indeed it was. Both instances suggest that Kennedy's piracy was at least in part a raging rebellion against the powerlessness he had suffered as a working sailor.[5]

Sailing now with Bartholomew Roberts (after the death of Davis), Kennedy soon decided to separate. His opportunity came when Roberts took off after a prize, leaving Kennedy, as lieutenant, in charge of one of the ships, in which he promptly sailed away (in turn leaving Roberts with a certain aversion to Irishmen ever after). Kennedy was "now chosen Captain of the revolted Crew," even though he had small skill in navigation. (He was apparently "preferred to the Command merely for his Courage.") But the crew itself decided to disband "and every Man to shift for himself, as he could see Occasion." Kennedy ended up shipwrecked in Scotland, where he either spent his gold or was robbed of it, then shipped out to Ireland and eventually to London, although several of his gang got themselves captured and hanged in Edinburgh. He soon kept a bawdy house on Deptford Road and indulged in an occasional robbery on the side until one of the women of the house informed on him and got him committed to the Bridewell (a workhouse), where the mate of a ship he had plundered found him and had him committed to Marshalsea Prison on capital charges of piracy. He was convicted by a judge of the Court of Admiralty, whose symbolic silver oar lay on the table during the proceedings.[6]

Once in prison, Kennedy did all he could to save his own life, including snitching on his comrades. He presented a list of thirteen men to the authorities, but since he had no idea where many of them were, only one was taken up, and even he was subsequently reprieved. The rest were "not to be found." The sellout was to no avail, and to have done so may have taken its own toll: "After sentence [of death], he showed much less concern for life than is usual for persons in that condition. He was so much tired with the miseries and misfortunes which for some years before he had endured, that death appeared to him a thing rather desirable than frightful."[7]

When he heard that one of his fellow pirates, John Bradshaw—who had also gotten death—had his sentence commuted to convict transportation, Kennedy "expressed great satisfaction" and was happier than "if he himself had received mercy." He worried, *"should I be banished into America as he is, 'tis highly probable I might be tempted to my old way of life, and so instead of reforming, add to the number of my sins."* As he was carried by cart to his execution, trailing the silver oar of the Admiralty, the pirate who had shared in gold and silver plunder spoke these words to someone who accompanied him to the gallows: *"when we go to death, we have not wherewith to purchase a coffin to bury us."* He had come home: he was hanged at Execution Dock in Wapping, the neighborhood of his birth, on July 21, 1721. He was twenty-six years old.[8]

The last point to be made is that Kennedy loved stories; he loved to hear about Henry Avery and no doubt others and loved to tell tales of his own piracies. He "took a particular delight in relating what happened to him in [his piratical] expeditions, even after they had brought him to misery and confinement." Storytelling was a sailor's art, as noted by the writer who met with Kennedy and told his story in a chapbook hawked about the streets after his execution: "Men of that profession have usually good memories with respect, at least, to such matters" as the history of piracy.[9]

One of the stories he told was about self-government among the pirates. The writer of his life called it "that form of rule which these wretches set up, in imitation of the legal government, and of those regulations there made to supply the place of moral honesty." As Kennedy explained,

> They chose a captain from amongst themselves, who in effect held little more than that title, excepting in an engagement, when he commanded absolutely and without control. Most of them [the pirates] having suffered formerly from the ill-treatment of their officers, provided carefully against any such evil, now they had the choice in themselves. By their orders they provided especially against quarrels which might happen among themselves, and appointed certain punishments for anything that tended that way; for the due execution thereof they constituted other officers besides the captain, so very industrious were they to avoid putting too much power into the hands of one man.[10]

In the end, Walter Kennedy was not only a pickpocket, a housebreaker, and a proprietor of a whorehouse; not only a rebel full of courage and rage, solidarity and treachery; not only a force of destruction against the slave trade; but a seafaring storyteller, and one with ideas, even a political philosophy that was not, as we will see, an imitation of "the legal government" but rather a critique of it. To what extent and in what ways he was a typical pirate will become clear in this chapter as we explore the social origins of those who sailed under the black flag.

Who became a pirate after the War of Spanish Succession? Almost all who went "upon the account" had labored as merchant seamen, Royal Navy sailors, privateersmen, fishermen, or "Baymen" (sailors turned lumberjacks).[11] The vast majority came from captured merchantmen as volunteers, for reasons suggested by Samuel Johnson's observation that "no man will be a sailor who has contrivance enough to get himself into a jail; for being in a ship is being in jail with the chance of being drowned.... A man in jail has more room, better food, and commonly better company."[12] Many sailors, of course, had made the comparison themselves, waking up punch drunk or just plain drunk in the jails of the port cities or in the holds of outward-bound merchant ships. Johnson's point, however, was that the lot of the merchant seamen in the early eighteenth century was a difficult one. Sailors suffered cramped, claustrophobic quarters, "food" that was often as rotten as it was meager, and more. They experienced as a matter of course devastating disease, disabling accidents, shipwreck, and premature death. They faced discipline from their officers that was brutal at best and often murderous. And they got small return for their death-defying labors, for peacetime wages were low and fraud in payment was frequent. Seamen could expect little relief from the law, whose purpose in the eighteenth-century Atlantic was, according to Jesse Lemisch, "to assure a ready supply of cheap, docile labor." Merchant seamen also had to contend with impressment as practiced by the Royal Navy.[13]

Some pirates had served in the navy, where conditions aboard ship were no less harsh. Wages, especially during wartime, were lower than in the merchant service, and the quantity and quality of food aboard the ship, although sometimes better than what could be had in the merchant service, were consistently undermined by corrupt pursers and officers. Organizing cooperation and maintaining order among the huge number of maritime workers on naval vessels required violent discipline—replete with intentionally spectacular executions—that was considerably more severe than on merchant ships. Another consequence of the numbers of sailors crowded onto ill-ventilated naval ships was the omnipresence of disease, often of epidemic proportions.

In an irony pirates would have savored, one official reported that the navy had trouble fighting freebooters because the King's ships were "so much disabled by sickness, death, and desertion of their seamen."[14] In 1722 the Crown sent the *Weymouth* and the *Swallow* in search of a pirate convoy. Surgeon John Atkins, noting that merchant seamen were frequently pressed, underlined precisely what these sailors had to fear when he recorded that the "*Weymouth*, who brought out of *England* a Compliment [*sic*] of 240 Men," had "at the end of the Voyage 280 dead upon her Books."[15] Epidemics, consumption, and scurvy raged on royal ships, and the men were "caught in a machine from which there was no escape, bar desertion, incapacitation, or death." Robert Deal of Port Royal, Jamaica, was one of many who deserted naval vessels for the pirates. John Upton, an old salt who had spent twenty-eight years aboard a man-of-war, finally had had enough and in 1725 joined the crew of the pirate captain Joseph Cooper aboard the *Night Rambler*.[16]

Life was a little better on a privateering vessel; the food was superior, the pay was higher, the work shifts were shorter, and the power of the crew in decision making was greater. But privateers were not always happy ships. Some captains ran their ships like naval vessels, imposing rigid discipline and other unpopular measures that occasionally generated grievances, protests, and even outright mutinies. Woodes Rogers, gentleman captain of a hugely successful privateering voyage in 1708 and later the scourge of the pirates of the West Indies as royal governor of the Bahama Islands (with whom Kennedy sailed), clapped into irons a man named Peter Clark, who had wished himself "aboard a Pirate" and said that "he should be glad that an Enemy, who could over-power us, was a-long-side of us." One privateering crew, learning of a peace that happened to break out, "sett their Captain ashore and turned Pirate." John Atkins, the naval surgeon, spoke of the transition from privateer to pirate as going from "plundering for others, to do it for themselves."[17]

The fisheries of Newfoundland also served as recruiting

grounds for pirates in the early eighteenth century, explained Captain Charles Johnson. Vessels from the west of England (Topsham, Barnstaple, Bristol) "transport over a considerable Number of poor Fellows every Summer, whom they engage at Low Wages, and are by their Terms to pay for Passage back to *England.*" These men, because of "the Hardness of their Labour" and "the Chillness of the Nights," drank lots of "black strap" (made of rum, molasses, chowder, and beer), which was sold to them by the merchants at exorbitant rates. They inevitably fell into debt and were forced to indenture themselves; many of them ran away to join the pirates at the first opportunity. Richard Neal, a young Irishman without education and born in Cork, had been a fisherman but ended up becoming a fellow mutineer to Philip Roche in 1721. John Rose Archer, who had sailed with Blackbeard in 1718, tried to avoid the gallows by lying low, working in the Newfoundland fisheries. But in 1723, when John Phillips began to cruise the region under the black flag, Archer could not resist returning to what Kennedy called "his old way of life." The decision would, in turn, cost him his life.[18]

Some pirates had been "Baymen," or logwood cutters, a rugged occupation at the edge of the empire, in the Bay of Honduras or the Bay of Campeche, on the eastern and western sides of the Yucatán Peninsula. Both places were inhabited by mariners, renegades, and castaways who cut logwood in the mangrove swamps to sell to Jamaica merchants, who would in turn ship it to Europe for use as a dye in the textile industry. These people lived after the collectivist seafaring tradition of "one and all," holding all things "in common," sharing their provisions and especially their liquor. They were famous for their drinking bouts. They devised their own autonomous government and social rules, one of which prohibited capital punishment. When Spanish authorities attacked both logging settlements in retribution for piracies that had occurred up to 1717, they made the problem worse, for themselves and everyone else, since the men who were once employed, reported a royal official in Jamaica, "turn'd pirates and infested all our seas." Pirates such as Edward Low and George Blacketer came from this seafaring-gone-ashore milieu.[19]

Other pirates had been indentured servants, especially the fourteen-year variety, which meant that they had been transported to the colonies in punishment for crimes committed in England. Governor Nicholas Lawes of Jamaica complained to the Council of Trade and Plantations in 1718:

> Those people have been so farr, from altering their evil courses and way of living and becoming an advantage to us, that the greatest part of them are gone and have induced others to go with them a pyrating, and have inveglied and encouraged severall negroes to desart from their masters and go to the Spaniards in Cuba, the few that remains proves a wicked lazy and indolent people, so that I could heartily wish this country might be troubled wth. no more [of] them.

Most of these runaways had probably been sailors, and indeed this underlines the main point about the occupational background of those who went "a pyrating": they came overwhelmingly from seafaring employments. Most had been merchant seamen, many had been in the navy and/or privateering, some had been fishermen, baymen, or servants, and a few had been bargemen and turtlers. Piracy emphatically was not an option for most landlubbers, since sea robbers "entertain'd so contemptible a Notion of Landmen." Men who went "upon the account" were familiar with a single-sex community of work and the rigors of life—and death—at sea.[20]

There were two fundamental ways of becoming a pirate. The more spectacular but less common was Walter Kennedy's way, by mutiny, during which sailors boldly and collectively seized control of a merchant vessel, drew up articles, stitched together a Jolly Roger, and "declared War against all the World." At least thirty-one mutinies erupted on merchant ships during the 1710s and 1720s, many of them on vessels involved in the African slave trade. Roughly half of these crews moved into piracy. Phineas Bunce and Daniel Macarty organized a mutiny aboard a vessel in the Caribbean in 1718; it commenced when the crew began to sing "Did not you promise me, that you would marry me?" Other rebellious crews who turned pirate were led by Howell Davis (1718), George Lowther (1721), Philip Roche (1721), John Phillips (1723), John Gow (1725), and William Fly (1726), almost all of whom would subsequently be killed in action or hanged on the gallows. (George Lowther committed suicide.) The names of the leaders of several other mutinous crews are lost to us. Since there were about eighty pirate ships for the period 1716–26, it would seem that roughly one in five ships—and probably one in five pirates—got its start in shipboard insurrection, a revolution in miniature.[21]

Most men, it follows, became pirates the second way, by volunteering when their merchant vessels were taken. Colonel Benjamin Bennett wrote to the Council of Trade and Plantations in 1718, setting forth his worries about freebooters in the West Indies: "I fear they will soon multiply for so many are willing to joyn with them when taken." Governor Spotswood of Virginia feared the same thing: the numbers of pirates were growing even though "they will force no man into their service." The pirates with Thomas Cocklyn told captive William Snelgrave that when they took ships, they met with no resistance, "For the People were generally glad of an opportunity of entring with them." How this happened is illustrated by the case of a sailor named Samuel Fletcher, who "was always Grumbling when order'd to any Duty, and several times wished to God Almighty they might meet the Pyrates." Pirate captain Edward England's crew took nine vessels off the coast of Africa in the spring of 1719 and found 55 of the 143 seamen ready to sign their articles. Such desertion to piracy was common, especially between 1716 and 1722.[22]

The seizure of a merchant ship was followed by a moment of confrontational drama. The pirate quartermaster, who had led the boarding party, assembled and asked the seamen of the captured vessel who among them would serve under the death's head and black colors, and frequently, as suggested by the commentators above, several stepped forward to join up. But some men, as it happened, wanted to volunteer without actually volunteering—in other words, they wanted to go with the pirates, but at the same time they wanted to pretend that they were forced so that they would have an alibi should they ever be captured. When Bartholomew Roberts gathered together the crew of the prize vessel *Onslow* in 1721 and "asked who was willing to go, and who not, for he would force nobody," he found that many of the men "had a Petitioning Countenance," which caused him to cry, no doubt with a wry smile, "I must oblidge these Fellows with a Shew of fforce." Men like Peter Scudamore said he "wou'd go with all his Heart with these Pyrates if he cou'd avoid Signing their Articles." When William Phillips joined a pirate crew, he expressed his hope that someone "wou'd put him in the News Paper." If anyone did, it was to no avail, as Phillips was captured and hanged at Cape Coast Castle in 1722.[23]

Pirates always preferred volunteers, vigorous and enthusiastic ones at that, who would create social cohesion within the group, stronger self-defense, and ultimately greater success in plundering on the high seas. Sam Bellamy's crew "forced no Body to go with them, and said they would take no Body against their Wills." A witness testified in court that "it was the Custome among the Pyrates to force no prisoners, but those that remained with them were Voluntiers." One sailor reported that when Francis Spriggs asked him if he wanted to join the pirates and was refused, he "bid me to go to the Devil, for he would force no man." Several captains thus "did not press any body (nor indeed is it credible they would)." Yet there were instances when skilled workers were detained. One man was held "because he was a Carpenter and a Singleman," for his talents were essential to those who lived in a wooden world. This policy against forcing men, however, began to change in the early 1720s. As the number of seamen willing to join dwindled, pirates increasingly coerced crew members of captured vessels, seizing labor power by impressment like the Royal Navy's and likewise engendering deadly resistance. During the last couple of years of piracy, "forced men" led dramatic mutinies of their own against pirate captains such as John Phillips, who was beheaded in 1724, and William Fly, who was captured and subsequently hanged in Boston in 1726.[24]

How old were those who became pirates? The ages of 169 pirates who were active between 1716 and 1726 are known. The range was 14 to 50 years, the mean being 28.2 and the median 27; the 20–24 and the 25–29 age categories had the highest concentrations, with 57 and 39 men respectively. Almost three in five pirates were therefore in their twenties. Compared with merchant seamen more broadly in the first half of the seventeenth century, there were fewer teenagers and more men in their thirties among the pirates, but not many. The age distribution among the outlaws was similar to that of the larger community of labor, suggesting that piracy held roughly equal attraction for sailors of all ages.[25]

It is important to emphasize that a sailor or pirate in his late twenties was not, by the standards of his occupation, a young man. His was a dangerous job, as suggested earlier, with a high risk of death by disease, accident, or military action. A seafaring man of this age was already a man of the world—experienced, knowledgeable, and cosmopolitan. Almost all pirates had been working in a seafaring occupation, probably for several years, before making the decision "to go upon the account."

Although evidence is sketchy, most pirates seem not to have been bound to land and home by familial ties or obligations. Samuel Cole, the thirty-seven-year-old quartermaster on the *Fames' Revenge* with William Fly, left a wife and seven children when he was executed in 1726, but he was an exception. Wives and children were rarely mentioned in the records of trials of pirates, and pirate vessels, to forestall desertion, often would "take no Married Man." This was true of Edward Low and several other pirate leaders, who sought, as Kennedy explained, to provide "especially against quarrels which might happen among themselves." A few pirates used their families to plead for mercy when facing the gallows, but the infrequency of the bid supports the conclusion that most were not married.[26]

Finally, but not least important, pirates almost without exception came from the lowest social classes. Like the larger body of seafaring men of which they were a part, they were poor and had worked in the most proletarian of occupations. They were, as a royal official condescendingly observed, "desperate Rogues" who could have little hope in life ashore. Philip Roche, a sailor who led a mutiny and turned pirate in 1721, was "brought up to a seafaring life," as were numerous poor, often orphaned boys. Many of those who sailed in pirate ships were men of "no property."[27]

Indeed, the number of pirates in this generation who could be considered propertied was exceptionally small by any standard. Among them were two "gentlemen"—Stede Bonnet, who was considered by many to be insane, and Christopher Moody, whose "gentleman-like" demeanor caused his crew to remove him from his command. Two other captains, Edward England and Henry Jennings, were said to be educated, and the same would have been true of the handful of surgeons who sailed with the pirates. A few skilled workers—mates, carpenters, and coopers—who turned pirate might have had modest comforts in life, but the overwhelming majority of pirates were common seamen, men like Walter Kennedy who had much to gain and little to lose by turning pirate.

Where did these pirates come from? What were their geographic origins? The simplest answer is that we do not know. The occupations of these poor seafaring men scattered them to the seven seas, kept them always in motion from one port city to the next, and in the end caused most of them to die young; they left behind little or no property and few documents by their own hands. They were rolling stones who gathered no moss, and because they were always rolling, they are hard to "fix" in geographic terms.

And yet the authorities of the day tried, recording places beside the names of many of the pirates they captured. These places are known for 348 pirates who were active between 1716 and 1726. The problem is, we rarely know the pirate's actual relationship to the recorded place. Was it a place of birth? A place of ancestral connection? Was it a place where he or she grew up? Or was it rather the *home* port, the base from which the seafarer always shipped out, a community of family and friends and neighbors? Or was it merely the *last* port out of which the seaman had sailed, one of an endless series of sailor towns where he had collected his pay and spent it as "the lord of six weeks" before shipping out again? Or was it simply something made up on the spot to mislead the authorities and thereby protect loved ones from the ignominy of impending execution? It is likely that the places with which the authorities associated the pirates were all of these and more. We must therefore, for these reasons and others yet to be explored, treat this evidence with special caution.[28]

One thing is clear: many, if not most, of the pirates were of British descent (though we must bear in mind that Britishness was a new invention in their day and they probably did not think of themselves in such terms). To be more precise, the majority of the pirates were descended from people who had lived in England, Ireland, Scotland, and Wales. Almost half (47.4 percent) were connected specifically to England, and roughly a third of these to Greater London, the vortex of the empire, especially its seafaring neighborhoods, Wapping, Stepney, Shadwell, and Rotherhithe (though most had only London listed rather than a specific neighborhood). About a quarter of the English were linked to other major port cities—Bristol, Liverpool, Plymouth. The rest were attached to counties: Devonshire, Kent, Somersetshire, and Cornwall, sometimes with a provincial port such as Bideford or Falmouth designated, but more commonly without. Roughly one pirate in ten (9.8 percent) was in some manner Irish; one in fourteen (6.3 percent) was Scottish; and one in twenty-five (4.0 percent) was Welsh. Not surprisingly, they, too, often came from the ports: Dublin, Cork, Aberdeen, and Glasgow. The Welsh numbers are modest, but two of the most popular and successful freebooting captains of this generation, Howell Davis and Bartholomew Roberts, were Welsh.

About one-quarter of the pirates were broadly American— that is, associated with the West Indies or North America. A huge majority of the West Indians were linked to the two historic strongholds of piracy, the Bahama Islands and Jamaica, and a few were connected to smaller islands such as Barbados, Martinique, and Antigua. The North Americans were more widely dispersed, the greatest number coming from Massachusetts (mostly Boston) and a smattering from almost everywhere else, from Rhode Island south to New York, on to South Carolina (probably Charleston), and many places between them. Six Native Americans were also involved.

From this fragmentary evidence about geographic association, we may hazard a second generalization: pirates were for the most part formerly deep-sea sailors, the ones who had taken off from the port cities on long voyages to distant parts of the world. Wherever they got caught, most of them were a long way from home, whatever that may have meant.

The evidence on place speaks to one last issue: that some of the pirates were not English or British and indeed came from numerous parts of the world such as Holland, France, Portugal, Denmark, Belgium, Sweden, and several parts of Africa— Calabar, Sierra Leone, and Whydah. According to the documents produced largely by court scribes and other officials, these international connections represented 6.9 percent of the total, but this proportion is misleading. For some reason, record keepers simply did not pay much attention to the pirates from foreign lands. Fortunately we may correct the misimpression by looking at other evidence, which strongly and more accurately conveys the motley, multinational character of the pirate ship.

Governor Nicholas Lawes of Jamaica echoed the thoughts of royal officials everywhere when he called pirates a "banditti of all nations." Another Caribbean official agreed: they were composed of "all nations." Black Sam Bellamy's crew of 1717 was "a Mix't Multitude of all Country's," including British, French, Dutch, Spanish, Swedish, Native American, African American, and two dozen Africans who had been liberated from a slave ship. In the same year Captain Candler of HMS *Winchelsea* wrote to the Admiralty that pirates "are compounded of all Nations." The main mutineers aboard the *George Galley* in 1724 were an Englishman, a Welshman, an Irishman, two Scots, two Swedes, and a Dane, all of whom became pirates. Benjamin Evans's crew consisted of men of English, French, Irish, Spanish, and African descent. Pirate James Barrow illustrated the reality as he sat after supper "prophanely singing . . . Spanish and French Songs out of a Dutch prayer book." Governments often told pirates that "they have no country," and pirates agreed, as we saw in chapter 1. A colonial official reported to the Council of Trade and Plantations in 1697 that pirates "acknowledged no countrymen, that they had sold their country and were sure to be hanged if taken, and that they would take no quarter, but do all the mischief they could." And as a mutineer had muttered in 1699, "it signified nothing what part of the World a man liv'd in, so he Liv'd well." The mixture of nationalities reflected the global nature of seafaring work.[29]

Most fully hidden by the legal record keeping is the important place that hundreds of people of African descent found on pirate ships. Colonial officials often refused to give black pirates a trial, preferring to profit by selling them into slavery rather than hanging them, with a few notable exceptions. Several maritime men of color ended up "dancing to the four winds," like the mulatto who sailed with Black Bart Roberts and was hanged for it in

Virginia in 1720. Another "resolute Fellow, a Negroe" named Caesar, stood ready to blow up Blackbeard's ship in 1718 rather than submit to the Royal Navy; he too was hanged.[30]

Even though a substantial minority of pirates had worked in the slave trade and had therefore been part of the machinery of enslavement and transportation, and even though pirate ships occasionally captured (and sold) cargo that included slaves, Africans and African Americans both free and enslaved were numerous and active on board pirate vessels. Black crewmen made up part of the pirate vanguard, the most trusted and fearsome men designated to board prospective prizes. The boarding party of the *Morning Star* had "a Negro Cook doubly arm'd"; more than half of Edward Condent's boarding party on the *Dragon* was black.[31] In 1724 a "free negro" cook divided provisions equally so that the crew aboard Francis Spriggs's ship might live "very merrily." "Negroes and Molattoes" were present on almost every pirate ship, and only rarely did the many merchants and captains who commented on their presence call them slaves. Black pirates sailed with Captains Bellamy, Taylor, Williams, Harris, Winter, Shipton, Lyne, Skyrm, Roberts, Spriggs, Bonnet, Phillips, Baptist, Cooper, and others. In 1718, 60 of Blackbeard's crew of 100 were black, and Captain William Lewis boasted "40 able Negroe Sailors" among his crew of 80. In 1719 Oliver LaBouche's ship was "half *French*, half Negroes."[32] Black pirates were common enough to move one newspaper to report that an all-mulatto band of sea robbers was marauding the Caribbean, eating the hearts of captured white men![33] In London, meanwhile, the most successful theatrical event of the period was prevented from portraying the reality of black pirates, as the Lord Chamberlain refused to license *Polly*, John Gay's sequel to *The Beggar's Opera*, which had ended with Macheath about to be hanged for highway robbery. In *Polly* he was transported to the West Indies where he escaped the plantation, turned pirate, and, disguising himself as Morano, "a negro villain," became the principal leader of a gang of freebooters. Polly

Peachum dressed herself as a man seeking her hero and the pirates by saying, "Perhaps I may hear of him among the slaves of the next plantation."[34]

Some black pirates were free men, like the experienced "free Negro" seaman from Deptford who in 1721 led "a Mutiney that we had too many Officers, and that the work was too hard, and what not." Others were escaped slaves. In 1716 the slaves of Antigua had grown "very impudent and insulting," causing their masters to fear an insurrection. Historian Hugh Rankin writes that a substantial number of the unruly "went off to join those pirates who did not seem too concerned about color differences."[35] They were more concerned with who would make a committed pirate, and of course escaped slaves fitted the bill. Just before the events in Antigua, Virginia's rulers had worried about the connection between the "Ravage of Pyrates" and "an Insurrection of the Negroes." Soon after, Lieutenant Governor Benjamin Bennett of Bermuda expressed his worries about the "negro men" who had grown "soe very impudent and insulting of late that we have reason to suspect their riseing." He was also sure, moreover, that if pirates should attack, the slaves would not defend the island but would join the invaders. The sailors of color captured with the rest of Black Bart's crew in 1722 grew mutinous over the poor conditions and "thin Commons" they suffered at the hands of the Royal Navy, especially since many of them had lived long in the "pyratical Way." This meant, to them as to others, more food and greater freedom.[36]

Such material and cultural contacts were not uncommon. A gang of pirates settled in West Africa in the early 1720s, joining and intermixing with the Kru, who were known for their skill in things maritime (and, when enslaved, for their leadership of revolts in the New World). And, of course, for many years pirates had mixed with the native population of Madagascar, helping to produce "a dark Mulatto Race there." Cultural exchanges among European and African sailors and pirates were extensive, resulting, for example, in the well-known similarities of form between

African songs and sea shanties. In 1743 some seamen were court-martialed for singing a "negro song" in defiance of discipline. Mutineers also engaged in the same rites performed by slaves before a revolt. In 1731 a band of mutineers drank rum and gunpowder, and on another occasion a sailor signaled his rebellious intentions by "Drinking Water out of a Musket barrel." Piracy clearly did not operate according to the black codes enacted and enforced in Atlantic slave societies. Some slaves and free blacks found freedom aboard the pirate ship, which, apart from the maroon communities, was no easy thing to find in the pirates' main theater of operations, the Caribbean and the American South. Indeed, pirate ships themselves might be considered multiracial maroon communities, in which rebels used the high seas as others used the mountains and the jungles. The ship of pirate captain Thomas Cocklyn was named the *Maroon*, and pirates frequently called themselves "marooners."[37]

What motivated the motley crew to turn pirate? Why did they risk their necks to sail under the Jolly Roger? The motivations were various. Some were escaping bad situations at home. Captain William Snelgrave wrote of Simon Jones, one of his own seamen who had elected to join the pirates: "His circumstances were bad at home: Moreover, he had a Wife who he could not love; and for these Reasons he had entered with the Pirates, and signed their Articles." The bold woman pirate Anne Bonny went to sea to escape her father's stifling ways. Stede Bonnet was a propertied man from a ruling family in Barbados; he was said to be in flight from his wife. Many others were no doubt burdened by debt or being hunted for crime. But these were not the most common motivations.[38]

Traditional explanations of why people turned to piracy have emphasized greed, and there is certainly truth to this. Many who worked the pirate ship wanted money, which as dispossessed proletarians they desperately needed to live. But the struggle for money is more complex than simple greed, as pirates themselves made clear. Money meant simply getting a living, as pirate

Stephen Smith explained in a deferential letter to the governor of Jamaica in 1716. It meant subsistence for poor families as pirates explained to Colonel Bennett of Bermuda in 1718. It meant escaping the brutalities of life at sea "as long as they lived," as pirates explained to prisoner Joseph Hollett in 1721. They were now "Gentlemen of ffortune."[39]

Recent interpretations have concentrated on the social causes of piracy, emphasizing the working conditions on merchant and naval ships.[40] This is no recent discovery (although it seems to have been forgotten for two and half centuries). Such causes were known by 1716, when Atlantic piracy erupted on a massive scale. One who knew all of the causes was the anonymous author of the pamphlet *Piracy Destroy'd,* an "Officer of an East India Company Ship" who had conversed "with several of those that have been concerned in the late Piracies in the East Indies" in the 1690s. He believed that the causes of piracy were the "general depravation of Seamens manners, and their little or no sense of religion," but he also relayed the reasons pirates had given, all of which turned on the brutalities of work at sea: impressment, beatings, poor food, and the disabling and deadly effects of these on themselves and their families. Some pirates cited "being drubb'd and beaten unmercifully by their Officers." "Such as had Sail'd in Merchants Ships," the officer continued, "complain'd of the barbarity of their Commanders, especially in depriving them of their sustenance, not allowing them half of what was necessary to preserve their Bodies in health, they frequently suffering extream thirst by denying them Water, notwithstanding many Tuns [casks] left when they came into Port." Admiral Edward Vernon agreed in 1720 that many sailors turned pirate because merchant shipowners did not provide adequate victuals for their crews.[41]

The knowledgeable officer pointed toward, but in the end did not specify, the essential point: the thirst, hunger, wounds from lashings, and premature death that these helped to engender were central to deep-sea faring in this period, and even more central to the decision to go "upon the account." Seafaring was one of the most dangerous occupations of a dangerous occupational age, with causes both natural and man-made. A common saying among sailors was, "There was the pox above-board, the plague between decks, hell in the forecastle, and the devil at the helm." We do not have a broad and reliable statistical picture of the mortality of deep-sea sailors in this period, but we do know that in the deadly African slave trade the rates for seamen were equal to or higher than those of the formally enslaved. And we know that sailors who had worked in the slave trade made up a substantial minority of pirates. Moreover, in this period dangers of the sailors' workplace produced an endless array of mutilated bodies, evident in every port city as sailors lame and crippled begged hither and yon.[42]

Many sought to escape the dreadful working conditions prevailing between 1716 and 1726. John Phillips ranted and raved against captured merchant John Wingfield; he "abused him calling him a Super Cargo Son of a B—h that he starved the Men, and that it was such Dogs as he as put men on Pyrating." John Jessop preferred the "jovial Life" among the pirates, "swearing 'twas better living among them than at Cape Coast Castle," the infamous and deadly British slave-trading fortress in West Africa. On the gallows of Providence in the Bahama Islands, pirate Daniel Macarty "began to rattle, and talk [with other pirates] with Great Pleasure, and much boasting of their former Exploits when they had been Pyrates, crying a Pyrate's Life to be the only one for a Man of any Spirit." Enslaved Africans, as we have seen, sought to escape slavery; fishermen sought to escape peonage; transported felons sought to escape long terms of servitude; and sailors sought to escape impressment or deadly conditions aboard ship.[43]

Some mariners cast their lot with pirates in order to escape any sort of work at all. A transatlantic merchant ship of 250 tons, which would have had a working crew of 15 to 18 "hands," would, if taken and refitted by pirates, have been manned by 80 to 90 men, each of whom, accordingly, had much less work to do. As

pirate Joseph Mansfield said in 1722, "the love of Drink and a
Lazy Life" were "stronger Motives with him than Gold."
Admiral Vernon knew of such motives and sought to address
them in his own way. From Jamaica jails he took sixteen sus-
pected pirates aboard his man-of-war and immediately assigned
them to backbreaking work at the pump, thinking "it might be
of service to carry them out of the way of falling into their old
Courses," and, moreover, "might be a Means to learn them ...
Working," which "they turned Rogues to avoid." Woodes
Rogers, governor of the Bahamas and another man who knew
pirates well, noted that when it came to work, "they mortally hate
it." Samuel Buck knew the pirate community in the Bahamas
before Rogers arrived and echoed the governor's words: "working does not agree with them."[44]

In the end, Walter Kennedy was a typical pirate in several key
respects. He was born into poverty in a port city; he was experienced in the rough conditions of life at sea, in both the navy and
the merchant service; he was apparently unmarried; and he was
in his mid-twenties. These traits served as bases of unity with
others when, in search of something better, he decided to become
a pirate. And yet he, like the others, was not merely escaping oppressive circumstances. He was escaping *to* something new, a
different reality, something alluring about which he had heard
tales in his youth.

Chapter Four

"THE NEW GOVERNMENT
OF THE SHIP"

BARNABY SLUSH, A "SEA-COOK," knew sailors; he
knew pirates; and he knew why the one became the other. This
sage but anonymous commentator on life at sea in the early eighteenth century explained that those who risked their lives to sail
under the Jolly Roger were motivated by more than greed. They
sought to live in a new social order, under different governing
assumptions.

> Pyrates and Buccaneers, are Princes to [Seamen], for there, as none
> are exempt from the General Toil and Danger; so if the Chief have
> a Supream Share beyond his Comrades, 'tis because he's always the
> Leading Man in e'ry daring Enterprize; and yet as bold as he is in
> all other attempts, he dares not offer to infringe the common laws of
> Equity; but every Associate has his due Quota . . . thus these Hostes
> Humani Generis as great robbers as they are to all besides, are pre-
> cisely just among themselves; without which they could no more
> Subsist than a Structure without a Foundation.[1]

Those demonized by the rulers of society as the "common enemies of mankind," he suggested, were heroes to the common
sailor. One major reason was how the outlaws organized their
ships, which attracted many seamen. How did poor, motley, and
single seafaring workers from many parts of the world equalize
"the General Toil and Danger"? How did the "Chief" pirate lead
in "e'ry daring Enterprize"? How did the comrades divide their
shares? How did "every Associate" get his "due Quota"? What
were "the common laws of Equity," and how did pirates imple-
ment them? How did they manage to be "precisely just among

themselves"? What did justice mean to those whom the law sought to "bring to justice" by hanging?

This chapter explores these questions within a larger social and cultural history of the pirate ship, focusing on its social organization and the relations among the people who sailed it. It argues that piracy, for the most part, represented a way of life voluntarily chosen by large numbers of men who directly challenged the ways of the society from which they excepted themselves. Beneath the Jolly Roger, "the banner of King Death," and far beyond the reach of traditional authority, a new social order took shape once pirates had, as Walter Kennedy put it, "the choice in themselves."[2]

The seafaring experience of work, class, and power described in the previous chapters had a vital bearing on the ways pirates organized their daily activities. Contemporaries who claimed that pirates had "no regular command among them" mistook a different social order—different from the ordering of merchant, naval, and privateering vessels—for disorder. This new social order, articulated in the organization of the pirate ship, was conceived and deliberately constructed by the pirates themselves. Its hallmark was a rough, improvised, but effective egalitarianism that placed authority in the collective hands of the crew, which is to say that the core values of the broader culture of the common sailor were institutionalized aboard the pirate ship. It was a world turned upside down, as we will see in examining how pirates made decisions, how they designed and selected their leaders, and how they organized the distribution of plunder, food, and discipline—how, in short, they created and perpetuated their culture. They—and all of their formidable adversaries—were conscious that pirates had created "a new government of the ship."[3]

If the social order of the pirate ship represented something new in the early eighteenth century, it was nonetheless a long time in formation. Piracy itself was ancient and had changed over time. In the British Atlantic, piracy had long served the needs of the state and the merchant community. But there was a long-term tendency for the control of piracy to devolve from the top of society to the bottom, from the highest functionaries of the state (late sixteenth century), to big merchants (early seventeenth century), to smaller, usually colonial merchants (late seventeenth century), and finally to the common men of the deep (early eighteenth century). When this devolution reached bottom, when seamen—as pirates—organized a social world apart from the dictates of mercantile and imperial authority and used it to attack merchants' property (as they had begun to do in the 1690s), then those who controlled the state resorted to massive violence, both military (the navy) and penal (the gallows), to eradicate piracy, as we will see in chapters 7 and 8.[4]

It took a long time for seamen to obtain autonomous control of the ship and to organize its miniature society as they wanted. The struggles that sailors waged in revolutionary England in the 1640s and 1650s over subsistence, wages, and rights and against impressment and violent discipline took a new, more independent form among the buccaneers in America. Even as buccaneering benefited the upper classes of England, France, and the Netherlands in their New World struggles against their common enemy, Spain, ordinary seamen were building a tradition of their own, which at the time was called the Jamaica Discipline or the Law of the Privateers. The tradition, which the authorities considered the antithesis of discipline and law, boasted a distinctive conception of justice and a class hostility to shipmasters, owners, and gentlemen adventurers. It also featured democratic controls on authority and provision for the injured.[5] In fashioning their own social order, buccaneers drew on the peasant utopia called the Land of Cockaygne, where work had been abolished, property redistributed, social distinctions leveled, health restored, and food made abundant. They also drew on international maritime custom, in which ancient and medieval seafarers divided their money and goods into shares, consulted collectively and democratically on matters of the moment, and elected consuls to adjudicate differences between captain and crew.[6]

{ 63 }

The early makers of the tradition were what one English official in the Caribbean called "the outcasts of all nations"—convicts, prostitutes, debtors, vagabonds, escaped slaves and indentured servants, religious radicals, and political prisoners, all of whom had migrated or been exiled to the new settlements "beyond the line." Another royal administrator explained that the buccaneers were former servants and "all men of unfortunate and desperate condition." Many French buccaneers, like Alexander Exquemelin, had been indentured servants and before that, textile workers and day laborers. Most of the buccaneers were English or French, but Dutch, Irish, Scottish, Scandinavian, Native American, and African men also joined up, often after they had, in one way or another, escaped the brutalities of the Caribbean's nascent plantation system.[7]

These workers drifted to uninhabited islands, where they formed maroon communities. Their autonomous settlements were multiethnic and organized around hunting and gathering—they hunted wild cattle and pigs and gathered the king of Spain's gold. These communities combined the experiences of peasant rebels, demobilized soldiers, dispossessed smallholders, unemployed workers, and others from several nations and cultures, including the Carib, Cuna, and Moskito Indians.[8] One of the most potent memories and experiences that underlay buccaneer culture, writes Christopher Hill, was the English Revolution: "A surprising number of English radicals emigrated to the West Indies either just before or just after 1660," including Ranters, Quakers, Familists, Anabaptists, radical soldiers, and others who "carried with them the ideas which had originated in revolutionary England." A number of buccaneers hunted and gathered while dressed in the "faded red coats of the New Model Army." One was "a stout grey-headed" and "merry hearted old Man," aged eighty-four, "who had served under Oliver in the time of the Irish Rebellion; after which he was at Jamaica, and had followed Privateering ever since." In the New World such veterans insisted on the democratic election of their officers just as they had done in a revolutionary army on the other side of the Atlantic. Another source of buccaneering culture, according to J. S. Bromley, was a wave of peasant revolts that shook France in the 1630s. Many French freebooters came, as *engagés*, "from areas affected by peasant risings against the royal *fisc* and the proliferation of crown agents." Protesters "had shown a capacity for self-organization, the constitution of 'communes,' election of deputies and promulgation of *Ordonnances*," all in the name of the "Commun peuple." Such experiences, once carried to the Americas, shaped the lifeways among the buccaneering "Brethren of the Coast."[9]

The early experiences were passed on to later generations of sailors and pirates by the hearty souls who survived the odds against longevity in seafaring work. When a privateering captain took on board four seasoned buccaneers in 1689, he designated them "to be a mess by themselves, but the advantage of their conversation and intelligence obliged him afterward to disperse them amongst the Shipps Company." Some of the old-timers served on Jamaican privateers during the War of Spanish Succession, then took part in the new piracies after the Treaty of Utrecht. The Jamaica Discipline and the exploits it made possible also lived on in folktale, song, ballad, and popular memory, as we saw in the case of Walter Kennedy, not to mention the popular published (and frequently translated) accounts of Alexander Exquemelin, Père Jean-Baptiste Labat, and others who knew life among the buccaneers firsthand.[10] Therefore when sailors encountered the deadly conditions of life at sea in the late seventeenth and early eighteenth centuries, they had an alternative social order within living memory.

The codes of the buccaneers evolved into the articles of the later pirates, among whom a striking uniformity of rules and customs

prevailed. Each ship functioned under the terms of these com-
pacts, drawn up at the beginning of a voyage or upon the election
of a new captain and agreed to by the crew. By these written
agreements, crews allocated authority, distributed plunder, food,
and other resources, and enforced discipline.[11] These arrangements made the captain the creature of his crew, or, as Captain
Charles Johnson put it, "They permit him to be Captain, on
Condition, that they may be Captain over him."[12]

Demanding someone both bold of temper and skilled in navigation, the men elected their leader. They wanted leadership by
example, not leadership by ascribed status and hierarchy. They
therefore gave the captain few privileges; he "or any other Officer
is allowed no more [food] than another man, nay, the Captain
cannot keep his Cabbin to himself."[13] Some pirates "messed with
the Captain, but withal no Body look'd on it, as a Mark of Favour,
or Distinction, for every one came and eat and drank with him
at their Humour." A merchant captain held captive by pirates
noted with displeasure that crew members slept on the ship
wherever they pleased, "the Captain himself not being allowed a
Bed." Pirates took "the liberty of ranging all over the ship," a
practice called "laying rough." The determined reorganization of
space and privilege aboard the ship was crucial to the remaking
of maritime social relations.[14]

The crew granted the captain unquestioned authority "in
fighting, *chasing*, or *being chased*," but "in all other Matters whatsoever" he was "governed by a Majority."[15] A scandalized merchant captain noted, "The Captain seems to have no Manner of
Command, but in time of Chace or Engaging, then [he] is absolute." As the majority elected, so did it depose. Captains
were snatched from their positions for cowardice, cruelty, or
refusing "to take and plunder English Vessels."[16] One captain
incurred the class-conscious wrath of his crew for being too
"Gentleman-like."[17] Occasionally, a despotic captain was summarily executed. Recall Walter Kennedy's comment that most
sea robbers, "having suffered formerly from the ill-treatment of
their officers, provided carefully against any such evil" once they

arranged their own command. The democratic selection of officers stood in stark, telling contrast to the near-dictatorial arrangement of command in the merchant service and Royal Navy.[18]

To prevent the misuse of authority, pirates elected an officer called the quartermaster, whose powers counterbalanced those of the captain. William Snelgrave explained that the quartermaster "has the general Inspection of all Affairs, and often controuls the Captain's Orders: This Person is also to be the first Man in boarding any Ship they shall attack; or go in the Boat in any desperate Enterprize." Another prisoner, Captain Richard Hawkins, called the quartermaster the "chief Director" of the pirate ship. Captain Charles Johnson wrote, "The Quarter-Master's Opinion is like the Mufti's among the *Turks;* the Captain can undertake nothing which the Quarter-Master does not approve. We may say, the Quarter-Master is an humble Imitation of the *Roman* Tribune of the People; he speaks for, and looks after the Interest of the Crew." Johnson also called the quartermaster a "civil Magistrate" and a "prime minister." Like a mufti, the quartermaster was the keeper of pirate tradition, the one who issued final judgments about cultural practice. Like a tribune (originally, the leader of a tribe) in ancient Rome, he protected the people from the powerful, the plebeians from the patricians. The quartermaster, who was considered not an officer in the merchant service but rather just a "smart" (that is, knowledgeable, experienced) seaman, was elevated among the pirates to a supremely valued position of trust, authority, and power.[19]

One of the quartermaster's main purposes was to prevent the galling and divisive use of privilege and preferment that characterized the distribution of "the necessaries of life" in other maritime occupations. He dispensed food among the crew equally and fairly, an especially important practice when provisions were scarce and the crew on short allowance. "Then they put all under the care of their Quarter-master, who discharges all things with an Equality to them all, every Man and Boy faring alike," wrote seaman Clement Downing.[20] As the most trusted man on board the ship, the quartermaster was placed in charge of all booty, from its initial capture, to its transit and storage aboard the pirate ship, to its disbursement to the crew. This responsibility began with the selection and organization of the boarding party that would attack a prospective prize or board a vessel that had already surrendered. Since members of the boarding party got special privileges—a choice of the best weapon on board (usually a pistol) or a new shift of clothes—the men sometimes "tangled among themselves" for the right to go aboard. The quartermaster therefore had to regulate access in the fairest way possible. On some ships the quartermasters kept "watchbills," or lists, so as to give everyone an equal chance to board prize vessels. On others they simply called out, "Who will go on board?" and selected the party from among the volunteers; newcomers to the crew were usually excluded. At times the volunteers were so numerous that they almost sank the boats.[21]

Once on board, the quartermaster took charge of the prize vessel, assembling the sailors and asking them, as we will see, how their captain treated them. He would also use the occasion to ask the sailors who among them wished to join the pirate ship, and he usually got several volunteers. He then toured the prize vessel, looking over the cargo, deciding "what he thinks fit for the Company's use," and directing its movement from one ship to the other. Back aboard his own ship, he "kept a book" in order to account properly and fairly for everyone's share. Sam Bellamy's quartermaster, who oversaw £20,000 to £30,000 worth of gold and silver, "declared to the company, that if any man wanted Money he might have it." Peter Hooff testified that aboard the *Whydah*, "Their money was kept in Chests between Decks without any Guard, but none was to take any without the Quarter Masters leave." On another ship loot was kept in an "iron bound Chest which was called the Company's Chest." The quartermaster was the keeper of "the common Chest."[22]

The use of the quartermaster to contain authority within a

dual and representative executive was a distinctive feature of social organization among pirates, and one that influenced the formation of new ships. The quartermaster, who was part tribune, part mediator, part treasurer, and part keeper of the peace on one ship, often became the captain of a new one when a prize vessel was taken and converted because the original vessel was overcrowded or divided by discord. Calico Jack Rackam, Paul Williams, and several other pirate captains had been quartermasters first and had thereby gained the trust—and votes—of their crews. In this way the limits pirates placed on authority were institutionalized and transmitted from ship to ship.[23]

And yet neither the captain nor the quartermaster represented the highest authority on the pirate ship. That honor belonged to the common council, which met regularly and included every man from captain to foremast man. The decisions that had the greatest bearing on the welfare of the crew were taken up in open meetings that featured lively, even tumultuous debate. In making the crew sovereign, pirates drew on an ancient maritime custom that had lapsed by 1700, in which the master of a merchant vessel consulted his entire crew (who were often part owners of the cargo) in making crucial decisions. Freebooters also knew of the naval tradition—the council of war—in which the top officers in a ship or fleet met to plan strategy, and they democratized the naval custom. The floating town meeting acknowledged the truth of the old proverb "We are all in this boat together."[24]

The main purpose of the council, as suggested earlier, was to elect officers, especially the captain and quartermaster and lesser officers as well, particularly if a crew had more than the minimum number of skilled workers such as carpenters. One crew carried the logic so far as to elect a boatswain's mate! The council also determined such matters as where the best prizes could be taken and how any disruptive dissension was to be resolved. When Edward England proposed that he and his consort ship attack Portuguese Goa on the western coast of India, the men

gathered in council and debated the matter, but "they could not
agree on it, so proceeded to the southward." What happened
with England and his crew was not uncommon, for rank-and-
file pirates frequently carried the day against the wishes and judgments of their officers. In one instance Captains Sam Bellamy
and Paul Williams were "for giving [merchant captain Samuel]
Beer his Sloop again after they had took out her Loading, but the
Ships Crew ordered her to be sunk." The same thing happened
to Edward Low and Francis Spriggs, who found themselves
"overpower'd by Votes." Pirates also voted on punishments to be
doled out to those who violated the articles, and on the requests
of forced men and prisoners to be released, sometimes granting
their requests, sometimes denying them.[25]

The decisions the council made were sacrosanct. Even the
boldest captain dared not challenge its power. Indeed, councils
removed a number of captains and other officers from their positions. Thomas Anstis lost his position as captain; he was, as the
pirates put it, "turn'd before the Mast," that is, made a common
seaman on the ship he had once commanded. Charles Vane was
labeled a coward by his crew and removed from his captaincy.
Captain Charles Martel's company deposed him on account of
his cruelty in the treatment of crew and captives and chose a
"more righteous" man in his place. A majority of Bartholomew
Roberts's crew thought that David Simpson, an "old pirate," had
grown vicious as quartermaster; he was "turn'd out by them."
Shipboard democracy, especially to those who had labored long
and hard in a totalitarian work environment, could be intoxicat-
ing. Some crews continually used the council, "carrying every
thing by a majority of votes"; others set up the council as a court.
They loved to vote, claimed a captured captain, "all the Pyrates[']
Affairs being carried by that." Indeed, there was "so little
Government and Subordination" among pirates that "they are,
on Occasion, all Captains, all Leaders." Naval captain Humphrey Orme, who captured and interrogated a gang of pirates in
1723, summed up the situation succinctly: "the enjoyment of

posts aboard them [pirate ships] are very precarious, depending wholly upon the will and pleasure of the crew."[26]

The distribution of plunder was regulated explicitly by the ship's articles, which allocated booty according to a crewman's skills and duties. Pirates used the precapitalist share system to apportion their take. The captain and the quartermaster received between one and a half and two shares; gunners, boatswains, mates, carpenters, and doctors, one and a quarter or one and a half; all the others got one share each.[27] This pay system represented a radical departure from the practices in the merchant service, Royal Navy, and privateering. It leveled an elaborate hierarchy of pay ranks and decisively reduced the disparity between the top and the bottom of the scale. Indeed, this must have been one of the most egalitarian plans for the disposition of resources to be found anywhere in the early eighteenth century. If (as Philip Gosse, a noted historian of piracy, suggested) "the pick of all seamen were pirates," the equitable distribution of plunder and the conception of partnership may be understood as the work of men who valued and respected the skills of their comrades. By expropriating a merchant ship (after a mutiny or a capture), pirates seized the means of maritime production and declared it to be the common property of those who did its work. They abolished the wage relation central to the process of capitalist accumulation. So rather than work for wages using the tools and machine (the ship) owned by a merchant capitalist, pirates commanded the ship as their own property and shared equally in the risks of their common adventure.[28]

The articles, or in some cases pirate customs, carefully regulated the distribution of food and drink aboard ship, for these very items had, for many, figured crucially in the decision to "go upon the account" in the first place. A mutinous sailor aboard the *George Galley* in 1724 responded to his captain's orders to furl the mizzen top by saying "in a surly Tone, and with a kind of Disdain, So as we Eat so shall we work." Other mutineers simply insisted that "it was not their business to starve," and that if a captain was making it so, hanging could be little worse. It was on old joke among underfed, angry sailors that should mutiny fail, the weight of their bodies would not be enough to hang them.[29]

Sailors, as pirates, changed all this. Those who had long suffered short or rotten provisions in other maritime employments ate and drank "in a wanton and riotous Way," which was indeed their custom. They conducted so much business "over a Large Bowl of Punch" that sobriety sometimes brought "a Man under a Suspicion of being in a Plot against the Commonwealth." Shipmates ribbed an always-sober man named Thomas Wills by nicknaming him "Presbyterian." The very first item in Bartholomew Roberts's articles guaranteed every man "a Vote in Affairs of Moment" and "equal Title" to "fresh provisions" and "strong Liquors," showing how political and economic democracy might be linked. For one man (and probably a great many more) who joined the pirates, drink was more important than the wealth he might gain. Most would have agreed with the motto *"No Adventures to be made without Belly-Timber."*[30]

Not surprisingly, many observers of pirate life noted the carnivalesque quality of pirate occasions—the eating, drinking, fiddling, dancing, and merriment—and some considered such "infinite Disorders" inimical to good discipline at sea. They had a point; shipboard life did sometimes get out of control, but then again that *was* the point, for pirates were under no one's control but their own. Captain Snelgrave commented on the ferocious ways in which the pirates with Howell Davis took food and drink from a prize vessel. They "made such Waste and Destruction" during their pillage that Snelgrave was sure that a more "numerous set of such Villains would in a short time, have ruined a great City." Using winches and tackle, they hoisted from belowdecks "a great many half Hogsheads of *Claret*, and *French Brandy*." They promptly "knock'd their Heads out, and dipp'd Canns and Bowls into them to drink out of." As soon as these casks were empty, they hoisted up more. Soon they were throwing "full Buckets" of claret and brandy on each other, and at the end of the day they "washed the Decks with what remained in the Casks." They were no more restrained in their handling of bottled liquor. They "would not give themselves the trouble of drawing the cork out, but nick'd the Bottles, as they called it, that is struck their necks off with a Cutlace; by which means one in three was generally broke." In short, "they made such havock" of the bottled liquor that "in a few days they had not one Bottle left." Something similar went on among Edward England's crew, who kept Christmas "in a most riotous manner" for three days, destroying about two-thirds of their fresh provisions. Such wastefulness no doubt led to greetings like the one reported between pirates and Captain John Brett on a recently captured prize vessel in June 1716: the outlaws "damn'd the Depnt. and bid him bring his Liquor onboard."[31]

Pirates thus made merry. Indeed, "merry" is the word most commonly used to describe the mood and spirit of life aboard the pirate ship. This was inadvertently made clear in testimony given in the 1718 trials of Stede Bonnet and his men in Charleston, South Carolina. As James Killing fingered various pirates for execution, he testified that these men had tried to cheer him up after his capture. "They asked me [why] I would not come and eat along with them?" Killing, upset, had replied, "I told them I had but little stomach to eat." They would not give up. "They asked me, why I looked so melancholy?" Killing answered, "I told them I looked as well as I could." They then turned their attention from changing his mood to changing their own: "They asked me what Liquor I had on board? I told them some rum and sugar." The pirates fetched these items, made bowls of punch, drank toasts, and "sung a song or two." Captain Peter Manwaring, who for ten weeks was a prisoner among Bonnet's crew, confirmed the picture conveyed by the morose Killing. "They were civil to me, very civil," testified Manwaring. They "were all very brisk and merry; and had all Things plentiful, and were

a-making Punch and drinking." Another merchant captain recalled that the crew of Captain Francis Spriggs drank hot punch
every morning, and that "They live merrily all Day; at Meals
the Quarter-Master overlooks the Cook, to see the Provisions
equally distributed to each Mess." When a knowledgeable but
initially reluctant seaman finally decided to sign Spriggs's articles, huzzahs filled the air, cannon boomed, and a day was spent
in "boysterous Mirth, roaring and drinking of Healths."[32]

The merriness of the pirate ship had its downside. The endless drinking easily led to fights, which in turn sometimes became brawls engulfing the entire ship. Worse, drunkenness
could lead to disaster. Sam Bellamy's crew "regaled themselves so
liberally with Madera that they all got drunk and run their vessel on shoar." Nor did prolonged merriness make for battle readiness. For example, when the time came for engagement with
HMS *Swallow*, numerous men aboard Bartholomew Roberts's
ship were drunk. One of these was Joseph Mansfield, who "came
up [on deck] vapouring with his Cutlash" after his own vessel had
already struck her colors and surrendered. He wanted to know
"who would go on board the Prize; and it was some Time before
they could perswade him into the Truth of their Condition."[33]

It is astonishing to think that in devising their shipboard social order pirates anticipated a modern idea that many consider
one of the most humane of our times: creating their own social
security system. The popular image of the pirate as a man with a
patched eye, a peg leg, and a hook for a hand is not wholly accurate, but it speaks an essential truth: sailoring was a dangerous
line of work, destructive to the human body. Pirates therefore addressed the issues of health, safety, and security in their articles,
making it a point to allocate a portion of all booty to a "common
fund" to provide for men who had sustained injury of lasting
effect, whether the loss of eyesight or a limb. Pirate Jeremiah
Huggins claimed that he had been given 14 gold pistoles, 7½
ounces of gold dust, 82 pieces of eight, and 17 ounces of silver bul-
lion "by reason of his being wounded among them." Moreover,

those who suffered accidents and the resulting disabilities did not face discrimination aboard the pirate ship. Indeed, the one-armed John Fenn became a captain, as did John Taylor, who was "lame of his Hands." By guaranteeing food and drink and creating a sort of welfare system, pirates attempted to protect their health, enhance recruitment, and promote loyalty within the group.[34] One of the most dramatic acts undertaken by pirates was Blackbeard's blockade of Charleston Harbor in the fall of 1718. The reason for the action that brought trade to a standstill was that the pirates needed medicines to treat their sick.[35]

Another area of social life in which pirates appear modern is their sense of sexual liberty, which their articles did little to regulate. Seventeenth-century buccaneers had practiced *matelotage*, a relationship of shared property and mutual obligation that existed between two men, or in some instances, between a man and a youth. Such practices reflected personal choice but also the skewed sex ratio of the Caribbean, where women were scarce. Only two crews of early-eighteenth-century pirates were known to have included anything about sexual relations in their articles. One was a prohibition enacted by the crew of Bartholomew Roberts around 1720: "No Boy or Woman to be allowed amongst them." The second, established by the pirates with John Phillips in 1723, outlawed "meddling" with a "prudent Woman" without her consent. None of the articles mentioned anything about sexual relations among men or about sodomy, suggesting that pirates were free to do as they liked. It is, however, too much to state, as historian B. R. Burg has done, that pirates organized themselves as a "sodomitical society." For as the literary historian Hans Turley has written, "The evidence for pirate sodomy is so sparse as to be almost non-existent." And yet there are suggestive shards. In July 1723, during the trial of thirty-six freebooters in Newport, Rhode Island, John Wilson testified that pirate Thomas Powell had said to him, "I wish you and I were both ashore here stark naked." In the sermon given before Powell and twenty-five others were hanged, Cotton Mather called attention to "the abominable Sin of Uncleanness," a phrase that suggested sex with prostitutes or other men. In a homosocial and hyper- {75} masculine world, one that valued strength, stamina, toughness, courage, and aggressiveness, the choice was for a sexual liberty that transgressed the polite standards of the day.[36]

The articles also regulated discipline aboard ship, though "discipline" is perhaps a misnomer for a system of rules that left large ranges of behavior uncontrolled. Less arbitrary than that of the merchant service and less codified than that of the navy, discipline among pirates always depended on a collective sense of transgression. Many misdeeds were accorded "what Punishment the Captain and Majority of the Company shall think fit," and it is noteworthy that pirates did not often resort to the whip. Their discipline, if no less severe in certain cases, was generally tolerant of behavior that provoked punishment in other maritime occupations.[37]

Three major methods of discipline were employed, all conditioned by the fact that pirate ships were crowded; an average crew numbered nearly eighty on a 250-ton vessel. The articles of Bartholomew Roberts's ship revealed one tactic for maintaining order: "No striking one another on board, but every Man's Quarrels to be ended on Shore at Sword and Pistol." The antagonists were to fight a duel with pistols, but if both missed their first shots, they would then seize swords, and the first to draw blood would be declared the victor. By taking such conflicts off the ship (and symbolically off the sea), pirates promoted harmony in the crowded quarters belowdecks.[38]

The ideal of harmony was also reflected when pirates made a crew member the "Governor of an Island." Men who were incorrigibly disruptive or who transgressed important rules were marooned. For defrauding his mates by taking more than a proper share of plunder, for deserting or malingering during battle, for keeping secrets from the crew, or for stealing, a pirate risked being deposited "where he was sure to encounter Hardships."[39]

The ultimate method of maintaining order was execution. This penalty could be imposed for bringing on board "a Boy or a Woman" or for meddling with a "prudent Woman" on a prize ship, and in extreme cases for desertion if it was believed that by fleeing, a pirate had put the entire company in danger. Such would appear to have been the case when in 1722 Bartholomew Roberts's crew executed two crew members for desertion. Each man was allowed to choose his own executioner, was then tied to the mainmast, and was shot. On another occasion, a deserter who was recaptured was given two lashes by each member of the crew. In the end, execution was most commonly invoked to punish a captain who had abused his authority.[40]

Crewmen also intervened against their leaders in lesser, but equally telling ways. In 1719 pirate captains Howell Davis, Oliver LaBouche, and Thomas Cocklyn designed one evening to go ashore to visit "the *Negroe-Ladies*" in Sierra Leone. Wanting to look their best, they took from the store of plundered goods some fancily embroidered waistcoats. But they did not have permission to do this from the quartermaster, whose job it was to keep track of all such items in the "common Chest." When the crew learned what the captains had done, they were outraged. They immediately confiscated the clothes and put them back in the chest, insisting that they would be sold at the mast, by auction, to the highest bidder. As they explained to William Snelgrave, "If they suffered such things, the Captains would for the future assume a Power, to take whatever they liked for themselves." In this instance as in all others, whether the infraction was large or small, the crew declared itself to be sovereign. Captain Richard Hawkins spoke of the essential point about discipline: "If anyone commits an Offense, he is try'd by the whole Company." By the articles of a pirate ship, even a sea cook could govern.[41]

Some crews attempted to circumvent disciplinary problems by taking "no Body against their Wills."[42] By the same logic, they would keep no unwilling person. The 1718 confession of pirate Edward Davis indicates that oaths of honor were used to cement the loyalty of new members: "at first the old Pirates were a little shy of the new ones, ... yet in a short time the *New Men* being sworn to be faithful, and not to cheat the Company to the Value of a *Piece of Eight*, they all consulted and acted together with great unanimity, and no distinction was made between *Old* and *New*."[43]

This passage raises a question: how did pirates create and re-create their culture? The answer depends on the way in which a gang of pirates formed. Mutineers had to organize a founding moment, and already-constituted pirate ships devised rituals of integration for volunteers. The mutiny on the *Buck* was an important example of the former, as it represented the origin of the lineage that would lead to Bartholomew Roberts and his capture of four hundred vessels between 1719 and 1722. Mate Howell Davis knew that many former pirates and other hands were "ripe for Rebellion" aboard the ship and easily organized the mutiny, which proved successful. The outlaws immediately called a "Counsel of War," a meeting of all members of the ship, over "a large Bowl of Punch," to choose a commander. They voted for Davis "by a great Majority," and eventually "all acquiesced in the Choice." The next step was constitutional, the drawing up of articles, the rules by which they would operate, "which were signed and sworn by himself [Davis] and the rest." The new pirate commander then "made a short speech, the sum of which was a Declaration of War against the whole World." Then they "consulted" about where to go and what to do, and soon they were off on their adventure.[44]

Other mutinous crews did the same. Edward Worley and his crew made "a black Ensign, with a white Death's Head in the middle of it," signed articles, and "bound themselves under a solemn Oath, to take no Quarters, but to stand by one another to the last Man." The rebels on the Royal African Company ship the *Gambia Castle* met with leaders George Lowther and John Massey. They "agreed to go a pirating and took Oaths & entered into Articles in writing for that purpose & prepared black

Figure 3. George Lowther; Captain Charles Johnson,
A *General History of the Lives and Adventures of the Most Famous
Highwaymen, Murderers, Street Robbers, &c.* (London, 1734).

Colours." They also "knocked down the Cabins, made the Ship
flush fore and aft," and renamed her the *Delivery*. Things worked
similarly when a ship divided and a new captain was elected and
installed. Such was the case with Francis Spriggs, whose crew
created its own Jolly Roger and fired their guns to salute the new
captain.[45]

How did pirates integrate newcomers into the life and work
of the ship? This was especially important because a large majority of pirates had not been mutineers but had joined as vol-

unteers from captured vessels. The initiation process usually included signing the articles and taking an oath to "swear to true to the Crew" as, for example, carpenter John Haswell did when he joined the crew of Howell Davis. Newcomers then had to demonstrate their commitment to the enterprise, and this usually took time. Pirate captain Thomas Cocklyn apparently felt that the "new-entered men" would not truly be part of the pirate community until they had seen action in battle. They must, he said, "learn to smell gunpowder." Cocklyn was said to use the boatswain's rattan cane on the new men, and Israel Hynde, boatswain on Roberts's ship *The Ranger*, "was always swearing and cursing at the new Pyrates." James Phillips often tried "to terrifie new Comers if they offer'd to Speak saying that they ought to serve their time first."[46]

The older pirates placed restrictions on the new ones until the latter had proved that they were "trusty" men or "brisk hands." On several ships, "no new-Comer amongst the Company were suffered to goe a plundering of any Prize." Thomas Davis testified that men were excluded from democratic discussion and decision making on Bellamy's ship until they had signed the articles: "When the company was called to *Consuls* [councils], and each Man to give his Vote, they would not allow the forced Men to have a Vote." On the *Cassandra*, "the Surgeons had no vote," presumably because their class background (or forced status) made them untrustworthy. The process of integration was not without tension. "The old Pyrates were always jealous of the new Comers, and consequently observant of their Behaviour; this was done with the utmost Caution." They imposed a public inspection of all formal communication: "no Man was suffered to write a word, but what was Nailed up to the Mast."[47]

The transmission of pirate culture through space and time was linked closely to their success in attracting new recruits and to their democratic—one might say anarchic—form of self-organization. As more and more volunteers joined the pirates, and as the ship became more crowded, the moment inevitably

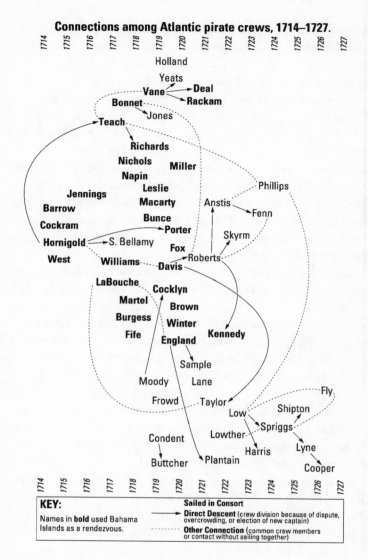

Figure 4. Connections among pirate crews, 1714–1727.

arrived when the crew would split. When a suitable vessel was taken (one with the appropriate size, speed, and ordnance), those who wanted to set up independently would draw up their own articles, elect a captain, and constitute themselves as a new crew. Another common reason for splitting was a developing conflict within an existing crew—over leadership, where to cruise, and so on—whereupon a dissident portion would elect its own captain and sail away from their former mates. The social organization constructed by pirates was flexible, but it could not accommodate severe, sustained conflict. Those who had experienced the claustrophobic and authoritarian world of the merchant ship cherished the freedom to separate. The pirates' democratic exercise of authority had both negative and positive effects. Although it produced a chronic instability, it also guaranteed continuity; the very process by which new crews were established helped to ensure a cultural continuity among the pirates.[48]

The mechanism for the continuity can be seen by charting the connections among pirate crews. The accompanying diagram, arranged according to vessel captaincy, demonstrates that by splintering, by sailing in consorts, or by other associations, roughly thirty-six hundred pirates—about 90 percent of all those active between 1716 and 1726—fitted into two main lines of genealogical descent. Captain Benjamin Hornigold and the pirate rendezvous in the Bahamas stood at the origin of an intricate lineage that ended with the hanging of John Phillips's crew in June 1724. The second line, spawned in the chance meeting of the lately mutinous crews of George Lowther and Edward Low in 1722, culminated in the executions of William Fly and his men in July 1726. It was primarily within and through this network that the social organization of the pirate ship took on its significance, transmitting and preserving customs and meanings, and helping to structure and perpetuate the pirates' social world.[49]

What was spreading, hydralike, in the division of pirate crews was a radical democratic social order and culture, with distinctive social attitudes and relations, both within the group and without. One aspect was especially troubling to authorities, as described by Governor Alexander Spotswood as he sought "some safe opportunity" to sail from Virginia to London in 1724. He discovered that he could do so only in a well-armed man-of-war:

> Your Lordships will easily conceive my Meaning when [you] reflect on the Vigorous part I've acted to suppress Pirates: and if those barbarous Wretches can be moved to cut off the Nose & Ears of a Master for but correcting his own Sailors, what inhuman treatment must I expect, should I fall within their power, [I] who have been markt as the principle object of their vengeance, for cutting off their arch Pirate Thatch [Teach, or Blackbeard], with all his grand Designs, & making so many of their Fraternity to swing in the open air of Virginia.[50]

Spotswood knew these pirates well. He had authorized the expedition that returned to Virginia boasting Blackbeard's head as a trophy. He had done his share to ensure that many pirates would swing on Virginia gallows. He knew that pirates had a fondness for revenge, that they often punished ship captains for "correcting" their crews, and that a kind of "fraternity" prevailed among them. He had good reason to fear them, as we will see in the following chapter.

Chapter Five

"TO DO JUSTICE TO SAILORS"

IN 1720, AS EDWARD ENGLAND and Oliver LaBouche and their crews prowled the western Indian Ocean around the island of Johanna, off Madagascar, they spied a vessel that proved to be the *Cassandra*, commanded by James Macrae. Little did the pirates know it, but Macrae, who worked for the East India Company, was coming after them. He and the captain of another ship had concluded that "it might be of great Service to the *East-India* Company to destroy such a Nest of Rogues" who had disrupted the lucrative commerce of the region. When the pirates approached and ran up the dreaded Jolly Roger, Macrae did not surrender as most merchant captains would have done in such a situation. Rather, he and his crew announced their intentions with their cannon, beginning a hot three-hour engagement that would make the decks of both ships slick with blood and littered with dead bodies. The pirates at some point raised their red or "bloody" flag, as they called it, indicating that they would neither take nor give quarter. It would be a fight to the death.[1]

Eventually the pirates prevailed, not least because two consort ships whose captains had vowed to fight with Macrae against the pirates lost heart and sailed away. Macrae himself, bleeding profusely from a wound to his head by a musket ball, nonetheless managed to gather the survivors into a long boat and row ashore to King's Town, Johanna. But now there was no escaping the pirates, who anchored offshore and put out word that they would pay a ten-thousand-crown bounty to anyone who would deliver Macrae to them. They wanted his head. It was their customary practice to torture and kill those who dared to resist them, to teach them a lesson by terror, especially when the blood of their own comrades had been spilled in battle. When Macrae was finally taken aboard England's ship, he must have assumed that he was going to his death.

As the drama concerning his fate unfolded on the quarterdeck, there suddenly appeared "A fellow with a Terrible Pair of Whiskers, and a wooden Leg," a pirate who had come up from belowdecks. He was "stuck round with Pistols, like the man in the Almanack with Darts." He lurched along, swinging his peg leg, "swearing and vapouring," and asked, "in a damning Manner, which was Captain *Mackra*." The very sight of the man nearly scared the captain out of his wits; he was sure that "this Fellow would be his Executioner."

But when the fierce man came near Macrae, "he took him by the hand, swearing, damn him he was glad to see him." As it happened, this particular pirate, like several others, "had formerly sail'd with him" and took the opportunity to announce to the assembled crew that Macrae was "an honest Fellow." For good measure, he added (no doubt with a few salty oaths), "*shew me the Man ... that offers to hurt Captain* Mackra, *for I'll stand by him*." He had invoked the strongest expression of seafaring solidarity—to stand by someone, a favorite among pirates—and he meant it in a confrontational way. Anyone who wished to get at Macrae would have to go through him. The magnanimous gesture earned the captain a reprieve until the matter could be taken up in a common council. Macrae himself had no illusions, as he later noted: "several of the Chief of them knew me, and some of them had sailed with me, which I found of great Advantage; because, notwithstanding their promise [of his personal safety], some of them would have cut me, and all that would not enter with them, to Pieces."

The pirates then held a "Consultation amongst themselves," at which the bewhiskered peg leg and many others had their say. They concluded: "considering the gallant Behaviour of Capt. Mackray"—they admired his pluck—"and what a good Character he bore Amongst his Men"—he was "an honest Fellow"—they would not only let him live, but decided "to return him another ship in room of his own," which had been severely damaged in battle. His life saved and the gift ship accepted, Macrae sailed away, his pluck intact, to obtain reinforcements, and he soon returned to engage the pirates in battle once again and try to kill or capture them. The pirates must have been stunned, but soon disbelief turned to white-hot rage. One of them remarked that Macrae's actions represented an abuse of "civillity," and he vowed never to let a merchant captain off the hook ever again.[2]

The story of Captain Macrae among the pirates raises an issue to be probed in this chapter: why did pirates care whether he or any other ship captain happened to be "an honest Fellow"? Why did it matter to them "what a good Character he bore Amongst his Men"? Having explored the social origins and self-organization of pirates aboard their ship, we now move to their social relations. This is an important topic because pirates constructed their own social order in defiant contradistinction to the ways of the world they had left behind. They had special contempt for the merchant captain, the royal official, and the system of authority those figures represented and enforced. In 1718, when eight pirates were tried in Boston, merchant captain Thomas Checkley told of the capture of his ship by pirates, who "pretended," he said, "to be Robbin Hoods Men." Herein lies a clue about their self-perception and their relations to others.[3]

Robin Hood was, of course, the legendary figure who in late medieval England "robbed from the rich and gave to the poor." He was the preeminent social bandit, the man who was, to the upper classes of his day, a criminal, but at the same time a hero to the lower orders. Historian Eric Hobsbawm has described social banditry as a "universal and virtually unchanging phenomenon," an "endemic peasant protest against oppression and poverty: a cry for vengeance on the rich and the oppressors." Its goal is "a traditional world in which men are justly dealt with, not a new and perfect world"; Hobsbawm calls its advocates "revolutionary traditionalists." The pirates who emerged after the War of Spanish Succession were not peasants, of course, but they certainly did, as we have seen, protest against oppression and poverty as they built a new world aboard their ships. Of special importance was their "cry for vengeance."[4]

When Governor Alexander Spotswood spoke of pirates as "barbarous Wretches [who] can be moved to cut off the Nose & Ears of a Master for but correcting his own Sailors," and of himself as "the principle object of their vengeance" for having killed Blackbeard and hanged others, he articulated the fears of royal officials and merchant captains everywhere about the pirates and their fondness for revenge.[5] The very names of pirate ships made the same threat. Blackbeard's vessel was named *Queen Anne's Revenge*; other notorious craft were Stede Bonnet's *Revenge*, John Cole's *New York Revenge's Revenge*, and William Fly's *Fames' Revenge*.[6] The foremost target of vengeance was the merchant captain. Frequently, "in a far distant latitude," as one seaman put it, "unlimited power, bad views, ill nature and ill principles all concur[red]" in a ship's commander. Here was a man "past all restraint," who often made life miserable for his crew.[7] In 1722 merchant captains Isham Randolph, Constantine Cane, and William Halladay petitioned Spotswood "in behalf of themselves and other Masters of Ships" for "some certain method ... for punishing mutinous & disobedient Seamen." They explained that captains faced great danger "in case of meeting with Pyrates, where we are sure to suffer all the tortures w[hi]ch such an abandoned crew can invent, upon the least intimation of our Striking any of our men." Pirates acted the part of a floating mob, a "flying gang," as they called themselves, with its own distinctive sense of popular justice.[8]

Upon seizing a merchantman, pirates often administered the "Distribution of Justice," "enquiring into the Manner of the Commander's Behaviour to their Men, and those, against whom Complaint was made" were "whipp'd and pickled."[9] The practice of investigating the master's usage of his men was so widespread that it was called a "Custom" among the pirates. Bartholomew Roberts's crew considered such inquiry so important that they formally designated one of their men, George Willson, as the "Dispencer of Justice." In 1724 merchant captain Richard Hawkins described another form of retribution, a torture known as the "Sweat": "Between decks they stick Candles round the Mizen-Mast, and about twenty-five men surround it with Points of Swords, Penknives, Compasses, Forks &c in each of their hands: *Culprit* enters the Circle; the Violin plays a merry Jig; and he must run for about ten Minutes, while each man runs his Instrument into his Posteriors."[10] Many captured captains were "barbarously used," and some were summarily executed. Pirate Philip Lyne carried this vengeance to its bloodiest extremity, confessing when apprehended in 1726 that "during the time of his Piracy" he "had killed 37 Masters of Vessels."[11] The search for vengeance was in many ways a fierce, embittered response to the violent, personal, and arbitrary authority wielded by the merchant captain.

Still, the punishment of captains was not indiscriminate, as the case of Captain Macrae suggests. A few captains were singled out for reward by pirates. The best description of pirates' notions of justice comes from merchant captain William Snelgrave's account of his capture in 1719. On April 1 Snelgrave's ship was seized by Thomas Cocklyn's crew of rovers at the mouth of the Sierra Leone River. Cocklyn was soon joined by men captained by Oliver LaBouche and Howell Davis, and Snelgrave spent the next thirty days among 240 pirates. His account is one of the most insightful ever written about social attitudes and practices among the pirates. Let us examine it carefully.[12]

The capture was effected when twelve pirates in a small boat came alongside Snelgrave's ship, a large vessel manned by forty-five sailors, plenty to mount a stiff resistance. Snelgrave ordered his crew to arms. They refused, but the pirate quartermaster heard the command and was infuriated by it. Once the pirates boarded, without resistance, their leader drew a pistol and, according to Snelgrave, "with the but-end endeavoured to beat out my Brains." Some of Snelgrave's crew came to his defense; they "cried out aloud 'For God sake don't kill our Captain, for we never were with a better Man.'" The quartermaster heard their plea and stopped the beating. Snelgrave noted, "he told me, 'my Life was safe provided none of my People complained against me.' I replied, 'I was sure none of them could.'"[13]

Snelgrave was taken to Cocklyn, who told him, "I am sorry you have met with bad usage after Quarter given, but 'tis the Fortune of War sometimes.... [I]f you tell the truth, and your Men make no Complaints against you, you shall be kindly used." Howell Davis, commander of the largest pirate ship, apparently continued the interrogation of Snelgrave's men. He later reprimanded Cocklyn's men for their roughness and, by Snelgrave's account, expressed himself "ashamed to hear how I had been used by them. That they should remember their reasons for going a pirating were to revenge themselves on base Merchants and cruel commanders of Ships.... [N]o one of my People, even those that had entered with them gave me the least ill-character.... [I]t was plain they loved me."[14]

Indeed, Snelgrave's character proved so respectable that the pirates proposed to give him a captured ship with full cargo and to sell the goods for him. Then they would capture a Portuguese slaver, sell the slaves, and give the proceeds to Snelgrave so that he could "return with a large sum of Money to London, and bid the Merchants defiance."[15] Pirates hoped to show these merchants that good fortunes befell good captains. The proposal was "unanimously approved" by the pirates, but fearing a charge of complicity, Snelgrave hesitated to accept it. Davis quickly interceded, saying that he favored "allowing every Body to go to the Devil in their own way" and that he knew that Snelgrave feared for his reputation. The refusal was graciously accepted, Snelgrave claiming that "the Tide being turned, they were as kind to me, as they had been at first severe."[16]

Snelgrave later wrote of pirates to merchant Humphrey Morice, "they pretend one reason for these villainies is to do justice to sailors." He related another incident to prove that it was not merely pretense. While Snelgrave remained in pirate hands, a decrepit schooner belonging to the Royal African Company sailed into Sierra Leone and was taken by his captors. Simon Jones, a member of Snelgrave's crew who had volunteered to join Cocklyn and his gang, urged his mates to burn the ship, since he had been poorly treated while in the company's employ. The pirates were about to do so when another of them, James Stubbs, protested that such action would only "serve the Company's interests," since the ship was worth little. He also pointed out that "the poor People that now belong to her, and have been on so long a voyage, will lose their Wages, which I am sure is Three times the Value of the Vessel." The pirates concurred and returned the ship to its crew, who "came safe home to England in it." Captain Snelgrave also returned to England soon after this incident, but eleven of his seamen remained behind as pirates. Snelgrave's experience revealed how pirates attempted to intervene against— and modify—the standard brutalities that marked the social relations of production in merchant shipping. That they sometimes chose to do so with brutalities of their own shows how they could not escape the system of which they were a part.[17]

Snelgrave seems to have been an exceptionally decent captain. Captain Skinner had a rather different experience, although he was, like Snelgrave, a slave trader and, again like him, captured off the coast of Sierra Leone by pirates. Skinner struck the colors of his vessel, the *Cadogan,* a snow out of Bristol, to the same freebooters, captained by Edward England and Oliver LaBouche, who would later capture Macrae. Ordered to come aboard one of the pirate ships in his boat, he complied. As soon as he got there, the "Person that he first cast his eye upon, proved to be his old Boatswain," a man who had sailed with him on a previous voyage. The bosun "star'd him in the Face like his evil genius, and accosted him in this Manner.—*Ah, Captain Skinner! Is it you? The only Man I wished to see; I am much in your Debt, and now I shall pay you all in your own Coin.*"[18]

As it happened, on that previous voyage Skinner and several of his men had quarreled, and the captain had "thought fit to remove these fellows on board a Man of War"—something captains often did with sailors they considered mutinous—and put them in a floating prison. Skinner "at the same Time refused them their Wages," another practice not uncommon at the time. Soon after, the sailors "found means to desert that Service" and secured berths aboard a sloop to the West Indies, where they were taken by pirates. They apparently joined the brotherhood and sailed to Providence in the Bahamas, a pirate rendezvous, where they enlisted "upon the same Account along with Captain England" and soon set sail for West Africa.

Skinner probably thought, and surely hoped, he would never see these sailors again. But there they were, and the circumstances were rather different from the last time he had seen them. According to Captain Charles Johnson, who probably talked to an eyewitness, "The poor Man trembled [in] every Joint, when he found into what Company he had fallen, and dreaded the Event, as he had Reason enough so to do." The boatswain "immediately called to his Consorts, laid hold of the Captain, and made him fast to the Windless." His former seamen proceeded to pelt him "with Glass Bottles, which cut him in a sad Manner." Then they pulled out the lash and "whipp'd him about the Deck, till they were weary." All the while they were "deaf to all his Prayers and Entreaties." At last, they announced with sarcasm that "because he had been a good Master to his Men," he "should have an easy Death, and so [they] shot him thro' the Head." Such was the grim moment of truth for a captain who bore a rather different character from Snelgrave, even on board a pirate ship whose captain (England) was known to be good-natured, "always averse to the ill Usage Prisoners received."[19]

Numerous sailors, once they became pirates, seized their new and unusual circumstances to settle old scores in vengeful ways. The slave-trading captain Thomas Tarlton, writes historian Stanley Richards, "was beaten unmercifully by Bartholomew Roberts himself, who detested the dictatorial methods and brutalities of these same merchant captains." Roberts knew them well, for he had labored under them in the slave trade. When Charles Vane's crew captured merchant captain Alex Gilmore in 1718, a crew member named Robert Hudson, who had sailed with Gilmore, threatened, "Damn your blood, I'll kill you, for sending me on the Main-Yard in the storm." (In this instance Vane protected the captain against the wrath of his former crew member.) In January 1722, when pirates approached Joseph Traherne's ship, the *King Solomon* of the Royal African Company, his boatswain, William Phillips, refused to fight. Once the pirates boarded, Phillips used the occasion to make a complaint. He used "threatning Language against the officers because his Captain had once threatened to cut off his ears for cutting Cordage without his Order." He later joined the pirates, and Traherne survived to testify against the pirates and watch many of them, Phillips included, dangle from the gallows.[20]

Once pirates determined the "character" of the captured captain, they decided what to do with his ship. A poor reputation among his seamen would lead to the destruction, usually burning or sinking, of the vessel. When Captain Thomas Grant was captured on the coast of Africa in July 1719, he suffered the wrath of Walter Kennedy, who punched him in the mouth for a previous offense and urged his comrades to kill him. They saved his life but condemned and sunk his ship, apparently to appease Kennedy. A similar situation developed when Edward England and his crew captured a Captain Creed and discovered that England's brother, John, had once been mistreated by the man who was now a prisoner. This "occasion'd the sd Pyrates to misuse the sd Capt Creed and to burn his ship the Coward." These deliberations could also work the other way, as suggested earlier in the account of Snelgrave and again in the case of the *Elizabeth*, captured by Roberts and his crew in January 1722. Some of the pirates "hindered the Cargoe's being plundered" and suggested that the ship "be restored to the Second Mate" because the captain and the first mate had died. This they proposed "out of respect to the generous Character [the ship] Owner bore, in doing good to poor Sailors." The fate of a ship and its cargo frequently depended on the pirates' investigation of the character of the ship's captain and owner.[21]

The "Distribution of Justice" could occasion debate among pirates. After the process was under way aboard a prize vessel in 1723, pirate captain John Evans intervened and asked of his own rank-and-file mates, *What have we to do to turn Reformers, 'tis Money we want?*" He then turned to the sailors of the captured vessel, and "he asked them, *Does your Captain give you Victuals enough?* And they answering in the affirmative: *Why, then,* said he, *he ought to give you Work enough.*" But this is the exception that proves the rule, not least because Evans himself proved to be a tyrannical captain who was subsequently killed by a member of his own crew after giving out a beating that the victim considered an insult to his dignity. In any case, money and "reform" were not incompatible objectives, as numerous pirate crews made clear.[22]

The idiom of reform is worth noting. When merchant captain Fowle willingly came aboard the ship of Bartholomew Roberts, the pirates said "they were sure he was an honest Fellow that never abused any Sailors." They continued: "had he been a Rogue, he would never have come on board to them." As it happened, one of the pirates knew Fowle "and swore to the Company that he was an honest Fellow, which hinder'd her [Fowle's ship] from being burnt." On another occasion, a Captain Cain was captured by pirates who "whipp'd him barbarously, and told him their reason for doing so was, to make him honest." Captain Macrae was said to be "an honest Fellow." And of course the pirates considered themselves "honest men," as explained by William Fly, who, facing the gallows, commented on the hundreds of pirates who had already met their ends; the authorities, he explained, have "hanged many an Honest Fellow already." Honesty was a watchword for the fair and decent treatment of sailors.[23]

Pirates like Howell Davis claimed that the more "dishonest" masters of merchantmen ("base" and "cruel," as he called them) —the Tarltons and the Skinners rather than the "honest" Macraes and Snelgraves—had contributed mightily to seamen's willingness to become sea robbers. John Archer, whose career as a pirate dated from 1718 when he sailed with Edward Teach, uttered a final protest before his execution in 1724: "I could wish that Masters of Vessels would not use their Men with so much Severity, as many of them do, which exposes us to great Temptations." Fly, as we saw in chapter 1, made an even angrier indictment, as did many others. John Gow, facing the gallows for mutiny and murder in 1726, insisted that "the captain's inhumanity had produced the consequences which had happened." To pirates revenge was justice; punishment was meted out to barbarous captains, as befitted the captains' crimes.[24]

Pirates also reserved choice words for governmental officials they considered their enemies. While making merry by eating, drinking, and toasting, Charles Vane's crew lustily chanted "Damnacon to King George." They added, for good measure, "Dam the Governour," probably referring to the recently established Woodes Rogers, who had ended their rendezvous in the Bahama Islands. And in case their drift remained unclear, they added, "Curse the King and all the Higher Powers." Some of the pirates executed by Rogers in the Bahamas in December 1718 "reflect[ed] on the king and Government" in what must have been uncomplimentary ways. Other pirates, such as the crew of Stede Bonnet, rattled the nerves of the authorities by drinking to the health of "the Pretender," James II, "and hoped to see him King of the *English* nation." One observer noted that such actions made him see that pirates were "doubly on the side of the Gallows, both as Traitors and Pirates."[25]

In 1718, at the trial of Bonnet and thirty-three members of his crew at Charleston, South Carolina, Richard Allen, attorney general of South Carolina, told the jury that "pirates prey upon all Mankind, their own Species and Fellow-Creatures without Distinction of Nations or Religions." Allen was right in claiming that pirates did not respect nationality in their plunders, that they could no longer be trusted to attack only the vessels of Catholic Spain, and that they attacked British ships. But he was absolutely wrong in claiming that they did not respect their "Fellow-Creatures." Pirates did not prey on one another. Rather, they consistently showed solidarity for each other, a highly developed group loyalty. Here I turn from the external social relations of piracy to the internal in order to examine this solidarity for their "fellow creatures" and the collectivistic ethos it expressed.[26]

Pirates had a profound sense of community. They showed a recurring willingness to join forces at sea and in port, even when the various crews were strangers to each other. In April 1719, when Howell Davis and his gang aboard the *Rover* sailed into the Sierra Leone River, the pirates who were already there, captained by Thomas Cocklyn, prepared to fight—to defend themselves if it should prove to be a naval vessel and to attack if a merchant ship. But when they saw on the approaching ship "her Black Flag," "immediately they were easy in their minds, and a little time after," the crews "saluted one another with their Cannon." Other crews exchanged similar greetings and, like Davis and Cocklyn, who combined their powers, frequently invoked an unwritten code of hospitality to forge spontaneous alliances.[27] Such a combination transcended nationality. French, Dutch, Spanish, and British pirates not only cooperated on the same ship, as we saw in chapter 3, but usually did the same when a ship manned primarily by one nationality met another of a different nationality. Such solidarity limited the amount of discord between different pirate crews.[28]

This communitarian urge occasionally took landed form,

for example, in the pirate strongholds of Madagascar and Sierra Leone. Sea robbers occasionally chose more sedentary lifeways in regions far from imperial power, on various thinly populated islands, and they contributed a notorious number of men to the community of logwood cutters at the Bay of Campeche in the Gulf of Mexico. In 1718 a royal official complained of a "nest of pirates" in the Bahamas "who already esteem themselves a community, and to have one common interest." Pirates had, since the time of the buccaneers, considered themselves "the brethren of the coast." In the 1722 trials at Cape Coast Castle, Thomas Howard called pirates "the Brotherhood"; others called each other "Brother Pirate."[29]

The pirates' sense of brotherhood or fraternity, which Spots-wood and others noted, was nowhere more forcefully expressed than in the threats pirates made and the acts of revenge they took. Theirs was truly a case of hanging together or being hanged separately. In April 1717 the pirate ship *Whydah* was wrecked near Boston. Most of its crew perished, and the survivors were jailed. In July, Thomas Fox, a Boston ship captain, was taken by pirates, who "Questioned him whether anything was done to the Pyrates in Boston Goall," promising "that if the Prisoners Suffered they would Kill every Body they took belonging to New England."[30] Shortly after this incident, Teach's sea rovers captured a merchant vessel and, "because she belonged to Boston, [Teach] alledging the People of Boston had hanged some of the Pirates, so burnt her." Teach declared that all Boston ships deserved a similar fate.[31] The fearsome Charles Vane "would give no quarter to the Bermudians" and punished them and "cut away their masts upon account of one Thomas Brown who was (some time) detain'd in these Islands upon suspicion of piracy." Brown apparently planned to sail as Vane's consort until foiled by his capture.[32]

Acts of revenge could be more daring—and more frightening to colonial authorities. In September 1720, pirates captained by Bartholomew Roberts "openly and in the daytime burnt and destroyed our vessels in the Road of Basseterre [Saint Kitts], and had the audaciousness to insult H. M. Fort," avenging the execution of "their comrades at Nevis." Roberts then sent word to the governor that "they would Come and Burn the Town [Sandy Point] about his Ears for hanging the Pyrates there."[33] In 1721 Spotswood relayed information to the Council of Trade and Plantations that Roberts "said he expected to be joined by another ship and would then visit Virginia, and avenge the pirates who have been executed here."[34] The credibility of the threat was confirmed by the unanimous resolution of the Virginia Executive Council that "the Country be put into an immediate posture of Defense." Lookouts and beacons were quickly provided, and communications with neighboring colonies effected. "Near 60 Cannon," Spotswood later reported, were "mounted on sundry Substantial Batteries."[35]

In 1723 pirate captain Francis Spriggs vowed to find a Captain Moore "and put him to death for being the cause of the death of [pirate] Lowther," his "friend and Brother"; shortly after, he similarly pledged to go "in quest of Captain Solgard," who had overpowered a pirate ship commanded by Charles Harris.[36] In January 1724 Lieutenant Governor Charles Hope of Bermuda wrote to the Board of Trade that he found it difficult to procure trial evidence against pirates because residents "feared that this very execution wou'd make our vessels fare the worse for it, when they happen'd to fall into pirate hands." Walter Kennedy, as we saw in chapter 3, led a devastating attack on the slave-trading fortress on the Princes Islands in West Africa after the governor there had ambushed his comrade Howell Davis. The threats of revenge were sometimes effective.[37]

Fear of retaliation not only terrified Governor Spotswood of sea travel unless he was in a man-of-war, it also drove some to retire from seafaring altogether. Nicholas Simons, who had killed three members of Shipton's crew in 1725, begged relief of the Massachusetts government because he "is now under a necessity to leave off his Employment of a Mariner for Fear of Sd Pirates."

He found himself "in low Circumstances" and had to seek "a new Employment ... for his Support." Captain Luke Knott faced a similar dilemma. After playing a critical role in fingering, convicting, and hanging eight pirates in Virginia in 1720, he petitioned the government for relief, "his being obliged to quit the Merchant Service, the Pirates threatning to Torture him to death if ever he should fall into their hands." He chose to give up his maritime career. As it happened, none other than the prime minister of Great Britain validated the threat; Robert Walpole personally intervened to give Knott £230 for both his service to the state and his simultaneous loss of his means of subsistence.[38]

Pirates also affirmed their unity symbolically. Evidence suggests that sea robbers may have had a sense of belonging to a separate, in some manner exclusive, speech community. Philip Ashton, who in 1722–23 spent sixteen months among pirates, noted that "according to the Pirates usual Custom, and *in their proper Dialect*, asked me, If I would sign their Articles."[39] Many sources suggest that cursing, swearing, and blaspheming may have been defining traits of this style of speech, to an even greater extent than among the larger population of seafaring men. For example, near the Sierra Leone River a British official named Plunkett pretended to cooperate with, but then attacked, the pirates with Bartholomew Roberts. Plunkett was captured, and Roberts,

> upon the first sight of Plunkett[,] swore at him like any Devil, for his Irish Impudence in daring to resist him. Old Plunkett, finding he had got into bad Company, fell a swearing and cursing as fast or faster than Roberts; which made the rest of the Pirates laugh heartily, desiring Roberts to sit down and hold his Peace, for he had no Share in the Pallaver with Plunkett at all. So that by meer Dint of Cursing and Damning, Old Plunkett ... sav'd his life.

The pirates with George Lowther apparently engaged in similar palavers. During their Christmas celebrations, they played the dozens, "striving who should outdo one another in new invented Oaths and Execrations." It may not be surprising that

Cotton Mather was shocked by the language that William Fly employed, but it surely must be so that Captain Snelgrave, who had spent a lifetime around foul-mouthed sailors, was nonetheless taken aback by the speech of the freebooters with Thomas Cocklyn. It appears that the symbolic connectedness among pirates extended into the domain of language.[40]

The best-known symbol of piracy, the Jolly Roger, also illustrates the strong sense of community among the pirates. Of first importance is that the flag was very widely used; no fewer, and probably a great many more, than twenty-five hundred men sailed under it. So general an adoption indicates an advanced state of group identification.[41] The flag itself was a "black Ensign, in the Middle of which is a large white Skeleton with a Dart in one hand striking a bleeding Heart, and in the other an Hour Glass." The flag varied from ship to ship, but almost all were black, adorned with white representational figures, sometimes an isolated human skull, or "death's head," but more frequently an entire skeleton, or "anatomy." Other recurring items were a weapon—cutlass, sword, or dart—and an hourglass. The main purpose of the flag was to terrify the pirates' prey, but its triad of interlocking symbols—death, violence, limited time—simultaneously pointed to meaningful parts of the seaman's experience. Seamen who became pirates escaped from a deadly work situation to the freer, more hopeful world symbolized by the Jolly Roger. Under the somber colors of "King Death," they fought back against captains, merchants, and officials who waved banners of authority.[42]

Pirates thus regarded certain social groups as their enemies, but they got support and material assistance from people at all levels of society, as they had done for decades. Piracy had long served as an informal arm of English state policy against Spain in the New World. Some of the more spectacular raids carried out by the buccaneers in the seventeenth century had been organized with the assistance of the colonial government of Jamaica. Sea robbers had also served vital economic functions, providing,

for example, gold and silver to specie-starved colonial economies. In 1704 the pirate John Quelch made the point, in astonishment, as he stood on the gallows of Boston. He warned those
assembled not to bring hard currency into New England because
they would be hanged for it! Colonial officials had long connived
at such purposes. Governor John Hope of Bermuda recalled this
legacy in his letters of 1723 and 1724 to royal officials in London,
explaining how piracy was as popular in his colony as smuggling
was in Britain. When he engaged an "honest man" in discussion
about how to stop the concourse with pirates, he was told, "Sr.
(sayd he) you'l have business enough upon your hands if you go
about to rectifie that, for, there is not a man that sails from hence
but will trade with a pyrate etc." Hope added later that "Pyrates
in former days were here made very welcome, & Governours
have gain'd Estates by them." The same was true in Jamaica, New
York, North Carolina, and other places, although such attitudes
among officials began to change with a broad reorganization of
the empire in the 1670s and with a crackdown against piracy in
the 1690s.[43]

Yet many people, a few of them among the wealthier sectors
of society, continued to cooperate with pirates. Spotswood put
his finger on the reason: "People are easily led to favour these
Pests of Mankind when they have hopes of Sharing in their
ill-gotten Wealth." In 1718, when he organized an expedition
against Edward Teach and his gang, it required, Spotswood
wrote, "such Secresy that I did not so much as communicate to
his Maj'ty's Council here, nor to any other Person but those who
were necessarily to be employed in the Execution, least among
the many favourers of Pyrates we have here in these Parts some
of them might send intelligence to Tach." Pirates themselves explained in 1718 that without merchants in Rhode Island, New
York, and Pennsylvania who sold them ammunition and provisions, "they could never have become so formidable, nor arriv'd
to that degree that they have." At the trial of Stede Bonnet and
his gang in 1718, Attorney General Richard Allen noted that

some in Charleston had spoken in favor of the pirates, and he expressed his hope that there were no such people among the property-owning jurors.[44]

Much of the support took the form of conveying what Spotswood and others called intelligence to pirates—especially information about the comings and goings of merchant ships and the deployment of naval vessels. An official from Saint Kitts wrote that Roberts and his crew had "intelligence of this Island in particular that I am surprised at." Governor Hope hinted at the same practice when he wrote to his superiors, "I am sorry to say it; but those People [of Bermuda] do not look upon those Monsters with that Abhorrence which they ought to do: And I find that when we do fall into those Villains hands, Our treatment is not so rough as that which other people meet with." Admiral Edward Vernon complained that pirates had "daily intelligence" from supporters in Jamaica, which made it impossible to catch them. The intelligence was provided by small merchants and ship captains who fenced the pirates' goods, but, more important, it was passed along by working sailors, some of whom joined up, some of whom were sympathetic, and others of whom used the information as bargaining chips in the hope that, when captured, the pirates would treat them better.[45]

Some of the "poorer sort" in the port cities supported pirates in their own ways. According to historian Shirley Carter Hughson, Charleston churned with tension in the period leading up to the trial of Bonnet and others in 1718: "There had been rioting by night, threats of burning the town, and intimidation of the officers of the law, and the government was almost powerless to preserve the safety of the citizens of the province." Some of the solidarity was practical as Bonnet and another man escaped from prison. Other mobs demonstrated in favor of pirates in Port Royal, Jamaica, and Providence in the Bahama Islands, showing that the law does not a criminal make. Pirates, according to Barnaby Slush, were "Princes" to the common sailor. And they would remain so long after the propertied elements of society turned against pirates as soon as their cooperation was criminalized by the death penalty in 1721.[46]

Pirates perceived themselves and their social relations through a collectivistic ethos that had been forged in their struggle for survival, first as seamen, then as outlaws. They had reasons for what they did, and they expressed them clearly, consistently, confidently, and even, on occasion, with a degree of self-righteousness. In and through their social rules, their egalitarian social organization, and their notions of revenge and fairness, they tried to establish a world in which people "were justly dealt with." And although what they did could be described as revolutionary, it was hardly "traditionalist." By walking "to the Gallows without a Tear," by calling themselves "Honest Men" and "Gentlemen," and by speaking self-servingly but proudly of their "Conscience" and "Honor," pirates flaunted their certitude.[47]

Bartholomew Roberts clearly expressed this lofty self-conception, all within the idiom of revenge, in one of the very few documents we have that was written by a pirate's hand. Roberts had apparently requested a meeting with Lieutenant General William Mathew, presumably to discuss the recent hanging—"barbarous usage"—of two pirates in Nevis. When Mathew did not appear, Roberts and his crew sailed into Basseterre, Saint Kitts, and burned several ships; he then sent a letter chastising Mathew for his rudeness, and, by implication, his cowardice: "This comes expressly from me to lett you know that had you come off as you ought to a done and drank a glass of wine with me and my company I should not [have] harmed the least vessell in your harbour." Roberts had apparently planned to come ashore and wanted the general to know that "it is not your gunns you fired yt. affrighted me or hindred our coming on shore but the wind not proving to our expectation that hindred it." He explained that the pirates had a new ship, and "for revenge you may assure yourselves here and here after not to expect anything from our hands but what belongs to a pirate as farther Gentlemen." For good measure, he added a threat: "that

poor fellow you now have in prison at Sandy point is entirely ignorant and what he hath was gave him and so pray make conscience for once let me begg you and use tht man as an honest
man and not as a C[riminal?] if we hear any otherwise you may
expect not to have quarters to any of your Island." The letter was
signed "yours," "Bathll. Roberts."[48]

When, in 1720, ruling groups concluded that "nothing but
force will subdue them," many pirates responded by intensifying
their commitment.[49] This was the moment at which the preservation of the pirate way of life, with all of its freedoms, comforts,
and supposed moral superiority, began to take precedence
over all other motivations among maritime brigands. In 1724
Edward Low's crew swore, "with the most direful Imprecations,
that if ever they should find themselves overpower'd they would
immediately blow their ship up rather than suffer themselves
to be hang'd like Dogs." These sea robbers would not "do Jolly
Roger the Disgrace to be struck." Their attitude of death before
dishonor was one more example of their own vaunted selfconception.[50]

Chapter Six

THE WOMEN PIRATES:
ANNE BONNY AND MARY READ

JAMAICA'S MEN OF POWER gathered at a Court of Admiralty in Saint Jago de la Vega in late 1720 and early 1721 for a series of show trials. Governor Nicholas Lawes, members of his Executive Council, the chief justice of the Grand Court, and a throng of minor officials and ship captains trumpeted the gravity of the occasion by their concentrated presence. Such officials and traders had recently complained of "our Coasts being infested by those Hell-hounds the Pirates." In this, Jamaica's coasts were not alone; pirates had plagued nearly every colonial ruling class as they made their marauding attacks on mercantile property across the British Empire and beyond. The great men had come to see a gang of pirates "swing to the four winds" upon the gallows. They would not be disappointed.

Eighteen members of Calico Jack Rackam's crew had already been convicted and sentenced to hang, three of them, including Rackam himself, afterward to dangle and decay in chains at Plumb Point, Bush Key, and Gun Key as moral instruction to the seamen who passed that way. Once shipmates, now gallows mates, they were meant to be "a Publick Example, and to terrify others from such-like evil Practices."[1]

Two other pirates were also convicted, brought before the judge, and "asked if either of them had any Thing to say why Sentence of Death should not pass upon them, in like manner as had been done to all the rest." These two pirates, in response, "pleaded their Bellies, being Quick with Child, and pray'd that Execution might be staid." The court then "passed Sentence, as in Cases of Pyracy, but ordered them back, till a proper Jury should be appointed to enquire into the Matter."[2] The jury in-

Figure 5. Anne Bonny and Mary Read;
Captain Charles Johnson, *A General History of the Robberies
and Murders of the Most Notorious Pyrates* (London, 1724).

quired into the matter, discovered that they were indeed women, pregnant ones at that, and gave respite to these two particular "Hell-hounds," whose names were Anne Bonny and Mary Read.

This chapter explores some of the meanings of the lives of the two women pirates, both during their own times and after. It surveys the contexts in which Bonny and Read lived and discusses how these women made a place for themselves in the rugged, overwhelmingly male worlds of seafaring and piracy. It concludes by considering their many-sided and long-lasting legacy. Any historical account of the lives of Anne Bonny and Mary Read must in the end be as picaresque as its subjects, ranging far and wide across the interrelated and international histories of women, seafaring, piracy, labor, literature, drama, and art. To an even greater extent than their male counterparts, theirs was ultimately a story about liberty, whose history they helped to make.[3]

Much of what is known about the lives of these extraordinary women appeared originally in *A General History of the Pyrates*, written by Captain Charles Johnson and published in two vol-

umes in 1724 and 1728. Captain Johnson recognized a good story
when he saw one. He gave Bonny and Read leading parts in his
account, boasting on the title page that the first volume contained "The remarkable Actions and Adventures of the two female Pyrates, Mary Read and Anne Bonny." *A General History*
proved a huge success; it was immediately translated into Dutch,
French, and German, published and republished in London,
Dublin, Amsterdam, Paris, Utrecht, and elsewhere, by which
means the tales of the women pirates circulated to readers around
the world. Their stories had doubtless already been told and re-
told in the holds and on the decks of ships, on the docks, and in
the bars and brothels of the sailor towns of the Atlantic by the
maritime men and women of whose world Bonny and Read had
been a part.[4]

According to Johnson, Mary Read was born an illegitimate
child outside London; her father was not her mother's husband.
To obtain support from the husband's family, Read's mother
dressed her to resemble the recently deceased son she had by
her husband, who had died at sea. Read apparently liked her
male identity and eventually decided to become a sailor, enlist-
ing aboard a man-of-war, and then a soldier, fighting with distinction in both infantry and cavalry units in Flanders. She fell
in love with a fellow soldier, allowed him to discover her secret,
and soon married him. But he proved less hardy than she, and
before long he died. Read once again picked up the soldier's gun,
this time serving in the Netherlands. At war's end she sailed in
a Dutch ship for the West Indies, but her fate was to be captured
by pirates, whom she joined, thereafter plundering ships, fighting duels, and beginning a new romance. One day her new lover
fell afoul of a pirate who was much more rugged than himself and
was challenged to go ashore and fight a duel in the pirates' customary way, "at sword and pistol." Read saved the situation by
picking a fight with the same rugged pirate, scheduling her own
duel two hours before the one that would involve her lover, and
promptly killing the fearsome pirate "upon the spot." Her mar-

Figure 6. Anne Bonny; Captain Charles Johnson,
Historie der Engelsche Zee-Roovers (Amsterdam, 1725).

tial skills were impressive, but they alone were no match for the
well-armed vessel that captured and imprisoned her and her
comrades in 1720.

Anne Bonny was also born an illegitimate child (in Ireland),
and she too was raised in disguise, her father pretending that
she was the child of a relative entrusted to his care. Her father
eventually took the lively lass with him to Charleston, South
Carolina, where he became a merchant and planter of considerable wealth and standing. Bonny grew into a woman of "fierce
and couragious temper." Once, "when a young Fellow would
have lain with her against her Will, she beat him so, that he lay

ill of it a considerable time." Ever the rebel, Bonny soon forsook her father and his fortune to marry "a young Fellow, who belong'd to the Sea, and was not worth a Groat." She ran away with him to the Caribbean, where she dressed "in Men's Cloaths" and joined a band of pirates that included Mary Read and, more important, Calico Jack Rackam, who was soon the object of Bonny's affections. Their romance too came to a sudden end, when one day in 1720 she and her mates fell into battle with a vessel sent to capture them. When they came to close quarters, "none [of the pirates] kept the Deck except Mary Read and Anne Bonny, and one more"; the rest of the pirates scuttled down into the hold in cowardice. Exasperated and disgusted, Read fired a pistol at them, "killing one, and wounding others." Later, as Rackam was to be hanged, Bonny answered his imploring look by saying, *"she was sorry to see him there, but if he had fought like a Man, he need not have been hang'd like a Dog."* Bonny, who had "fought like a Man," was forced to plead her belly to prolong her days among the living.

Of the existence of two women pirates by the names of Anne Bonny and Mary Read there can be no doubt, for they were mentioned in a variety of historical sources, all independent of *A General History of the Pyrates*. The names first appeared in a proclamation by Woodes Rogers, governor of the Bahama Islands, who on September 5, 1720, declared Jack Rackam and his crew to be pirates and warned all authorities to treat them as "Enemies to the Crown of *Great Britain*." He named the pirates involved and noted "Two women, by name, Ann Fulford alias Bonny, & Mary Read." The second mention came in a pamphlet, *The Tryals of Captain John Rackam and Other Pirates*, published in Jamaica in 1721. At about the same time Governor Nicholas Lawes wrote from Jamaica to the Council of Trade and Plantations that "the women, spinsters of Providence Island, were proved to have taken an active part in piracies, wearing men's clothes and armed etc." Finally, newspaper reports in the

Figure 7. Mary Read; Captain Charles Johnson,
Historie der Engelsche Zee-Roovers (Amsterdam, 1725).

American Weekly Mercury, the *Boston Gazette,* and the *Boston News-Letter* mentioned but did not name the two women pirates who were members of Rackam's crew.[5]

The Tryals of Captain John Rackam and Other Pirates presents testimony from the trial and verifies crucial parts of Johnson's *General History,* independently establishing Bonny and Read as fierce, swashbuckling women, genuine pirates in every sense.[6] One of the witnesses against Bonny and Read was Dorothy Thomas, who had been captured and made prisoner by Rackam's crew. She claimed that the women "wore Mens Jackets, and long

Trouzers, and Handkerchiefs tied about their Heads, and that each of them had a Machet[e] and Pistol in their Hands." {109} Moreover, at one point they "cursed and swore at the Men," their fellow pirates, "to murther the Deponent." "[T]hey should kill her," they growled, "to prevent her coming against them" in court, as was indeed happening before their very eyes. At the time, Bonny and Read were dressed as men, but they did not fool Thomas: "the Reason of her knowing and believing them to be Women was, by the largeness of their Breasts."[7]

John Besnick and Peter Cornelius, likewise captives of Rackam and his crew, testified that Bonny and Read "were very active on Board, and willing to do any Thing." Bonny apparently worked as a powder monkey in times of engagement: she "handed gun-powder to the Men."[8] When Rackam and his crew "saw any vessel, gave Chase or Attack'd," Bonny and Read wore men's clothes, but at other times, free of military confrontation, they wore women's clothes. According to these witnesses, the women "did not seem to be kept, or detain'd by Force," but rather took part in piracy "of their own Free-Will and Consent." Thomas Dillon, a captured master of a merchant vessel, added that they "were both very profligate, cursing, and swearing much, and very ready and willing to do any Thing on board."[9]

Despite the general authenticity of the tales,[10] many modern readers must surely have doubted them, thinking them descriptions of the impossible. After all, women never went to sea; seafaring was a man's world and a man's world only. But recent research throws doubt on such assumptions. Linda Grant Depauw has shown that women went to sea in many capacities: as passengers, servants, wives, prostitutes, laundresses, cooks, and occasionally—though certainly much less often—even as sailors, serving aboard naval, merchant, whaling, privateering, and pirate vessels.[11] Dianne Dugaw has written: "Perhaps the most surprising fact about eighteenth-century female soldiers and sailors is their frequency, not only in fiction but in history as well."[12] An anonymous British writer, possibly the dramatist and poet Oliver Goldsmith, wrote in 1762 that there were so many women in the British army that they deserved their own separate battalion, perhaps not unlike the contemporaneous women warriors who fought for the African kingdom of Dahomey.[13]

So Bonny and Read rigged themselves out in men's clothes and carried their bold imposture into the always rough, sometimes brutal world of maritime labor. Their cross-dressing adventures were not as unusual among early modern women as previously believed, but they were nonetheless direct challenges to customary maritime practice, which forbade women to work as seamen aboard deep-sea vessels of any kind. The reasons for the exclusion are not yet clear, but the evidence of it is incontrovertible: the ship was a sharply gendered workplace, reserved almost exclusively for male labor. Seafaring was a line of work long thought to "make a man" of anyone who entered.[14]

One reason women found no berth may have been the sheer physical strength and stamina required for early modern maritime labor. Employing at this time a low level of machine power, the ship depended on brute strength for many of its crucial operations—assisting in the loading and unloading of cargo (using pulleys and tackle), setting heavy canvas sails, and operating the ship's pump to eliminate the water that oozed through the seams of always-leaky vessels. A few women, obviously, did the work and did it well, earning the abiding respect of their fellow workers. But not everyone—certainly not all men—was equal to its demands. It was simply too strenuous, too hard on the body, leaving in its wake lameness, hernias, a grotesque array of mutilations, and often premature death.[15]

A second and perhaps more important reason for the segregation of the sexes was the apparently widespread belief that women and sexuality more generally were inimical to work and social order aboard the ship. Arthur N. Gilbert has convincingly shown that homosexual practice in the eighteenth-century British Royal Navy was punished ruthlessly because it was considered subversive of discipline and good order.[16] Minister John

Flavel made the same point when he wrote that the death of the "lusts" of seamen was a means of giving "life" to the merchant's trade, which made the saving of souls and the accumulation of capital complementary parts of a single disciplinary process.[17] But some version of his view apparently commanded acceptance at all levels of the ship's hierarchy. Many sailors saw women as objects of fantasy and adoration but also as sources of bad luck or, worse, dangerous sources of conflict, potential breaches in the male order of seagoing solidarity. Early modern seafarers seem to have agreed among themselves that some kind of sexual repression was necessary to do the work of the ship.[18]

The assumption was strong enough to command at least some assent from pirates, who, as we have seen, organized their ships in otherwise novel and egalitarian ways. The freebooters who sailed the Mediterranean in the early seventeenth century refused to allow women aboard the ships because their presence was "too distracting."[19] The refusal was continued into the eighteenth century. The articles drawn up by Bartholomew Roberts and his crew specified that no boy or woman was to be allowed on board. Moreover, should a woman passenger be taken as a captive, "they put a Centinel immediately over her to prevent ill Consequences from so dangerous an Instrument of Division and Quarrel." The crew of John Phillips reasoned likewise: "If at any Time we meet with a prudent Woman, that Man that offers to meddle with her, without her Consent, shall suffer present Death." Captain William Snelgrave added, "It is a rule amongst the Pirates, not to allow Women to be on board their Ships, when in the Harbour. And if they should Take a Prize at Sea, that has any Women on board, no one dares, on pain of death, to force them against their Inclinations. This being a good political Rule to prevent disturbances amongst them, it is strictly observed."[20]

Black Bart Roberts was straighter laced than most pirate captains (he banned gambling among his crew to reduce conflict), so it may be unwise to hold up his example as typical.[21] Another, perhaps more important doubt arises from evidence that Bonny and Read did not cross-dress all of the time aboard the pirate ship. As John Besnick and Peter Cornelius testified in court, they wore male attire during a chase or engagement, when a show of "manpower" might help to intimidate their prey and force a quick surrender. At other times, presumably during the daily running of the ship, they dressed as women.[22]

The strongest test of the attitudes of male pirates toward females is the actual number of women who appeared on the sea rovers' ships in the early eighteenth century; the surviving evidence suggests that few of them did. Two other women faced charges for piracy in this era, both in Virginia, where authorities tried Mary Harley (or Harvey) and three men for piracy in 1726, sentenced the three men to hang, but released the woman.[23] Three years later they tried a gang of six pirates, including Mary Crickett (or Crichett), all of whom were ordered to the gallows. Crickett and Edmund Williams, the leader of the pirates, had been transported as felons to Virginia aboard the same ship in late 1728.[24] It is not known whether Harley and Crickett cross-dressed to become pirates, nor if they were moved to do so by tales of Anne Bonny and Mary Read. The very presence of all four women among the pirates came to light only because their vessels were captured. Thus the pirate ship may have offered more room to women than either the merchant or the naval vessels of the day, but still it was little enough. And in any case, it existed only because radical female action created it in the first place.[25]

Bonny and Read were able to undertake such action in part because class experiences and personal characteristics enabled them to draw on and perpetuate a deeply rooted underground tradition of female cross-dressing, pan-European in its dimensions but especially strong in early modern England, the Netherlands, and Germany. Such disguise was usually, though not exclusively, undertaken by proletarian women.[26] Like other female cross-dressers, Bonny and Read were young, single, and humble of origin; their illegitimate births were not uncommon.

Moreover, Bonny and Read perfectly illustrated what historians Rudolf M. Dekker and Lotte C. van de Pol have identified as the two main reasons women cross-dressed in the early modern era; Read did it largely out of economic necessity, and Bonny, turning her back on her father's fortune, followed her instincts for love and adventure.[27]

Bonny may have been drawn to the sea and to piracy in particular by popular lore in her native Ireland about Grace O'Malley, a pirate queen who in the late sixteenth century marauded up and down the Emerald Isle's western coast. O'Malley was fierce of action and of visage; the face of this commanding figure had been badly scarred in her youth by the talons of an eagle. In 1577 Sir Henry Sydney wrote that O'Malley "was a notorious woman in all the coasts of Ireland." Such coasts would have included the port of Cork, where O'Malley had often attacked the merchant ships that sailed to the Iberian Peninsula and where Bonny was born to a family of seafaring experience.[28]

In any event, Bonny and Read became part of a larger tradition that included such famous women as Christian Davies, who, dressed as a man, chased her dragooned husband from Dublin to the European continent, survived numerous battles, wounds, and capture by the French, and returned to England and to military honors bestowed by Queen Anne.[29] Ann Mills went to sea "about the year 1740," serving as "a common sailor on board the Maidstone frigate" during the War of Austrian Succession. She distinguished herself in hand-to-hand combat against "a French enemy" and "cut off the head of her opponent, as a trophy of victory."[30] Perhaps the best-known cross-dressing sailor of the eighteenth century was Hannah Snell, who ran away to sea in 1745 in search of a seafaring husband who had abandoned her during pregnancy. Accounts of her life appeared in *Gentlemen's Magazine*, *Scots Magazine*, and in books long and short, in English and in Dutch.[31]

Women such as Christian Davies, Ann Mills, and Hannah Snell were also celebrated in popular ballads around the Atlantic.

Figure 8. Ann Mills; James Caulfield, *Portraits, Memoirs,*
and Characters of Remarkable Persons from the Revolution of
1688 to the End of the Reign of King George II (London, 1820).

A "semi-literate lower class" of "apprentices, servants, char-
women, farmworkers, laborers, soldiers, and sailors" sang the
glories of "warrior women" at the fairs, on the wharves, around
the street corners, and amid the mass gatherings at hangings.[32]
Bonny and Read came of age in an era when female warrior ballads soared to the peak of their popularity.[33]

Dianne Dugaw has pointed out that ballads about warrior
women gave "a surprisingly accurate, if conventionalized, reading of lower-class [female] experience," which as a matter of
course bred physical strength, toughness, independence, fear-
lessness, and a capability of surviving by one's wits. The prevailing material reality of working women's lives made it possible for
some women to disguise themselves and enter worlds dominated
by men; the same reality then ensured that such women would
be familiar enough within early working-class culture to be cel-

ebrated. Bonny and Read represented not the typical but the strongest side of popular womanhood.[34]

Their strength was a matter of body and mind, for the two women were well suited for maritime labor and piracy in ways both physical and temperamental. By the time she was a teenager, Read was already "growing bold and strong." Bonny was described as "robust" and of "fierce and couragious temper." In "times of Action, no Person amongst [the pirates] was more resolute, or ready to board or undertake any Thing that was hazardous" than Bonny and Read, not least because they had, by the time they sailed beneath the Jolly Roger, already endured all manner of hazards. Read's mother had been married to "a Man who used the Sea" but in the end was himself apparently used up by it; Anne Bonny's mother was a "Maid-Servant." As illegitimate children, both faced shifting, precarious circumstances early in life. The art of survival in a rough proletarian world included a capacity for self-defense, which both Bonny and Read had mastered.[35] Read's experience in the British infantry and cavalry helped make her a fearsome duelist among the pirates. Bonny's training was less formal but no less effective, as her would-be rapist would discover suddenly and painfully.[36]

Bonny and Read were thus well prepared to adopt the sailor's and even the pirate's cultural style, which they did with enthusiasm. They cursed and swore like any good sailor. They were, moreover, armed to the teeth, carrying their pistols and machetes like those well trained in the ways of war. They also affirmed one of the principal values and standards of conduct among both seamen and pirates, that is, an unwritten code of courage. Calico Jack Rackam got his big boost in the pirate world when his captain, Charles Vane, refused to engage a French man-of-war, which led immediately to charges of cowardice, a democratic vote of no confidence, and Rackam's promotion from quartermaster to captain. Among sailors and especially pirates, courage was a principal means of survival, and cowardice was an invitation to disaster and ultimately death.[37]

Courage was traditionally seen as a masculine virtue, but Read and Bonny proved that women might possess it in abundance. They demonstrated it in the mutinies that launched each of them into piracy and again in the skirmish after which they were captured, when they fired a pistol into the hold, aiming at their quivering comrades. Read dreaded to hear her lover called a coward; Bonny called her own lover as much while the noose tightened around his neck in Port Royal. The strongest evidence of the importance of courage came in Read's class-conscious answer to the question of a captive about her prospect of an "ignominious Death" on the gallows, when she gamely insisted "Men of Courage"—like herself—would not fear it. She indicted the cowardly rogues ashore who used the law as an instrument of oppression; in so doing she commented indirectly on the broad, violent redefinition of property relations that was taking place in her native England at the very moment that she uttered her condemnation.[38]

Read considered courage a resource, something akin to a skill that offered the poor some protection in a vicious labor market. The same idea was expressed more fully by pirate captain Charles Bellamy, who lectured a captured captain thus:

> damn ye, you are a sneaking Puppy, and so are all those who will submit to be governed by Laws which rich Men have made for their own Security, for the cowardly Whelps have not the Courage otherwise to defend what they get by their Knavery; but damn ye altogether: Damn them for a Pack of crafty Rascals, and you, who serve them, for a Parcel of hen-hearted Numskuls. They villify us, the Scoundrels do, when there is only this Difference, they rob the Poor under the Cover of Law, forsooth, and we plunder the Rich under the Protection of our own Courage.

Courage was thus the antithesis of law; proletarians had to have it in order to make their way in a world of sneaking puppies, hen-hearted numbskulls, crafty rascals, and scoundrels. This was the secularized eighteenth-century voice of the radical antinomian who had taken the law into his or her own hands during the English Revolution.[39]

An antinomian disdain for state authority was evident in another part of the class experience of Bonny and Read, that is, their marital and family situations. Both women engaged in what John Gillis has called the "proletarian practice of self-marriage and self-divorce." Read happily wedded herself to her husband. Bonny, once she had prospects for a life of some wealth and class privilege, promptly turned her back on them, married a poor sailor, and headed off to a place known to be "a Receptacle and Shelter for Pirates & loose Fellows." The property-preserving marriage practices of the middle and upper classes were not for her. Nor, apparently, was the marriage to James Bonny, for she soon tried, with the help of her new lover, Calico Jack Rackam, to arrange a popular form of divorce known as a "wife sale" in order to end an old relationship and begin a new one. Rackam was to give her husband "a Sum of Money, in Consideration he should resign her to the said *Rackam* by a Writing in Form, and she even spoke to some Persons to witness the said Writing." When Governor Woodes Rogers refused to recognize the validity of the popular custom, threatening to whip and imprison Bonny for such "loose Behaviour," she and Rackam, "finding they could not by fair Means enjoy each other's Company with Freedom, resolved to run away together, and enjoy it in Spight of all the World." Bonny and Read thus exercised marital liberty, the collective choice of which helped to generate the passage of England's Hardwicke Act of 1753, designed to restrict legal marriage to public ceremonies conducted in the church.[40]

Bonny and Read threw down their greatest challenge to state authority by choosing the life of the pirate, which was yet another class experience and no less, in its way, about liberty. Captain Charles Johnson recognized piracy as a "Life of Liberty" and made the matter a major theme of his book. Bonny and Read took part in the bold experiment beyond the reach of the traditional powers of family, state, and capital, one that was carried out by working men and, with their presence, at least a few women. They added another dimension altogether to the subversive appeal of piracy by seizing what was regarded as male liberty. In so doing they were not merely tolerated by their male compatriots, for they clearly exercised considerable leadership aboard their vessel. Although not formally elected by their fellow pirates to posts of command, they nonetheless led by example—in fighting duels, in keeping the deck in times of engagement, and in being part of the group designated to board prizes, a right always reserved to the most daring and respected members of the crew. They proved that a woman could find liberty beneath the Jolly Roger.[41]

Did Anne Bonny and Mary Read, in the end, make their mark on the world? Did their daring make a difference? Did they leave a legacy? Dianne Dugaw has argued that the popular genre of ballads about warrior women like Bonny and Read was largely suffocated in the early nineteenth century by a new bourgeois idea of womanhood. Warrior women, when they appeared, were comical, grotesque, and absurd, since they lacked the now-essential female traits of delicacy, constraint, and frailty. The warrior woman, in culture if not in fact, had been tamed.[42]

But the stubborn fact remained: even though Bonny and Read did not transform the terms in which the broader societal discussion of gender took place, and even though they apparently did not see their own exploits as a call for rights and equality for all women, their very lives and subsequent popularity represented a subversive commentary on the gender relations of their own times as well as "a powerful symbol of unconventional womanhood" for the future. The frequent reprinting of their tales in the romantic literature of the eighteenth, nineteenth, and twentieth centuries surely captured the imaginations of many girls and young women who felt imprisoned by the bourgeois ideology of femininity and domesticity.[43] Julia Wheelwright has shown that nineteenth-century feminists used the examples of female soldiers and sailors "to challenge prevailing notions

about women's innate physical and mental weakness." Bonny
and Read, like many others, offered ample disproof of then-
dominant theories on women's incapacity.[44]

Anne Bonny, Mary Read, and women like them captured
many an imagination in their own day, including those at work
in the realm of literature. Bonny and Read were real-life versions
of Defoe's famous heroine Moll Flanders. In fact, Bonny, Read,
and Flanders had a lot in common. All were illegitimate children, poor at birth and for years thereafter. All were what Defoe
called "the offspring of debauchery and vice." Flanders and
Bonny were born of mothers who carried them in the womb
while in prison. All three found themselves on the wrong side of
the law, charged with capital crimes against property, and facing
"the steps and the string," popular slang for the gallows. All experienced homelessness and roving transience, including trips
across the Atlantic. All recognized the importance of disguise,
the need to be able to appear in "several shapes." Flanders too had
cross-dressed: her governess and partner in crime "laid a new
contrivance for my going abroad, and this was to dress me up in
men's clothes, and so put me into a new kind of practice."[45]
Flanders even had a brush with pirates during her passage to
Virginia, though she encountered no women on board. Had she
decided to join up with those who sailed beneath the Jolly Roger,
the lives of Bonny and Read might be read as one possible outcome to the novel, which was published the year after our heroines' adventures.

Christopher Hill writes, "The early novel takes its life from
motion." Commenting on the seventeenth and early eighteenth
centuries, he concludes that "the novel doesn't grow only out of
the respectable bourgeois household. It also encompasses the pi-
caro, the vagabond, the itinerant, the pirate—outcasts from the
stable world of good householders—those who cannot or will
not adapt." Peter Linebaugh also emphasizes the proletarian origins of the picaresque novel in the early modern age, especially
in England, where the literary form "reached an apogee in the

publication of *Moll Flanders* in 1722." Thus the experiences of the teeming, often dispossessed masses in motion—people like Anne Bonny and Mary Read—were the raw materials of the literary imagination. Hannah Snell's contemporary biographer made the connection when he insisted that his subject was "the real *Pamella*," referring to Samuel Richardson's famous novel. The often desperate activity of working-class women and men in the age of nascent capitalism thus helped to generate one of the world's most important and durable literary forms, the novel, which indeed is inconceivable apart from it.[46]

Bonny and Read also affected another major area of literary endeavor: drama. It is widely known that John Gay's *Beggar's Opera* was one of eighteenth-century England's most popular and successful plays. It is less widely known that in 1728–29 Gay wrote *Polly: An Opera, being the Second Part of the Beggar's Opera.* The sequel's obscurity was a matter of political repression, for it was censored by none other than Prime Minister Robert Walpole, who was less than happy that he had appeared in *The Beggar's Opera* as Bob Booty. Disliking Gay's effort to establish moral equivalence between highway robbers and the prime minister's own circle in government and considering the new play a still-seditious continuation of the old, Walpole had *Polly* banned. But in so doing, he may have made *Polly* even more popular. Demand for the new play was clamorous; thousands of subscriptions brought Gay a handsome sum of money, though not nearly as much as would have been his had it not been for twenty-odd pirate printers and booksellers who produced and sold their own editions. *Polly* achieved a popular presence and visibility well before its first performance in 1777.[47]

The namesake of the play was the daughter of a Jonathan Wild–type character called Peachum. Polly came to the New World, the West Indies in particular, in search of her love, Macheath, the highwayman of *The Beggar's Opera*, who had been transported for his crimes. Macheath, Polly discovered, had turned pirate and was disguised as Morano, a "Negro villain" and captain of a crew of freebooters.[48] En route to America, Polly's money was stolen, which forced her to indenture herself as a servant. She was bought by a Mrs. Trapes, who ran a house of prostitution, then sold by the "madame" to a wealthy sugar planter, Mr. Ducat. Polly escaped the situation by cross-dressing "in a man's habit" and going to sea as a pirate in search of Macheath. She did it, she explained, "To protect me from the violences and insults to which my sex might have exposed me."[49]

The very act of writing a play that featured women pirates only a few years after Anne Bonny and Mary Read had stood trial suggests that Gay knew of and drew on the adventures of the real women pirates. The likelihood is made even stronger by specific similarities between the play and the freebooting reality of the Caribbean earlier in the decade. Jenny Diver, a prostitute in *The Beggar's Opera* and Macheath's (Morano's) "doxy" aboard the pirate ship, may have, in the new play, been modeled on Anne Bonny. Like Bonny, Jenny is the lover of the pirate captain; she also falls for another pirate, who turns out to be a woman in disguise, in this case the cross-dressed Polly rather than Mary Read. For her part, Polly resembles Mary Read in her modest, even "virtuous" sexual bearing.[50]

Bonny and Read may have influenced posterity in yet another, more indirect way, through an illustration by an unknown artist that appeared as the frontispiece of the Dutch translation of Captain Charles Johnson's *General History of the Pyrates*, now called *Historie der Engelsche Zee-Roovers*. It featured a bare-breasted woman militant, armed with a sword and a torch, surging forward beneath the Jolly Roger, the international flag of piracy. In the background at the left hangs a gibbet with ten executed pirates dangling; at the right is a ship in flames. Trampled underfoot are an unidentifiable document, perhaps a map or a legal decree; a capsizing ship with a broken mainmast; a woman still clutching the scales of justice; and a man, possibly a soldier, who appears to have his hands bound behind his back. Hovering at the right is a mythical figure, perhaps Aeolus, Greek god of the

Figure 9. An allegory of piracy (1725); Captain Charles Johnson, *Historie der Engelsche Zee-Roovers* (Amsterdam, 1725).

winds, who adds his part to the tempestuous scene.[51] Bringing up the rear of the chaos is a small sea monster, a figure commonly drawn by early modern mapmakers to adorn the aquatic parts of the globe.

The illustration is an allegory of piracy, the central image of which is female, armed, violent, riotous, criminal, and destructive of property—in short, the very picture of anarchy.[52]

The characteristics of the allegory of piracy were equally characteristic of the lives of Anne Bonny and Mary Read, who, not surprisingly, were featured prominently in the *Historie der Engelsche Zee-Roovers*, not only in its pages but in separate illustrations and even on the cover page, directly opposite the frontispiece, where the book proudly advertised its account of their lives. It seems almost certain that these two real-life pirates, who lived, as their narrative claimed, by "Fire or Sword," inspired the illustrator to depict insurgent piracy in the allegorical form of a militant, marauding woman holding fire in one hand and a sword in the other.

It is instructive to compare the work to a famous painting, Eugène Delacroix's *Liberté guidant le peuple* (Liberty leading the people), for the similarities are striking.[53] Compositionally the works are remarkably similar: a central female figure, armed, bare-breasted, and dressed in a Roman tunic, looks back as she propels herself forward, upward, over, and above a mass of bodies strewn below. The proletarian identity of each woman is indicated by the bulk, muscle, and obvious strength of her physique; Parisian critics in 1831 were scandalized by the "dirty" Liberty, whom they denounced as a whore, a fishwife, a part of the "rabble."[54] Moreover, flags and conflagrations help to frame each work: the Jolly Roger and a burning ship at the right give way to the French tricolor and a burning building in almost identical locations. An armed youth, a street urchin, stands in for the windmaker.[55] Where the rotting corpses of pirates once hung now mass "the people." Two soldiers, both apparently dead, lie in the forefront.

There are differences: Liberty now has a musket with bayonet rather than a sword and torch. She still leads but now takes her inspiration from the living rather than the dead. "The people" in arms have replaced "the people"—as a ship's crew was commonly called in the eighteenth century—who are hanging by the neck in the Dutch illustration.[56]

More important, Delacroix has softened and idealized both the female body and face, replacing anger and anguish with a tranquil, if determined, solemnity. His critics notwithstanding, Delacroix has also turned a partly naked woman into a partly nude woman, exerting over the female body an aesthetic control that parallels the taming of the warrior woman in popular

15. E. Delacroix, *Le 28 juillet: la Liberté guidant le peuple*

Figure 10. Eugène Delacroix, *Liberty Leading
the People* (1830); the Louvre, Paris.

balladry. Liberty thus contains her contradictions: she is both a
"dirty" revolutionary born of action and an otherworldly, idealized female subject combining a classical artistic inheritance and
a new nineteenth-century definition of femininity.[57]

It cannot be proven definitively that Delacroix saw the earlier
graphic and used it as a model. In 1824 the artist discontinued his
journal, where he might have noted such an influence, and did
not return to it until 1847. And in any case, both the Dutch and
the French artist probably drew on classical depictions of god-
desses such as Athena, Artemis, or Nike as they imagined their
subjects.[58] Regardless, there is a great deal of circumstantial evidence to suggest that the allegory of piracy may have influenced
Delacroix's greatest work.

First, it is well known that Delacroix drew on the experiences
of real people in his rendition of *Liberty Leading the People,* including Marie Deschamps, who during the hottest of the July
days seized the musket of a recently killed citizen and fired it
against the Swiss guards. Another subject familiar to the artist

was "a poor laundry-girl" known only as Anne-Charlotte D., who was said to have killed nine Swiss soldiers in avenging her brother's death.[59] These real women, like Anne Bonny and Mary Read, were bound to appeal to the romantic imagination.[60]

Second, Delacroix himself noted in his journal that he often studied engravings, woodcuts, and popular prints as he conceptualized his paintings and sought to solve compositional problems. By the time Delacroix composed his famous painting, in late 1830, at least twenty editions of *A General History of the Pyrates* had appeared, six (or more) of these in French and many containing the Dutch illustration. The majority of these editions, which, including the French, advertised the stories of Bonny and Read on their title pages, would have been available to the artist in Paris.[61]

Third, and most important, it can be established that piracy was on Delacroix's mind at the very moment he was painting *Liberty*. The English romantic poet Lord Byron was, according to the art historian George Heard Hamilton, "an inexhaustible source of inspiration" for the painter. Delacroix engaged the work of Byron intensely during the 1820s, exhibiting three major paintings on subjects from Byron's poetry in 1827 and executing several others on the Greek civil war, in which Byron ultimately lost his life. More crucially still, Delacroix was reading Byron's poem "The Corsair"—about piracy—as he was painting *Liberty*. In 1831, at the very same Salon in which he exhibited his greatest painting, Delacroix also entered a watercolor based on Byron's poem.[62]

The image of piracy (1725) preceded the image of liberty (1830) by more than a century. And yet it seems that the liberty seized by Anne Bonny and Mary Read—the liberty they found so briefly, so tantalizingly, beneath the Jolly Roger—took a strange, crooked path from the rough, rolling deck of a ship in the Caribbean to the polished, steady floor of an art salon in Paris. It was a case of liberty seized in action; of low culture affecting high culture; of New World struggles supplying and driving what once would have been seen as the genius and originality of European art and culture. It would be a fitting tribute to Bonny and Read if the example of these two women who seized liberty beneath the Jolly Roger in turn helped to inspire one of the most famous depictions of liberty the modern world has ever known.

Chapter Seven

"TO EXTIRPATE THEM
OUT OF THE WORLD"

ADDRESSING PIRATES WHO STOOD on the gallows of Boston in November 1717, Cotton Mather solemnly intoned: "All Nations agree to treat your Tribe, as the *Common Enemies of Mankind*, and [to] extirpate them out of the World." Mather told a threefold truth. The ruling classes of his day, representing, as they claimed, "All Nations," were in agreement about pirates; they did indeed regard them as *hostes humani generis* (the common enemies of mankind); and they would organize and carry out a campaign of extermination against them. They would, in short, produce a lurid and violent propaganda as part of the war against the pirates. They would make the pirate a villain on an international stage, not least because many of the people attending the drama of execution, as in Boston in 1717, did not share Mather's judgment.[1]

Now that we have seen who the pirates were (poor, working seamen), how they organized themselves (in egalitarian and democratic ways), and how they represented themselves (as "honest men" seeking justice for the common sailor), let us explore these issues from the other side, as taken up by those who sought not to understand them on their own terms but to obliterate them. The campaign to "cleanse the seas" was undertaken and supported by royal officials, attorneys, merchants, publicists, clergymen, and writers who created, through proclamations, legal briefs, petitions, pamphlets, sermons, and newspaper articles, an image of the pirate that would legitimate his annihilation. The rhetorical, military, and legal campaign would, in the end, be successful. Piracy would come to an end by 1726.

Before we discuss the image of the pirate drawn by his enemies, let us survey the interested parties who sought the extermination and in whose name they claimed to speak. Piracy was, first and foremost, a crime against property, more specifically, in almost every instance, the property of merchants, who traded across vast distances in national, imperial, and international commerce. Judge Nicholas Trott of the South Carolina Court of Admiralty stated bluntly that "the Law of Nations never granted to [pirates] a power to change the Right of Property." He was right. Pirates broke the law as they stole property, taking plunder in money and cargo, and as they destroyed property, throwing goods riotously into the sea, burning and sinking ships. They interfered with the very security of possessing property. These acts, according to the King's attorney in Massachusetts, carried "Destruction to the utmost parts of our Territories."[2] Pirates attacked intercolonial trade—in New England, the mid-Atlantic region, the Chesapeake, the lower South, the West Indies—and they assailed strategic trading areas such as West Africa and Spanish America, thereby damaging the interests of not only British merchants but "Trade and Commerce between Nation and Nation."[3] Pirates were accounted enemies of each law-abiding person, as stated by John Valentine as he prosecuted thirty-six pirates in Rhode Island in 1723: "This sort of Criminals are engag'd in a perpetual War with every Individual." As a foe to all of His Majesty's subjects, the pirate was someone with whom "no Faith, Promise, nor Oath is to be observed," someone "every Man may lawfully destroy." Ministers urged that children be protected from this disorderly round of life: they should be kept from going to sea.[4]

The pirate was an opponent of the government because, as one of the King's men in court explained in 1717, "*It is the Interest of the State that Shipping be improved.*" In this logic, attacks on trade "may justly be accounted Treason," as Sir Edward Coke had allowed in his seventeenth-century codification of English law. And of course no "wise or honest Men...who love their Country" would turn pirate, since maritime commerce had always produced the "Wealth, Strength, Reputation and Glory of the *English* Nation." In 1719 proclamations were sent around the empire offering rewards to anyone willing to serve king and country by apprehending or killing pirates. Pirates were declared enemies to the Crown of Great Britain because their disorders were "in Contempt and Defiance of His Majesty's good and wholesome Laws." And in 1722 the King made the antinational character of piracy explicit by announcing that persons injured in any battle against pirates "shall be provided for as if they were actually in the Service of the Crown."[5]

Yet the freebooter was more than an antagonist of the British merchant and government; he was "equally an Enemy and dangerous to all Societies," and to "every State, Christian or Infidel." Piracy was "Destructive of Government" in general, "in open violation of the Rights of Nations." Pirates could claim the benefit of no country because every nation was "threatened from the Combinations, Conspiracies, and Confederacies" of such "Profligate and Desperate Wretches." In 1717 a Boston prosecutor of eight sea robbers explained to the court the history of the word *pirate*. In "early and barbarous Ages," he claimed, the term had positive connotations, yet when nations settled into regular governments, the pirate soon became *hostes humani generis*, the common enemy of mankind. Since pirates tended to "Subvert and extinguish the Natural and Civil Rights of Mankind," they should therefore be eliminated in "the Interest of Mankind." The pirate was thus a threat to property, the individual, society, the colony, the empire, the Crown, the nation, the world of nations, and indeed all mankind. His villainy was complete.[6]

In 1718, in his opening remarks in the trial of Stede Bonnet and crew in Charleston, Richard Allen, attorney general of South Carolina, explained that piracy "is a Crime so odious and horrid in all its Circumstances, that those who have treated on that Subject have been at a loss for Words and Terms to stamp a sufficient Ignominy upon it." He outlined the task that would occupy men of his station for years to come. Which "Words and Terms" would be used to make the pirate ignominious and therefore hangable? How would the process of vilification work?[7]

Many writers, referring to pirates, agreed that "the name of Men they do not deserve." So they re-created the outlaws as subhuman beings—monsters, demons, and animals. Mather called them "Sea-Monsters, who have been the Terror of them that haunt the Sea." Others called them blood-lusting monsters, merciless monsters, cruel sea monsters, sea wolves, and hellhounds. They were feral and carnivorous, "full of Malice, Rage, and Blood." They were wild and savage beasts, like a menacing mountain lion, which everyone should destroy in the public interest. When the authorities were confident of success against the pirates, as they were after the *Winchelsea*, a man-of-war, had taken a pirate ship and several of its crew had been hanged in Curaçao in 1723, the sea robbers were merely "Vermin" to be cleared from the seas. The language of demonization predicted the violence of naval battle and hangings.[8]

These demons created vast disorder, in their own lives and through their depredations against others. "Oh! the *Folly*. Oh! the *Madness* of wicked men!" wailed Mather to a crowd that soon would observe a multiple hanging of pirates in 1723. As fools and madmen, pirates betrayed disorders of the mind. Philip Ashton, captured by a "mad, roaring, and mischevious Crew" of pirates in 1722, had to endure "a perpetual Din of Madness," much rage and dementia, while among them. Indeed, Ashton thought himself aboard a ship of fools. Others insisted that pirates were "mad fellows," that they had madness in their hearts, that they swore like madmen, and that each died "as a Fool dieth."[9]

Pirates were as disordered in their hearts as in their minds, their natural temperament being rage and fury. Ashton closed the account of his providential escape from Edward Low's pirates by thanking God for "saving me from the Rage of the Pirates." Frequently, a pirate's "too aspiring Temper" was behind his derangement. Indeed, such savage, villainous, fierce, and depraved tempers possessed by pirates were "often mistaken for a degree of madness." In 1720 the *Boston News-Letter* printed a lengthy account of the wanton ruination of a ship's cargo by pirates, who used cutlasses, axes, and any other tools at hand as they "cut, tore, and broke open Trunks, Boxes, Cases and Bales."[10] Such insane destructiveness was clearly incompatible with reason. Pirates "declared themselves to live in opposition to the rule of Equity and Reason"; they had "no rational prospect"; they were "unreasonable Men." The wickedness of their crimes was "evident to the Reason of all Men," as Judge Trott explained.[11]

Such disorders of mind and affection logically produced a disturbed way of life. "Riots, Revels, Debauches" among pirates were said to be commonplace. Indeed, as Captain Charles Johnson pointed out in 1724, "a riotous Manner of Living ... is the Custom of Pyrates"; there were "almost constant Noisy Revellings," which were abated only by sleep—a drunken sleep, since the unruly manner of living was organized around the incessant use of strong drink. Drunkenness was so common among pirates that "Sobriety brought a Man under a Suspicion of being in a Plot" against the group, and "he was looked upon to be a Villain that would not be drunk." Drink, according to a clergyman, "renders a Man a Monster," and drunkenness was "a beastly sin, a voluntary madness" that placed one below the brute beasts. Pirates were "almost always mad or drunk, [and] their Behaviour produced infinite Disorders." Alcohol, some said, led to rioting and civil disturbance. It also was "the great incendiary of Lust," which was the bodily parallel of the pirate's disorder of mind. The "infernal fire of Lust" mastered these criminals, producing in them "a desire of living after their own wicked inclinations." Pirates found "their Lusts perpetually Enslaving of them; their Passions throwing them into perpetual Disorders," making them slaves to Satan.[12]

The greatest disorder perpetrated by the pirate was violence. Writers reported "unheard of Barbarities"—that pirates slit the noses of captives, cut off ears, and used the whip, knife, and gun against their victims, which, as we have seen in previous pages, did happen, although usually with a causal logic that was omitted by the pirates' enemies. Violence was natural to those who lived without government, in a state of nature, abandoned to riotous living, lusts, and passions. In an execution sermon preached to pirates in 1726, Benjamin Colman observed: "What a fearful state and condition a state of Sin is: a state of nature which is a state of wrath." Pirates, their enemies never tired of saying, were cruel, barbarous, and bloody. These "Sons of Violence" transgressed the flesh. By emphasizing violence and by describing it in lurid detail, writers universalized piracy as a threat, creating a community of interest between merchants and investors on one hand and the broader public on the other. Yet some of the reported barbarities were "unheard of" because they were invented: the *Boston News-Letter* reported in April 1723 that a crew of black pirates recently executed in Jamaica "confessed" on the gallows that they had eaten the hearts of eleven white men![13]

Pirates were held up as the antithesis of the Christian way of life. They were possessed by Satan, "Led Captive by him to do his will." Pirates did not have the fear of God before their eyes and were instigated by the devil; they were "*Children of the Wicked One.*" As the Reverend John Barnard said to his congregation and to Philip Ashton in particular, who had escaped from pirates, "*Think what God has Delivered you from* ... a Herd of Wild Beasts; among whom ... prodigious Defiances of Heaven and Amazing Assurances of their own Damnation ... gave you the Liveliest Picture of Hell, and rendered your Companions no better than *Devils* Incarnate." Try as they might to run as far as they could from God, striving "to keep all Thoughts of God out of their Minds," pirates were, with providential assistance, captured. And when authorities and pirates came face to face, both seized the moment to explain how one came to travel "the Way of

Wicked Men." Pirate confessions were published, and even though many of them were too uniform in style and content to have been entirely authentic, the pattern of alleged lamentations nonetheless illuminates the representation of the pirate and his way of life.[14]

Pirates were said to regret their transgressions of godly speech, the Sabbath, acceptable sexuality, and legitimate authority. Pirates rued having been such vehement swearers, cursers, and blasphemers. As Cotton Mather put it, they were users of "Horrid *Oathes*, & the Language of Fiends." They voiced furious expressions, engaged in "monstrous Swearing and Cursing"; they had "Tongues set of Fire of Hell." They openly defied heaven, blasphemed like madmen, and sang "Bawdy & Filthy *Songs*, enough to infect the very air they are uttered in." They also desecrated the Sabbath, profaning the Lord's day, and "absenting themselves from the Public Worship of God." Their environment did not help, since "some of them scarce knew when it was the Lord's Day, (while they were on the Seas)."[15]

Pirates asked repentance for their "stings" of unchastity and uncleanness—their visits to the House of the Harlot, their "running after Lewd Women," their homosexuality, their wild debaucheries—for which they were reckoned more like "beasts than men. Yea, the Scripture compares them to the filthiest of beasts, even to Dogs."[16] Pirates also bemoaned their disobedience to their parents and other authorities. Mather wondered, "How often do you hear them Confessing; My Grieving & Leaving & Scorning of my Parents, has been that which has Brought the dreadful Vengeance of GOD upon me!" They also bid "monstrous Undutifulness to their Superiors" and were said to "Mock the Ministers and Messengers of God with outrageous Insolencies."[17]

The last two sins on the long list were greed and the forsaking of honest toil. Pirates were driven to their plunder by a "craving Appetite, and an insatiable Thirst after inordinate Gain."

They displayed an "Immoderate, Inordinate, Irregular Desire of *Worldly Possessions*." In 1726 Mather elaborated on the point by quoting lines written by Sir Richard Blackmore:

> To this vile Crue you may the PIRATE add
> Who puts to Sea the Merchant to invade,
> And reaps the Profit of another's Trade.
> He sculks behind some Rock, or swiftly flies
> From Creek to Creek, rich Vessels to surprize.
> By this ungodly Course the Robber gains,
> And lays up so much Wealth, that he disdains
> And mocks the poor, unprofitable Toil,
> Of those, who plant the Vine, or till the Soil.

The victims of piracy, explained the King's attorney in 1717, were merchants, "the most Useful and Beneficial to the Publick; whose indefatigable Industry conveys amidst innumerable Dangers, besides that of falling into the hands of Pirates, Blood into the veins of the Body Politick, and nourishes every Member." Many an exploited sailor would have stood astonished at the description, but such was part of the ruling rationale.[18]

The pirate's image was closely related to the space he occupied—the sea, a distant place full of dangers, a site of frequent disaster, a potential path of invasion to England and the colonies, and finally a natural space that was difficult if not impossible to control. Massachusetts governor Samuel Shute insisted in May 1717 that a primary concern of his colony was to create "some good posture of Defence . . . to secure our Sea Coast and Trading Places from such Danger & Violence by way of the Sea." Six years later Mather observed that "the Terrors of them that haunt the Sea are of late exceedingly multiplied." Both men were referring in some measure to piracy, but the sea was awe-inspiring in its own right. It was a "furious Creature," and, in Christian terms, was likened to "the Gulph of Despair." In 1726 John Flavel's *Navigation Spiritualized: or, a New Compass for Sea-Men* emphasized one of the principal dangers of the sea and revealed that it was nothing new. Flavel wrote that Plato had "diligently admonished all men to avoid the Sea; For (saith he) it is the School master of all vice and dishonesty." It was a place teeming with strange creatures, a place where sins proliferated and where death was omnipresent. Seamen, noted Flavel, are "to be numbered neither with the living nor the dead, their lives hanging continually in suspense before them." Sailors were liminal figures traveling upon a perilous space.[19]

The pirate's occupation of a space that was dangerous and distant from centers of authority was a vital element in his image. For as the King's attorney claimed in a 1717 trial, piracy was a singularly atrocious crime "Because it is done in remote and Solitary Places, where the weak and Defenceless can expect no Assistance nor relief and where these ravenous Beasts of Prey may ravage undisturb'd, hard'ned in their Wickedness with Hopes of Impunity, and of being Concealed for ever from the Eyes and Hands of avenging Justice." He continued, "*Those Crimes ought to be Punished with the utmost Severity, which cannot without the greatest difficulty be prevented.*" In 1720 a similar charge was made by another of the King's advocates: "The Crime of Pyracy... is of all other Robberies the most aggravating and inhumane, in that being...in remote and distant Parts, ye do in Wantonness of Power add Cruelty to Theft." The suggestion that distance from authority conferred power on the pirate illustrates a crucial point.[20]

But the sea created distance from authority in ways other than merely geographic, because it was not hospitable territory for the principal organizing institutions of early modern life: church, family, and labor. In 1725 the noted essayist Bernard Mandeville acknowledged that "Amongst our Seafaring Men, the practice of Piety is very scarce." He continued, "There are not many of them that are well-grounded in the Principles of their Religion." The seaman's mobility, long stints of work at sea, and his single-sex community of labor diminished the family's regulatory powers and encouraged other social bonds. And labor itself was none too reliable a mechanism given the tendency of seamen to mutiny and turn pirate. The disciplinary network that underlay the social order thus had a weak presence at sea.[21]

Numerous writers, citing the need of "Discipline of the Seas" for the betterment of trade, tried to compensate by telling the seaman (a potential pirate) that God will follow you "to the uttermost parts of the Sea"; that the religious "eye is continually upon you"; and that "all your Actions and Transactions are open and naked." In 1723 Cotton Mather indicated that those who "go to Sea should have their Sailing Orders from our SAVIOUR" and instructed the seaman to acknowledge in prayer "thine Eye is always upon me." These warnings tried to make it clear to sailors that the reach of certain authorities could not be lessened by distance. But most sailors knew otherwise.[22]

The discourse on piracy thus revealed and attempted to correct a serious disconnection between authority and life at sea. The sea had made available to "desperate, filthy fellows" like seamen a singular opportunity: they could, with a willingness to face danger, risk their lives, and forsake some fundamental social rules, escape conventional authority, manufacture their own power, and accumulate considerable wealth by turning pirate. They used the uncontrollable seas for their own purposes, but these would figure only obliquely in the public discussion. Indeed, the extremity of the demonization suggests that the alternatives and challenges that piracy posed to the prevailing power relations, both in seafaring and the larger class-based society, had to be answered by destruction.[23]

The image of the pirate evolved alongside and influenced a series of practical policies to eradicate robbery at sea. "A Proclamation for Suppressing of Pyrates" was issued by the royal government on September 5, 1717, offering a general amnesty for those who had committed piracies as well as rewards to any who might capture freebooters and turn them over to the government, dead or alive. Hundreds of freebooters accepted the pardon, but many of these returned immediately "to the Old Trade of Pyrating." Another act of grace, as it was called, was issued later that year, on December 5, with similar results. Meanwhile, the government acted on complaints about the pirate rendezvous in the Bahama Islands, sending Woodes Rogers to destroy it and put a proper English government in its place. He arrived, as we have noted, on July 20, 1718, and most of the pirates scattered in response. A final amnesty was issued on December 21, 1718, to be extended a few months into 1719 in the hope that pirates would wish to come in, accept the pardon, and sign onto privateers in the brief War of the Quadruple Alliance against Spain. Some did, but many of them seem to have taken the side of Spain. Throughout, some accepted the grace but refused to reform; others "seem'd to slight it," and the most defiant "used the King's Proclamation with great contempt, and tore it into pieces."[24]

{ 137 }

The attacks against trade continued, and transatlantic merchants who felt their sting began to petition the government for an alternative policy to the failing pardons. By 1720 ruling groups had decided to use force, and in two forms: more vigilant naval patrolling and ever-greater numbers of spectacular executions. Many merchants had a vested interest in eliminating piracy, but the final assault was launched in large measure as a response to demands by the increasingly powerful traders in West African slaves.[25]

A series of sailors' mutinies shook the slave trade between 1716 and 1726, a logical outcome of the chronic complaints about food, discipline, and the general conditions of the working life aboard the slave ships that left England and America for West Africa during these years. Sailors alleged in court that Captain Theodore Boucher of the slave ship *Wanstead* "did not allow victualls & liquor enough to support them & used them very barbarously and inhumanly in their diett." Other sailors complained of tyrannical discipline. Those who dared to resist shipboard conditions might find themselves "as Slaves linked and coupled by chains together & were fedd with Yams & Water the Usuall dyett for Slaves." In 1720 Francis Willis, a naval captain posted to the West African station, reported to the Admiralty that the sailors in the slave ships were "ripe for pyracy." He added, with discretion, "Whether it be occasioned by the masters' ill usage or their own natural inclination I must leave their Lordships to judge."[26]

Some mutinous sailors, however, averted a fate of chains by seizing their vessels and raising the black flag. When George Lowther and his comrades mutinied aboard the Royal African Company ship *Gambia Castle* in 1720, they "knocked down the Cabins, made the Ship flush fore and aft, prepared black Colours, new named her, the *Delivery*," and sailed away in triumph. Lowther and his crew may have taken inspiration from the hundreds of pirates who headed for the coast of Africa after the 1718 reestablishment of royal authority in the Bahama Islands, attacking poorly defended ships, seizing their cargo, and recruiting their crew members. Edward England and other pirate captains found the slavers to be excellent recruiting grounds. One slave trader testified that when his ship was taken, the pirates "diverted themselves" with the women slaves but also "Took off the Irons from all the [250] Negroes I had on board." Worse still, they "had armed the Negroes" with knives, leaving the captain in fear of deadly insurrection when he was allowed to retake control of the vessel.[27]

The pirates' interest in this region lay not in capturing ships full of slaves—there would have been few big merchants in the Americas willing to trade with them anyway—but in the ships themselves, which were on their way to trading for slaves. Several merchants pointed out that what pirates really wanted were "good Sailing Shipps well furnished with Ammunition, Provisions, & Stores of all Kinds, fitt for long Voyages."[28] Many sailors believed that slave ships—which were big, sturdy, seaworthy, and usually well armed with a variety of cannon—made the best pirate ships, or so suggested would-be mutineer Robert Sparks in a careful, somewhat elliptical comment to his fellow sailors aboard the *Abingdon* in 1719: "he believed that he could make the Ship go much better than she did." How would he do this, wondered John Whitcomb. Sparkes answered, "by Ripping off the upper Deck, and then she would be a Ship fit for Business." Mate John Bicknor asked "what business he meant." Sparkes replied: "she would make a good Pirate Ship, for he believed, that she would be stiffer and go better." Others apparently agreed, for several slave ships were captured and converted, including the shipwrecked and recently rediscovered *Whydah*, captained by Black Sam Bellamy and named for the slaving port in Benin.[29]

To make matters worse, pirates, as we saw in the biography of Walter Kennedy in chapter 3, did not restrict themselves to attacking only the shipping on the west coast of Africa. They also plundered the slave-trading fortresses, the vital nodes of human transshipment, as a group of merchants explained in a petition to the Admiralty in 720: pirates "sometimes land at the chief Factories and carry off what they think fit." Howell Davis and his crew attacked, plundered, and destroyed Gambia Castle in 1719, the fort at Sierra Leone soon after, and finally the Portuguese fort on the Princes Islands. These were serious, destructive, disruptive assaults, driven, as we have seen, by revenge but also by the knowledge that the Portuguese often paid for slaves and goods in gold.[30]

Davis and his successor, Bartholomew Roberts, were, with their crews of hundreds of pirates, the greatest plague to African merchants and their property. Between 1719 and 1722 they ranged up and down the African coast, "sinking, burning, and destroying such Goods and Vessels as then happen'd in [their] Way." As they sailed from Senegambia to the Gold Coast and back, the region most vital to British merchants in the 1720s, they "struck a Pannick into the Traders," observed naval surgeon John Atkins, who spent several months on the coast. Another writer estimated in 1720 that pirates had already done more than £100,000 worth of damage on the coast of Africa, and the greatest period of plunder in the region, over the next two years, was yet to come! In 1724

Figure 11. Captain Bartholomew and eleven captured
merchant vessels off the coast of West Africa; Captain
Charles Johnson, *A General History of the Robberies and
Murders of the Most Notorious Pyrates* (London, 1724).

an anonymous writer to the Board of Trade explained that pirates had taken "near 100 sail of Ships in the space of two years"
in the African slave trade. Things got so bad for traders that in
1720 the Royal African Company was forced to announce that
gratuities would be paid to officers and men injured in defense of
vessels attacked by pirates, and that larger sums would be paid to
their families in the event of their death.[31]

The extensive damage caused by pirates to the African trade
and the role its merchants played in suppression are demonstrated in the surviving papers of Humphrey Morice of London,
one of the leading slave traders of the time. Morice would eventually become a member of Parliament and, in 1727–29, governor of the Bank of England (from which he would swindle
£29,000). Between 1716 and 1732 (the year of his death), Morice
was personally responsible for the shipment of almost twenty
thousand Africans to the Americas. His small fleet of slave-

trading vessels made sixty-two voyages during these years. Drawing on letters from ship captains such as William Snelgrave (whom we met in chapter 5) and slave-trading officials such as James Phipps, chief factor at Cape Coast Castle, and an unnamed naval officer, Morice kept a close watch on the pirates. In 1718 he redirected one of his vessels to Maryland to avoid the freebooters swarming about Jamaica, but eventually the pirates captured three of his ships: the *Bird Galley*, captained by Snelgrave, the *Heroine*, captained by Richard Blincoe (both in 1719), and the *Princess*, captained by Thomas Wickstead (in 1722).[32]

Morice carefully recorded the damage being done by pirates, all the better with which to make a case for naval action by the British government. To summarize the dismal situation, he did an accounting for the five months between April and August 1719, bringing together three lists: "An Acct of Shipps taken by Pirates at Sierraleone on the Coast of Africa in April 1719," which was based on information sent to him in a letter by Captain Snelgrave on April 30, 1719; a second list merely entitled "Taken by said Pirates on the Gold Coast Whidah & Calabar"; and finally "A List of Ships taken at Gamba." Much to Morice's dismay, more than five hundred pirates sailed in "squadrons" with captains Howell Davis, Oliver LaBouche, Thomas Cocklyn, Edward England, Robert Sample, and a man known only as Lane, taking thirty-four ships in this brief period, several of which, like the *Robert & James*, they burned. He also gathered information from Captain John Daggs, who wrote to him in February 1720, "I was Informed att Barbados that the Pirates had taken upon the Coast of Guinea 38 Saile of Ships." Another captain, Jabez Biglow, relayed the boast (which was probably true) of Edward England's crew that they had (by April 1719) captured fifty vessels. In drawing up his own list, Morice made it his business to know the name of each ship and master taken and, no less, to know the names of the pirate captains, their vessels, and their strength in terms of cannon and number of men.[33]

Such information would lead Morice to draft two petitions,

one (undated) to the King on behalf of "Planters Merch[an]ts & Traders concernd in the West Indies," the other "The Memoriall of the Merchants of London Trading to Africa humbly Offered to the Rt. Hon.ble The Lords Commissioners for Executing the Office of Lord High Admirall of Great Brittaine &c.," during the early months of 1720. In the former, Morice warned that pirates "are so encreased in number that they are become dangerous to your Majesties plantations as well as destructive to the navigation of the West Indies." In the latter he expressed fear that pirates might in 1720 "do as much mischiefe as the others did the last year," when he personally lost two vessels. In both petitions Morice argued for naval force, and indeed he did not merely argue. He used political connections (with, for example, MP John Jennings) to help dispatch men-of-war to the African coast to protect the slave trade against the "terrour of ye Pirates." New tours began in 1719 and continued for several years.[34]

Merchants from Bristol, Liverpool, London, and many other British Atlantic ports, including those of the recently revitalized (though still declining) Royal African Company, formed a chorus around Morice, protesting their losses and demanding that Parliament take action to protect their trade, the plantation system, and the empire as a whole. Their cries fell on sympathetic ears. When two groups of merchants petitioned Parliament for relief in February 1721, at the very peak of Roberts's depredations, the House of Commons ordered an immediate drafting of another bill for the suppression of piracy, which, with Prime Minister Robert Walpole's assistance, was quickly passed.[35]

That same month a naval squadron under the leadership of Captain Challoner Ogle set sail for the African coast. (One crew member aboard one of the ships, the *Weymouth*, was Alexander Selkirk, the once-marooned sailor who was the prototype of Robinson Crusoe and who died on the voyage.) The convoy, led by the *Swallow*, arrived in Sierra Leone in April and Cape Coast Castle in June and began to patrol the coast. By January 1722 the *Weymouth* was disabled by sickness, but the *Swallow* eventually found and engaged the ships of Roberts, the first on February 5 and the second and larger of the two, on February 10. Many of { 143 } the pirates were drunk, and in any case they were no match for naval artillery. After grapeshot killed Roberts and a cannonball blew away his ship's mainmast, rendering it incapable of any offensive or defensive maneuver, the fight was over. The pirates took heavy casualties, a few escaped into the jungle, a select few were hanged aboard the *Weymouth* (to send a message), and a majority (more than 250) were captured and ordered to stand trial, if that's what the proceedings at Cape Coast Castle can be called. The pirates were held in the dungeons where enslaved Africans were customarily chained, marked with burning irons, fed, and held for the arriving slave ships. The pirates were tried within Cape Coast Castle's brick walls, which were fourteen feet thick and guarded by seventy-four mounted cannons, and fifty-two of them were executed and their chained corpses distributed along the coast in order to maximize the terror: nine at Cape Coast, four on the Windward Coast, two each at Acera, Calabar, and Whydah, and one at Winnebah. Another forty were sentenced to slavery, to work for the Royal African Company on ships or in gold mines; all of them apparently died in a matter of months. After his triumphant return to London, Challoner Ogle became, in May 1723, the first naval captain to be knighted for his actions against pirates. He was honored by King George I, whom Roberts and his fellow pirates had humorously ridiculed as "the turnip man."[36]

The defeat of Roberts and the subsequent eradication of piracy off the coast of Africa represented a turning point in the slave trade and even in the larger history of capitalism. Piracy and the slave trade had been linked for centuries, especially in the Mediterranean, where freebooters were a main source in supplying labor. Now pirates had interfered with the trade, and at a crucial moment. The end of the War of Spanish Succession brought a rich and shiny prize for British merchants: the *Asiento*, which gave these traders the legal right to ship forty-eight hundred slaves a year, and the illegal right to ship many more, to Spanish America through the South Sea Company. This incentive, coupled with the final deregulation of the African slave trade in 1712, when the chartered Royal African Company lost its battle against the free traders who had already begun to supply most of the slaves to American plantations, dramatically increased the importance of the slave trade in the eyes of British merchants and the state.[37]

Pirates now had to be exterminated for the new trade to flourish, a point made by William Snelgrave, who published *A New Account of Some Parts of Guinea and the Slave Trade*, dedicated to "the Merchants of London, trading to the Coast of Guinea." He divided the book into three sections, providing for his readers a "History of the late Conquest of the Kingdom of *Whidaw* by the King of *Dahomè*"; an account of the business practices and statistics of the slave trade; and "A Relation of the Author's being taken by Pirates" and the dangers posed thereby. But by the time Snelgrave published his book in 1734, piracy was dead, defeated by the terror of hanging and enhanced naval patrols, though occasionally the corpse would twitch with a mutiny here, an act of piracy there. In the immediate aftermath of the suppression of piracy, Britain consolidated its dominance on the west coast of Africa. As James A. Rawley has written, "In the decade of the 1730s England had become the supreme slaving nation in the Atlantic world, a standing she occupied until 1807." The slaves embarked on the trade had reached low points in 1720, 1721, and 1722, the years of greatest pirate activity, and surged upward immediately after their suppression, from 24,780 in 1720 to 47,030 in 1725 to a high of 49,130 in 1729. If the plantation capital of the Caribbean, allied with the merchant capital of the metropolis, killed the first generation of pirates—the buccaneers of the 1670s—and if the capital of the East India Company killed the pirates of the 1690s, when the company's ships were hothouses of mutiny and rebellion, it was the African slave-trading capital that killed the pirates of the early eighteenth century. Pirates had ruptured the Middle Passage, and this would not be tolerated. By 1726 the maritime state had removed a major obstacle to the accumulation of capital in its ever-growing Atlantic system.[38]

The image of the pirate and the military-legal campaign against them intersected in the courtroom and on the gallows, where members of Roberts's crew and hundreds of other pirates met their end. As we saw in chapter 1, and indeed throughout the book, executions of pirates were big events, and none was bigger than the execution of the most successful gang of pirates in recent memory. At this hanging as at others, multitudes of spectators gathered to hear official addresses, often a passionate sermon, and the last words of the condemned and to observe the villain's end, his *"awry Neck"* and *"Wet Pair of Breeches."*[39] The condemned pirate was meant to be awestruck, as a minister explained: "fearfulness and horror should overwhelm him; a dreadful sound should be in his ears of the Destroyer coming on him; Trouble and anguish shall make him afraid." He was to be silent, sober and sad, grave and serious, and consumed by sorrow and contrition. The place of execution afforded one last opportunity for the pirate to be orderly, to lament his transgression of the disciplinary institutions of church, family, and labor, and to prostrate himself before all authorities: God, minister, family, nation, and Crown. Some pirates complied, affirming the social order that they had, in their beastly criminality, undermined.[40]

Yet many pirates, as we have seen, refused to play the game; recall the pirates in Virginia who used the occasion of their hanging in 1720 to taunt the governor, pirates such as William Fly who in 1726 vented his rage against ship captains. A pirate facing execution in London in 1715, wrote the Reverend Paul Lorrain, rejected all admonitions and offered to kick the minister "downstairs." This fellow seemed to have "no Sense nor Principles of any Religion whatsoever, that could restrain him from Evil: And tho' one wou'd have thought he should have grown more rational and considerate at the approach of Death, yet he still retain'd his harden'd Temper and Irreligious and Impious Humour, who would neither hear the Word of GOD, nor make confession of, nor indeed seem'd in the least Sorry for his Sins." These pirates continued to oppose the authorities and attack the social order.[41] The impenitent and notorious were often hanged in chains, made "to stand like Marks or Fatal Rocks and Sands, to warn others from the same Shipwreck and ruin for the Future." The disorderly body that had allowed its lusts to rule and its temper to rage was put on display as a dead animal's carcass, now infused with symbolic power, carefully placed "within the Flux and Reflux of the Sea."[42]

Cotton Mather summed up the situation in 1726. Pirates, he said, were "Guilty of all Sins." Their detestable way of living "banished every Social Vertue." Having escaped the disciplinary effects of church, family, and labor, the pirate was denounced as bereft of wisdom and reason, possessed by madness, rage, temper, drink, and lust, behaving like a wild beast, and sowing massive disorder on distant but strategically important seas, especially the west coast of Africa. Stripped of all human characteristics, the pirate was now a wild fragment of nature that could be tamed only by death. According to the King's attorney, the pirate "can claim the protection of no Prince, the privilege of no Country, the benefit of no Law; *he is denied common humanity* and the very rights of Nature." Another added that pirates "have no country, but by their Guilt, separate themselves, renouncing the benefit of all lawful Society." The pirate's enemies had slowly but thoroughly disconnected him from the social order, showing him to be the enemy of all individuals, property owners, the colony, the empire, the King, the British nation, the world of nations, and all mankind. It remained for the pirate to be "hanged like a dog" and his corpse put on public display so that everyone could learn the lessons of property and order.[43]

Did the hanging work? It is impossible to be sure, but Admiral Edward Vernon, stationed in the West Indies, certainly thought so. In 1720 he wrote that "the fear of a Halter may effect what the fear of the Lord is ineffectual for among such abandoned Wretches." Five months later he added that the hanging of three pirates in Jamaica "has already made a great alteration in the behaviour of the Sea fareing People, who are become very Civill, and there has not been one Riot among them since which was their daily practice before." Another month later he observed, "These punishments have made a Wonderful reformation here." At the same time the punishments incited more violence and intensified the dialectic of terror. As more and more pirates were hanged, and as the likelihood of death for anyone who went "upon the account" increased, pirates responded by intensifying their commitment to each other, "one and all." And they did so with a laugh.[44]

Chapter Eight

"DEFIANCE OF DEATH ITSELF"

I BEGIN THE FINAL CHAPTER with tales of apocalypse, two stories told by men who had been captured by pirates. Samuel Cary, commander and probably the owner of a "rich ship" named the *Samuel,* which sailed out of London, gave the first account to an editor at the *Boston News-Letter.* His vessel had carried a cargo worth £8,000–9,000 until taken on July 13, 1720, off the coast of Newfoundland by the pirate crew of Black Bart Roberts. Captain Richard Hawkins told the second story, an "account of the Pirates in America," to a periodical called *The Political State of Great Britain,* recounting his capture in the Leeward Islands of the Caribbean on March 22, 1724, by Francis Spriggs and his gang of freebooters. Hawkins's cargo (logwood from Central America) was less lucrative, but his story was no less dramatic.

Cary watched in dismay as the pirates tore through his cargo like "a parcel of Furies," taking what they wanted and throwing the rest into the sea, threatening, swearing, cursing, and blaspheming all the while. The pirates were full of "madness and rage." He later heard them declare that "they would not go to Hope point in the River of Thames to be hung up in Gibbets a Sundrying as Kidd and Bradish's Company did, for if it should chance that they should be Attacked by any Superiour power or force, which they could not master, they would immediately put fire with one of their Pistols to their Powder, and all go merrily to Hell together!" Here they demonstrated their sense of humor, their knowledge of history, and their apocalyptic impulse. "Hope point" was their facetious term for Execution Dock in Wapping on the Thames, where for centuries pirates had been hanged or drowned. Pirates William Kidd and Joseph Bradish had been hanged there in 1701, their corpses enclosed in metal cages and suspended in public as a warning to others. Roberts and his crew vowed to blow themselves up rather than give the British state the satisfaction—and the terroristic propaganda value—of executing them.[1]

Hawkins went through "the utmost Confusion and Anxiety of Mind" during and after his capture by Spriggs and company. The pirates boarded his vessel and took what they wanted; "every Thing that pleased them not they threw over-board." Later, the pirates ate, drank, grew merry, and, seeking "Diversion, for Mischief is their sole Delight," decided to create for themselves a late-night fireworks show. They set Hawkins's ship aflame, and "in less than three Quarters of an Hour she was all of a Blaze, and down she went." He added, "They have no Thoughts of ever being taken; but swear, with the most direful Imprecations, that if ever they should find themselves over-power'd, they would immediately blow their Ship up, rather than do Jolly Roger the disgrace to be struck, or suffer themselves to be hang'd like Dogs." Like the crew of Roberts, they swore to control their own fate, even if it proved to be a fatal one.[2]

Such declarations were by no means unusual among pirates between 1716 and 1726. Indeed, many crews pledged to each other that "They would blow up rather than be taken." Two pirates transformed the vow into a personal ritual of friendship and devotion: they "took their Pistols, and laid them down by them, and solemnly swore to each other, and pledg'd the Oath in a Bumper of Liquor, that if they saw that there was at last no possibility of Escaping, but that they should be taken, they would set Foot to Foot, and Shoot one another, to Escape Justice and the Halter." John Gow and his fellow pirates also vowed to blow up—"as they had lived so they would die together." Captain Charles Harris and his crew "always kept a Barrel of Powder ready to blow up the Sloop rather than be taken." A favorite toast of Black Bart Roberts among these ever-toasting, ever-drinking sea robbers was "Damnation to him who ever lived to wear a halter." Coming as they did from a maritime culture suffused with death, and facing the gallows for their choice to break the maritime law of property, pirates defiantly embraced the destructive element.[3]

These were no idle boasts. Some of the members of Roberts's crew meant exactly what they said to Samuel Cary, and indeed they would soon prove it. When they met up with the *Swallow*, as described in the previous chapter, a hot engagement ensued. True to his toast, Roberts did not live to be hanged. Staying on the main deck with his men during battle, he was killed when grapeshot "struck him directly in the Throat." His comrades immediately honored a long-standing request: they threw his corpse, still armed, overboard. But once the commander was gone, their ship shattered, "all Hopes fled," and the cause lost, half a dozen pirates tried to make good on their collective promise to "put fire with one of their Pistols to their Powder, and all go merrily to Hell together!" They gathered around the gunpowder in the magazine in the steerage, into which John Morris fired an incendiary shot. As it happened, the long engagement had depleted the powder, which was now "too small a Quantity to effect any Thing more than burning them in a frightful Manner." Unable to ignite the apocalyptic explosion they had hoped for, Morris nonetheless managed to kill himself and two of his comrades. Meanwhile, on Roberts's consort ship, the *Ranger*, a similar drama was unfolding. James Phillips walked (a little drunkenly, it was said) "with a lighted match" toward the magazine, "swearing very profanely lets all go to Hell together." He and several others who wanted to carry out the common oath got into a skirmish with mates who found that the once-popular idea had suddenly lost some of its appeal and were prevented from lighting the gunpowder.[4]

Numerous other pirate crews of this generation also attempted to blow themselves up, and at least one of them succeeded. As Blackbeard and his fellow pirates began to lose their bloody, hand-to-hand battle with Lieutenant Robert Maynard

and his naval force off the coast of North Carolina at the end of
November 1718, a black pirate named Caesar, "a resolute fellow,"
tried to blow up the ship but was prevented "by two Prisoners
that were then in the Hold of the Sloop." When the pirate ship
commanded by Charles Harris was taken by Captain Philip
Solgard and H.M.S. *Greyhound* in late 1723, one freebooter made
his way toward the keg of powder to ignite the long-promised
blast; "being hindered," Captain Solgard reported, "he went forward, and with his Pistol shot out his own Brains." Another
group of pirates, captained by Joseph Cooper and sailing in the
West Indies in early 1726, had lost a battle with a ship of the Royal
Navy. When the officers of the victorious vessel tried to board,
Cooper and his mates blew up their ship, killing themselves.[5]

The death wish of pirates applied not only to moments of capture, as Captain William Snelgrave discovered, to his horror,
while a prisoner aboard Thomas Cocklyn's vessel, the *Rising Sun*,
in April 1719. A nameless pirate one day asked, said Snelgrave,
"Whether I was afraid of going to the Devil by a great Shot."
Snelgrave hardly knew what to say. He could only listen as the
pirate declared his own hope—that "he should be sent to Hell
one of these days by a Cannon Ball." Snelgrave replied weakly,
"I hoped that would not be my Road." But not long after, when
a fire broke out on the pirate ship, he thought his own road was
before him. He, like everyone else on board, knew that the ship
had thousands of pounds of gunpowder in its magazine. Soon he
heard "a loud shout upon the Main-deck." The "old harden'd
Rogues" among the crew, some of them drunk, had gathered
near the fire and begun to huzzah: *"For a brave blast to go to Hell
with."* This chant they "repeated several times," much to the terror of Snelgrave and the "new entered Pirates" who were fran-
tically trying to put out the blaze. The pirates were cheering,
lustily and repeatedly, for their own mutual destruction.[6]

It was a destruction designed to carry them to a specific destination. In announcing that they were on their way to hell, pirates affirmed what respectable, God-fearing people never tired

Figure 12. Edward Teach, a.k.a. Blackbeard; Captain Charles Johnson, A *General History of the Lives and Adventures of the Most Famous Highwaymen, Murderers, Street Robbers, &c.* (London, 1734).

of saying about them—that they were devils, all bound for hell. The captive Philip Ashton, for example, called Ned Low's crew "*Devils* Incarnate" who "gave you the Liveliest Picture of Hell." Judges and ministers routinely proclaimed that pirates had been "instigated by the devil." By agreeing, pirates inverted the values of Christianity and in various ways cast themselves as something their larger society understood to be evil. Here too they displayed an edgy sense of humor.

The maritime outlaws embraced Lucifer, the most rebellious of angels. Blackbeard, for example, consciously cultivated an image of himself as Satan, tying up his long black hair and beard in pigtails and inserting sparklers around his face to create an eerie, fiery glow when capturing prize vessels. When William Bell happened upon the tall, intimidating pirate on the Carolina coast and asked who he was and whence he came, Blackbeard replied that "he came from Hell and he would carry him [there] presently." William Fly taunted Puritan prelates Cotton Mather and Benjamin Colman by "wishing all the devils of hell would come and fly away with the Ship" in which he was captured. Another pirate explained to Snelgrave as he threw a captain's books overboard that such things bred mischief and might "prevent some of their Comrades from going on in their Voyage to Hell, whither they were all bound." Captain John Phillips spied a prospective prize and remarked to a bystander that he "want'd the damn'd thing just long enough to sail to Hell in."[7]

Captain Charles Johnson illuminated this mentality when he described a conversation between two pirates chained together in captivity on their way to being hanged. When one of them took to praying, the older pirate of the two, Thomas Sutton, swore at the younger man and asked him "what he proposed by so much Noise and Devotion." "Heaven, says the other, I hope." Sutton was aghast. "Heaven, you Fool, says Sutton, did you ever hear of any Pyrates going thither?" No, he said, "Give me H–ll, it's a merrier Place: I'll give Roberts a salute of 13 Guns at Entrance." When it became clear that his words had no effect, Sutton requested that the guard "either remove this Man, or take his Prayer-Book away, as a common Disturber."[8] Some pirates turned the religious world, like the social world, upside down. Hell was a merrier place than heaven, and pirates loved merriment.

In this chapter we listen to these cries from the dead zone, using them to explore the interrelated themes of death, apocalypse, hell, and self-destruction—fundamental matters of life and death and what they might have meant to these poor, motley, seafaring people in the early eighteenth century. Piracy in the early eighteenth century was, at bottom, a struggle for life against socially organized death. The contradictory, ironic, and humorous embrace of death by the pirates seems a good point of entry.

Pirates themselves made the point about the omnipresence of death, and made it repeatedly, in court, in petitions, and in mutinous action. A man from Aberdeen named William Scott, a member of Stede Bonnet's crew, gave a simple, quiet self-defense in his 1718 trial for piracy in Charleston, South Carolina: "What I did, was to keep me from perishing." When pirate Stephen Smith wrote a letter to a royal official requesting a pardon for his piracies, he explained, I am "now forced to go a pirateing to gett a living, which is much against my will." Finding himself aboard a death ship and contemplating mutiny and piracy in 1719, seaman Robert Sparks explained to his fellow tars that "they had better be dead than live in misery." William Mething agreed, adding, "Damn it, it was better to be hanged than [to] live so." In 1721, after organizing a successful mutiny aboard a Royal African Company ship, George Lowther spoke for all of the sailors: "it was not their Business to starve, or be made Slaves." Men who had sailed with Edward Condent in the Indian Ocean explained that they "had got enough & don their Busyness, & that they need not go to sea again as long as they lived." For many, piracy was an effort to escape the death trap, a desperate although contradictory choice for life.[9]

They found—and made—much life, if only for a short while, as we have seen. Once sailors got, as Walter Kennedy put it, "the choice in themselves"—that is, the autonomous power to organize the ship and its miniature society as they wanted—they built a better world than the one they had found on the merchant, naval, and privateering ships of the early modern Atlantic. They transformed harsh discipline into a looser, more libertarian way of running their ship that depended on "what Punishment the Captain and Majority of the Company shall think fit." They transformed the realities of chronically meager rations into ri-

otous chronic feasting, an exploitative wage relation into a collective risk bearing, and injury and premature death into active
health care and security. Their democratic selection of officers
stood in stark, telling contrast to the near-dictatorial arrangement of command in the merchant service and Royal Navy.
Building on the lower-class/lower-deck values of collectivism,
anti-authoritarianism, and egalitarianism, the pirates realized,
through their social order, tendencies that had been dialectically
generated and in turn suppressed in the normal course of alien-
ated work and life at sea. These signs of life flowered in the black
shadow of death, for if the dangers of the common seaman's life
were extreme, those surrounding the pirate, in battle, in prison,
or on the gallows, loomed even larger. They looked this grim reality in the eye and laughed.

A gang of pirates, five thousand miles from London, sat amid the
red mangrove trees on a deserted island off the southwestern
coast of Cuba, musing about life, death, justice, and the English
legal system. The year was 1722. Pirates with Captain Thomas
Anstis had retired to the island to live what they called "a marooning life." They hoped to be pardoned by King George II for
their piracies, which were many, and indeed they had written a
petition to him for that purpose. Now they would lie low while
awaiting an answer by way of a Jamaica merchant, in the mean-
time subsisting on turtle and diverting themselves as best they
could. They did what sailors usually did to pass the long, tedious
hours at sea: they danced, they sang, they told tales, and they performed plays.[10]

One of their favorite dramas was a "Mock Court of Judicature
to try one another for Pyracy." They created a *dramatis personae*
and allocated the roles. One pirate was selected to be the judge
to hear the case, another the attorney general to prosecute, others to be court officials and staff, yet others to make up the
jury, and several, finally, to be the accused. They improvised with

Figure 13. The mock trial performed by the crew of Thomas Anstis;
Captain Charles Johnson, *A General History of the Robberies and
Murders of the Most Notorious Pyrates* (London, 1724).

costumes, props, and sets. Lacking a black robe, the judge "had
a dirty Tarpulin hung over his Shoulders." Lacking a wig, he
stuck a thrum cap on his head. He put "a large Pair of Spectacles
on his Nose" and took his exalted place up in a tree so as to look
down on the proceedings from a position above it all. Scurrying
around below were "an abundance of Officers attending him,"
comically using ship's tools, "Crows, Handspikes, &c. instead of
Wands, Tipstaves, and such like." Soon "the Criminals were

brought out," probably in chains, "making a thousand sour Faces" as they entered the outdoor courtroom. The attorney general "opened the Charges against them." His speech, like all of the others in the play, was "very laconick," and the entire proceeding "concise." They apparently performed the play numerous times, changing the roles so that "he that was a Criminal one Day was made Judge another."[11]

News of the play eventually made its way from the Caribbean to London, to Captain Charles Johnson, who would include it in *A General History of the Pyrates,* the first volume of which was published in 1724. He wrote, "I had an Account given me of one of these merry Tryals, and as it appeared diverting, I shall give the Readers a short Account of it." It is not known whether the account "given" to Johnson was written or oral, though it was most likely relayed as a detailed story by a member of Anstis's crew who had been on the island, escaped subsequent shipwreck and capture, and returned secretly to England in October 1723. Johnson admitted knowing two members of the crew, whom, he explained, "I forbear to name, because, I understand they are at this day employed in an honest Vocation" in London. Johnson, who is widely regarded as a reliable chronicler, insisted on the authenticity of the play: "This is the Tryal just as it was related to me; the Design of my setting it down, is only to shew how these Fellows can jest upon things, the Fear and Dread of which, should make them tremble." This is precisely what makes the play so valuable for our purposes: it shows the pirate's ability to laugh in the face of his own death.

The play begins, and the courtroom comes to order.

ATTORN. GEN. *An't please your Lordship, and you gentlemen of the Jury, here is a Fellow before you that is a sad Dog, a sad sad Dog; and I humbly hope your Lordship will order him to be hang'd out of the Way immediately —He has committed Pyracy on the High seas, and we shall prove, an't please your Lordship, that this Fellow, this sad Dog before you, has escap'd a thousand Storms, nay, has got safe ashore when the Ship has been cast away, which was a certain sign he was not born to be drown'd; yet not having the Fear of Hanging before his Eyes, he went on robbing and ravishing Man, Woman, and Child, plundering Ships' Cargoes fore and aft, burning and sinking Ship, Bark, and Boat, as if the Devil had been in him. But this is not all, my Lord, he has committed worse Villainies than all these, for we shall prove, that he has been guilty of drinking Small-Beer, and your Lordship knows, there never was sober fellow but what was a Rogue.—My Lord, I should have spoke much finer than I do now, but that as your Lordship knows our Rum is all out, and how should a man speak good Law that has not drank a Dram —However, I hope, your Lordship will order the Fellow to be hang'd.*

JUDGE.—*Hearkee me, Sirrah,—you lousy, pittiful, ill-look'd Dog; what have you to say why you should not be tuck'd up immediately, and set a Sun-drying like a Scare-crow?—Are you guilty, or not guilty?*

PRIS. *Not guilty, an't please your Worship.*

JUDGE. *Not guilty! Say so again, Sirrah, and I'll have you hang'd without any Tryal.*

PRIS. *An't please your Worship's Honour, my Lord, I am as honest a poor Fellow as ever went between Stem and Stern of a Ship, and can hand, reef, and steer, and clap two Ends of a Rope together, as well as e'er a He that ever cross'd salt Water; but I was taken by one George Bradley [the name of him that sat as Judge] a notorious Pyrate, a sad Rogue as ever was un-hang'd, and he forced me, an't please your Honour.*

JUDGE. *Answer me, Sirrah, —How will you be tried?*

PRIS. *By G— and my Country.*

JUDGE. *The Devil you will.—Why then, gentlemen of the Jury, I think we have nothing to do but to proceed to Judgment.*

ATTOR. GEN. *Right, my Lord; for if the Fellow should be suffer'd to speak, he may clear himself, and that's an Affront to the Court.*

PRIS. *Pray, my Lord, I hope your Lordship will consider—*

JUDGE. *Consider!—How dare you talk of considering? —Sirrah, Sirrah, I never consider'd in all my Life. —I'll make it Treason to consider.*

PRIS. *But, I hope, your Lordship will hear some reason.*

JUDGE. *D'ye hear how the Scoundrel prates?—What have we to do with*

Reason?—I'd have you to know, Raskal, we don't sit here to hear Reason;—we go according to Law.—Is our dinner ready?

ATTOR. GEN. *Yes, my Lord.*

JUDGE. *Then heark'ee, you Raskal at the Bar; hear me, Sirrah, hear me.— You must suffer for three Reasons: First, because it is not fit I should sit here as Judge, and no Body be hang'd. —Secondly, you must be hang'd, because you have a damn'd hanging look. —And thirdly, you must be hang'd because I am hungry; for know, Sirrah, that 'tis a Custom, that whenever the Judge's Dinner is ready before the Tryal is over, the Prisoner is to be hang'd of Course. —There's law for you, ye Dog.—So take him away Gaoler.*

The scene no doubt dissolves into hilarity, which is, of course, the point of the gallows humor; the pirates imagined their own deaths and found comedy in it, or, to put the same point another way, they displayed the creative stubbornness of life in the face of extinction. They were not pondering an abstract proposition. Show trials of sea robbers had been taking place with increasing frequency since 1717, and by 1722 scores of those who sailed under the black flag had already been "launched into eternity." Their decaying bodies adorned the entrances to harbors around the Atlantic. We do not know if any of the members of Anstis's crew had attended or actually been prosecuted in any of these earlier trials, but at the very least we know that the stories of the trials had gotten around. And besides, the pirates, as seamen, would have had courtroom experience as defendants or witnesses, in disputes over wages, desertion, salvage, or mutiny. In any case, the pirates knew exactly what they wished to parody: first and foremost their object was the English legal system—the judge, the attorney, the law itself, and the class system they represented. But the pirates also reserved a few humorous, profane words for others: sober people, God, nation, even themselves.

The main purpose of the play was to expose—and satirize— England's pride, its legal system, the embodiment and protector of liberty, which is shown by the pirates to be a machinery of death; hanging is mentioned a dozen times in a short dialogue.

The fundamental class relationship is between the haughty, pretentious judge and the poor, *honest* sailor who stands accused of piracy. The judge is powerful enough to dispense with a trial altogether, arrogant enough to refuse to listen to reason, arbitrary enough to hang someone for no good cause, and gluttonous enough to put his next meal above someone's life. The poor pirate is stripped of his voice, as the attorney general explains: *"Right, my Lord; for if the Fellow should be suffer'd to speak, he may clear himself, and that's an Affront to the Court."* The hanging is therefore a foregone conclusion, a product of unreason and vulgar class bias. The judge solemnly intones: *"it is not fit I should sit here as Judge, and no Body be hang'd."* That is the purpose of the system, *"So take him away Gaoler."* The roles have been reversed, and the world has turned topsy-turvy. The judge is now the criminal.

The actors also make fun of the sober, straight-laced, and respectable type who drinks only "small-beer" and thereby brings great suspicion on himself in pirate society. They play with the popular saying about class fate: "He that's born to hang need fear no drowning." They poke fun at the pirate who seems to think that devotion to religion and nation can get him justice. With foolish hope, he asks to be tried *"By G— and my Country."* They ridicule the supplicant, calling him "a sad sad dog." But they go even further, showing that they know what they will do should they find themselves in court one day. They will, one after another, do as the poor prisoner does here; that is, claim to be "forced men." George Bradley *"forced me, an't please your Honour."* And most of them will be hanged anyway.

As indeed they were. A considerable number of the men on the island imagined their deaths correctly. Six members of Anstis's crew, including the one-handed leader John Fenn, were hanged at Antigua in May 1723. An unknown number, perhaps as many as a dozen, were executed in Curaçao in the same month and year. And in the following month, two more were "tuck'd up immediately" in Bermuda. One of these, it seems, was George

Bradley, the very man who played the callous judge in the pirate skit and dished out death himself, no doubt to the roaring, rib- ald laughter of his fellows. One wonders if he thought of this and took strength from it as he stood on the gallows of Bermuda in June 1723. He would have known that his corpse would be hanged in chains in the harbor as a warning to sailors. He would have known that he would, in the end, be "set a Sun-drying like a Scare-crow."[12]

Pirates also used real courtrooms to express humor about their deadly situation. Job Bayley, facing death for piracy in a Charleston courtroom in 1718, was asked by the attorney general of South Carolina why he and his fellow freebooters fought Colonel William Rhett and the vessels sent by the government against them. Bayley probably brought a roar of laughter from those attending the trial when he answered, "We thought it had been a pirate." The judge was not amused and ordered him hanged by the neck until "dead, dead, dead."[13]

Another pirate who had a sense of humor was John Walden. He sailed with Black Bart Roberts and was called "Miss Nanny" by his fellow pirates—"ironically it's assumed from the Hardness of his Temper." In 1722, when they captured a ship off the coast of West Africa and a gang of pirates began to weigh anchor, Walden promptly cut the cable and asked, why bother "straining in hot weather"? Turning to the captain of the merchant ship, Walden explained: "there are more Anchors at London, and besides, your ship is to be burnt." As it happened, the "bold and daring" Walden lost a leg to a cannonball during the engagement, in which he and his comrades were captured. He knew he was to be hanged, but he was nonetheless "undaunted" during his trial, more concerned to rest the stump of his leg than to answer the court's questions or defend himself. When the judge asked him what he would have done had the man-of-war proven to be an easily captured merchant ship, Walden answered with defiant humor, "I don't know what I would have done." He was hanged with fifty-one others.[14]

Perhaps the best example of the profane, seditious, and comical attitude of pirates toward the British government, and perhaps all governments, came in 1721 when Philip Lyne and his rather rugged crew captured a ship with a master out of Boston. As they plundered the vessel, the freebooters came across copies of official documents, correspondence involving the Lords of the Admiralty. They immediately put the papers to good use: "the pyrates wip'd their backsides" with them, adding, for contemptuous good measure, "that they were the Lords of the Sea."[15]

Pirates poked fun not only at the government but also at the practices of the market and commercial society, as demonstrated by a different sort of drama that Captain George Lowther and his crew enacted in June 1721. When they encountered a French ship off the western end of Hispaniola, they promptly disguised their own vessel, putting away the Jolly Roger, their cutlasses and pistols, and sending a swarm of pirates belowdecks—in short, doing everything they could to make the appearance of a working merchant ship. Concealing their identities (and their weapons), they sent a party aboard the French ship, as was customary, to greet and fraternize, exchange news, and conduct business. John Massey, dressed finely as a merchant, led the way. He proceeded to stroll around the decks of the French ship, inspecting the brandy, the wine, the chintz cloth, and other cargo. He "ask'd the price of one Thing and then another, bidding Money for the greatest part of the Cargo." Having taken stock of the ship and decided exactly what he wanted, he turned to the French captain and "whispered a Secret" in his ear: *they must have it all without Money.* The unsuspecting French captain must have been stunned but "presently understood his Meaning," probably at the very moment when the other pirates pulled out their guns to enforce the suggested terms of trade. The poor captain "unwillingly agreed to the Bargain." The pirates, probably doubled over with laughter, proceeded to haul away thirty casks of brandy, five hogsheads of wine, textiles, and "other valuable goods." Thinking that the captain had perhaps been treated unfairly, Lowther made a parting gesture: he "generously return'd five Pounds back to the French Master for his Civilities." To merchants and captains, the humor was cruel, but to pirates, who as common seamen had been frequently abused by these figures of power, it was a humorous moment of revenge.[16]

It has long been a commonplace among historians that nearly all pirates managed to escape their crimes with their booty and their lives.[17] Although this may have been true for the sixteenth and seventeenth centuries, when England, France, and the Netherlands supported or tolerated piratical attacks against Spain, it is false for the period under study here, when the numbers of pirates hanged were extraordinary by any measure. In a time when royal mercy and pardons in England routinely commuted death penalties to lesser sentences, especially one or another form of bound labor (after the Transportation Act of 1718), pirates rarely had their sentences lessened and instead were hanged in huge numbers and high percentages.[18] Between 1716 and 1726, no fewer than 418 were hanged, and in truth the actual number was probably one-third to one-half higher. This means that roughly one in every ten pirates came to an end on the gallows, a greater portion than many other groups of capital convicts, and vastly greater than what most historians have long believed. When we add the many hundreds of pirates who died in battle, in prison, by suicide, by disease, or by accident, it would seem that at least one in four died or was killed, and the number may have been as high as one in two. Premature death was therefore the pirate's lot; his was most decidedly not a romantic occupation. Cotton Mather wrote that "most [pirates] seemed to have no Thought of Returning from their Wicked Courses." Governor Walter Hamilton of Antigua saw that many pirates "seem'd resolved to live and dye by their Calling, or for it, as their Fate is likely to be." Captain Charles Johnson explained that most pirates did not live long enough to enjoy whatever riches they may have plundered. The state's campaign of extermination against them would have been visible to the eye of any seaman as he sailed into almost any port city during these years: in a prominent place dangled a gibbeted corpse of one who had sailed under the black flag, crows picking at the rotting flesh and bleaching bones.[19]

The omnipresence of death, the apocalyptic impulse, the heterodox belief, the gallows humor, and the centrality of these in the consciousness and culture of pirates show up in their symbolism, especially in the best-known emblem of piracy in this era or any other, the notorious black flag, which they called Old Roger or the Jolly Roger. A point to be emphasized is the significance of flags to the maritime world of the early eighteenth century. A dazzling array of flags, colors, standards, jacks, pennants, ensigns, and banners, especially those signifying nation and empire, were the most important means of communication among seafaring craft of all kinds. They were, at the most fundamental level, markers of property and sovereign power among the nations in oceanic zones of tremendous uncertainty. Pirates doubly defied the nationalist logic of this situation—first by forming themselves of the "outcasts of all nations" (mixing together the seafarers of all countries, as suggested earlier), and second by attacking vessels regardless of the flag flying at the mainmast, making all nations and their shipping equal prey. Every pirate ship worth its salt had a complete set of national flags, all the better with which to confuse prospective prizes and even naval vessels that might wish to chase them. But when pirates created a flag of their own, as they did for the first time in the early eighteenth century, they made a new declaration: they would use colors to symbolize the solidarity of a gang of proletarian outlaws, thousands strong and self-organized in daring ways, in violent opposition to the all-powerful nation-states of the day. By flying the skull and the crossbones, they announced themselves as "the Villains of all Nations."

The collective creation and affirmation of the black flag, as discussed briefly in chapter 4, was bound up in ritual on a pirate ship. In their founding moment, after a mutiny or when the crew

of an overcrowded vessel split and formed a new pirate ship, the
crew came together in a council to elect their captain, draw up
their articles, and declare to be true to each other and their flag,
all amid merriment, festivity, eating, drinking, and the firing of
cannon. One group of pirates "us'd to say [of their black flag] they
would live and die under it," and many others, as we saw at the
outset of this chapter, agreed. Like Francis Spriggs and his crew,
they swore never to allow the Jolly Roger to be struck. Those who
were overcome by force and captured tried to throw their colors
overboard to keep them out of the hands of authorities.[20]

Contemporaneous descriptions suggest that the Jolly Roger
was similar from ship to ship. Here are a few examples. The pirates aboard the *Revenge* (captained by Charles Martel) in 1716
"let fly her Jack, Ensign and Pendant, in which was the Figure of
a Man, with a Sword in his Hand, and an Hour-Glass before
him, with a Death's Head and Bones. In the Jack and Pendant
were only the Head and Bones." When the freebooters who had
sailed with Captain John Phillips were hanged in Boston in 1724,
the authorities placed at one end of the gallows "their own dark
Flag, in the middle of which [was] an Anatomy, and at one side
of it a Dart in a Heart, with Drops of Blood proceeding from it;
on the other side an Hour-glass, the sight dismal." Captain
Richard Hawkins, whom we have already met, wrote in 1724 that
Spriggs's crew "hoisted *Jolly Roger*, (for so they call their black
Ensign, in the Middle of which is a large white Skeleton, with a
Dart in one Hand, striking a Bleeding Heart, and in the other
an Hour Glass)."[21]

The primary symbolism of the flag was straightforward.
Pirates intended its symbols—death, violence, and limited time
—to terrify their prey, to say, unequivocally, to merchantmen
that their time was short, they must surrender immediately, or
they would die a bloody death. The idea was to intimidate the
crew of the ship under attack so that they would not defend their
vessel. Five men who mutinied and captured their ship in 1721
"sail'd away down the Coast" of West Africa, "making a black

Flag, which they merrily said, would be as good as fifty men more, i.e. would carry as much Terror." They knew whereof they spoke, as numerous merchant ship captains would attest in recounting their capture by pirates (see chapter 1). The sailors knew that if they did resist and were then overpowered, they would probably be tortured and killed, to teach them—and other sailors—a lesson. When a vessel of unknown origins and intentions bore down on a merchantman and finally raised the Jolly Roger at the mainmast, it was a chilling moment, a time of terror understood by all.

The pirate flag also conveyed a second set of meanings, which were commentaries on life and death at sea in this era. All of the chosen symbols on the black colors were rooted in the Christian cultures from which most of the pirates came. And even though both sailors and freebooters were quite irreligious (as ministers never ceased to point out in their gallows sermons), they nonetheless played with these godly symbols, drew on their power, manipulated and inverted them, and gave them new meanings derived from their own maritime experience. If the Jolly Roger symbolized the pirate as predator, it simultaneously and eloquently bespoke the pirate's own consciousness of himself as preyed upon in turn.

Pirates did not invent their symbols. All were common in the gravestone art of the late seventeenth and early eighteenth centuries. The skull, the crossbones, the skeleton, the hourglass, the dart, and even the color black suggested, in the Christian worldview, mortality, the transitoriness of life, and the swift passage of time. The skeleton, which was apparently assimilated from pagan into Christian iconography, represented the all-sovereign "King of Death," the "Grim Reaper," or "Father Time," who was depicted with a sword (or more commonly a scythe) and an hourglass.[22]

Pirates put their own profane touches on these religious symbols. One subtle way of doing so was to leave off the death's-head the customary wings that were intended to carry the soul of the

Figure 14. Death's-heads drawn in the log of
Captain Jacob Bevan; Jacob Bevan, "A Voyage to St. Jago,"
Sloane MS 854, f. 166, courtesy of the British Library.

departed to heaven. Pirates, as we saw earlier, declared a different
destination, and indeed they filled their flag with Satanic impli-
cations, calling it not only Jolly Roger but Old Roger, which was
a popular name for the devil. The skeleton or anatomy on the pirate flag was, in one of the representational meanings of the day,
a depiction of the devil himself. A Jolly Roger, therefore, was a
merry devil and more; a "roger," in the cant of the eighteenth-
century urban underworld, was "a man's yard" (penis), and "to
roger" was to copulate, which meant that the Jolly Roger was also
a happy phallus. Thus did life shadow death and Eros follow
its twin, Thanatos. The pirates jested with fear and dread, with
death itself.[23]

The death's-head had a particular meaning to seafaring people because ship captains used it "as a marginal sign in their logs
to indicate the record of a death."[24] The skull and crossbones
drawn in the captain's log were one of the few lasting marks of
the common sailor who died at sea, who was promptly sewn up
into an old canvas sail and dumped overboard to become "food
for the fishes of the deep." The "anatomy" had a similar social
meaning: it signified in this period "a living being reduced
to 'skin and bone'; a withered or emaciated creature, a 'walking

skeleton,'" the "withered lifeless form" of the human being, which is, as we have seen, precisely what many sailors, routinely denied "the necessaries of life," considered themselves to be. Living as they did in a shipboard regime of harsh, even brutal discipline, insufficient food, and hence regular, often preventable death, sailors who became pirates put the symbols of death, violence, and transient time on their flag. Common seamen thus escaped from a deadly system and marked the occasion, with irony and humor, by placing the symbol of "King Death" on their flag.[25]

Before, during, and after they died, these pirates said to their respectable contemporaries: whatever you fear—violence, destruction, the devil, death—we are that. We embrace it. We are the other. We are your nightmare. You have made us ugly, and we throw that ugliness in your face. The culture of pirates was deeply profane and blasphemous. Everything pirates did reflected their deep alienation from most aspects of European society. Unlike the generations of pirates before them, who called themselves privateers—in truth, anything *but* pirate for fear of the death penalty that soon came with the name—the freebooters of the early eighteenth century said yes, we are criminals, we are pirates, we are that name. Two men on the gallows in 1718 cried up, "A Pyrate's Life to be the only Life a Man of any Spirit." "Let us live while we can," said another. "A merry Life and short one" was one of their mottoes.[26]

They said these things with humor, but they also said them with rage. When asked to repent at his 1718 hanging, one pirate answered yes, "I do heartily repent; I repent I had not done more Mischief, and that we did not cut the Throats of them that took us, and [addressing the authorities] I am extreamly sorry that you an't hanged as well as we." Another pirate standing alongside him on the gallows piped up, "So do I." "And I," added a third. They "were all turned off, without making any other dying speeches." Note that in this instance the last wish of the three pirates was not for an exchange of places, not for the execution of the members of the colonial ruling class who presided over the grim occasion and the saving of themselves, but rather for a drowning destruction of all. Some pirates, it seems, wanted the ship to go down with everyone aboard.[27]

{ 169 }

Yet the deepest meaning of piracy was revealed when in February 1722 the Royal Navy captured the two ships of Black Bart Roberts on the coast of West Africa, after crew members had tried to blow up the ship and "all go merrily to Hell together!" Knowing their gallows fate and wanting to protect the Jolly Roger, the pirates aboard one of the ships threw the colors "over-board, that they might not rise in Judgment, nor be display'd in Triumph over them" at the hanging. Pirates aboard the other ship did not succeed in throwing the flag overboard, and indeed it was taken by the naval officers of the *Swallow* and eventually featured on the gallows built at Cape Coast Castle, the infamous slave-trading factory where fifty-two members of Roberts's crew met their end a month later. This particular flag "had the Figure of a Skeleton in it, and a Man pourtray'd with a flaming Sword in his Hand, intimating a Defiance of Death it self."[28] This was the meaning of the Jolly Roger, and perhaps of piracy altogether: a defiance of death itself.

BLOOD AND GOLD

IN ITS FINAL PHASE, the war turned savage. As naval captains and executioners killed more and more pirates, those who remained at large became more enraged, more desperate, more violent, and more cruel. The dialectic of terror with which I began this book reached a climax in carnage. The third and final stage in the history of pirates in the early eighteenth century commenced with the defeat and mass hanging of the pirates with Bartholomew Roberts at Cape Coast Castle in 1722 and ended in the near eradication of robbery at sea by 1726. The golden age had turned crimson.[1]

If Bartholomew Roberts, who took on himself the "distribution of justice," was the defining figure of the period between 1718 and 1722, the following phase was rather differently epitomized by the captaincy of Ned Low, who, after Roberts, probably captured more vessels than any other pirate commander. Low had worked as a merchant seaman out of London, a rigger in Boston, and a logwood cutter in Honduras. In late 1721 he led a mutiny aboard a small vessel, which launched a reign of terror that would last four years. In March 1724 Governor John Hart of Antigua provided a vivid account of Low and his murderous actions in a letter to the Council of Trade and Plantations. First he noted Low's isolation, which is important for understanding his actions: "I do not hear that there are any more pirates, except a ship commanded by one Lowe with about fifty pirates in his crew." Hart related that a portion of Low's crew had recently been captured by Captain Humphrey Orme aboard HMS *Winchelsea*, brought to Antigua, and hanged. Hart continued that Low's own quartermaster, Nicholas Lewis,

gave a most terrible relation of his barbarity and bloodthirsty temper; and that particularly in the Bay of Honduras he murder'd forty
five Spaniards in cold blood about twelve months past; and that
some time before, he took a Portugueze ship bound home from
Brazil; the Master of which had hung eleven thousand moydores of
gold in a bag out of the cabbin window, and as soon as he was taken
by the said Lowe, cutt the rope and lett them drop into the sea; for
which Lowe cutt off the said Masters lipps and broyl'd them before
his face, and afterwards murder'd the whole crew being thirty two
persons.

Just to be sure that his lordships did not think that Low was
acting out of national or Protestant zeal against Spanish and
Portuguese Catholic enemies, Hart added, "This Lowe is notorious also for his cruelty even to the subjects of the British Nation." He concluded that "a greater monster never infested the
seas," and that a special proclamation should be issued "offering
an ample reward to such as shou'd bring him in alive or dead."[2]

The special proclamation turned out to be unnecessary, for
Low's own crew rose up against him. Around the time of Hart's
letter, Francis Spriggs and others left him "on Account of the
Barbarity he used toward those he took." But some remained
with him, sailing on, leaving behind a bloody wake until they too
rebelled, throwing Low and his closest supporters into a boat,
without provisions, and abandoning them to their fate on the
open sea. And although representative of the last phase of piracy,
Low was by no means the only captain who practiced violence
on a greater scale than before. Indeed, almost all of the most violent pirate captains appeared in the final phase—Philip Roche,
William Phillips, John Gow, and William Fly, all of whom murdered their captains (Gow and Fly killed other officers too) in the
course of mutiny. And above (or below) all others stood Philip
Lyne, who carried the pirates' rage to its bloodiest limit. He
boasted on the gallows that he had killed thirty-seven masters
of vessels (he apparently kept a body count) as well as a number
of their crew members, probably those who had dared to resist

Figure 15. Ned Low in a hurricane; Captain Charles Johnson,
A *General History of the Lives and Adventures of the Most Famous
Highwaymen, Murderers, Street Robbers, &c.* (London, 1734).

capture. As the violence of the pirates and the violence of the
authorities against them swelled to a crescendo, the number of
seamen willing to sail under the black flag declined, which in
turn caused pirates to force more sailors aboard their vessels. This
impressment of sorts led to several mutinies aboard the pirate
ships (for example, Phillips and Fly), after which the pirates
were taken and executed. When royal officials hanged Gow,
Fly, Lyne, and Low (who was taken up by the French) in 1725
and 1726, the campaign of extermination came to a predictably

bloody end. Pirates stood indicted as monsters, beasts, and "the
common enemies of mankind."[3]

And yet, as we have seen, alongside this official view ran
another, quite different one, in the pirates' day and into our
own. This was perhaps originally and most clearly expressed by
Captain Charles Johnson in his book *A General History of the
Pyrates*, the first volume of which was published in 1724, while
pirates were still marauding on the high seas. According to
Johnson, pirates were not simply the common enemy of mankind, neither brutes nor beasts of prey, but rather "Marine
Heroes, the Scourge of Tyrants and Avarice, and the brave
Asserters of Liberty." He made the point with sarcasm, but the
implication was clear: many of his contemporaries held precisely
this view. Of Henry Avery, the "maritime Robin Hood," Johnson
wrote that there were among the people "Romantick Reports of
his Greatness." Cotton Mather acknowledged the same popular
image as he battled against it. Pirates and highwaymen, Mather
angrily preached, were "*Monsters*, whom we dignify with the title
of Hero's." In the popular mind, the pirate was not "the common
enemy of mankind" but rather the freest of mankind. This image
proved that the law did not a criminal make.[4]

The pirate, even in ignominious death, would be the stuff of
legend—immediately. Walter Kennedy was motivated to turn
pirate in 1718 by the stories of Henry Avery he had heard in his
youth. Endless tales surrounded Edward Teach, the fearsome
Blackbeard, whose villainous image suggested that he well understood his role in the play of early eighteenth-century life. A
young Ben Franklin wrote, published, and hawked about the
streets of Boston a ditty about Blackbeard not long after the
larger-than-life character had been killed in fierce hand-to-hand
combat, his head hung on the bowsprit of HMS *Pearl* as the vessel sailed from North Carolina back to Virginia. Bartholomew
Roberts cut a dashing figure as he strolled about the decks of
his ship "dressed in a crimson Damask Wastcoat and Breeches,
a red Feather in his Hat, a Gold Chain round his Neck, with a

Diamond Cross hanging to it." He cut no less a figure in the conversation of the day. As an anonymous pirate explained to a man who resisted capture, "don't you see says he them two Ships commanded by the famous Captain Roberts?" Even General Walter Hamilton of the West Indies referred to "the Great Pirate Roberts," who was rumored far and wide to have engaged and defeated numerous men-of-war, all the while threatening to ruin the entire colonies. Ballads of "Black Barty" were written and sung in Roberts's native Wales. And of course this was only the beginning. An entire romantic literature about pirates, for children and adults, has followed, as has a starry-eyed cinema.[5]

As it happens, the duality of perception—pirate as monster, pirate as hero—is almost as old as piracy itself, originating in the days of Greek and Roman antiquity and lasting down to the present. As the classical scholar Philip de Souza has shown, the image of the pirate in ancient Greece—in, for example, the writing of the great poet Homer—emphasized heroism and contained relatively few negative connotations. This image changed dramatically with the Romans, who as part of their imperial design sought to project their sovereignty over the seas and thus developed and enshrined within their legal codes the phrase *hostes humani generis* to describe pirates—the very phrase used by Judge Nicholas Trott and other judges almost two millennia later. Thus the term *pirate* has been highly ideological from antiquity forward, functioning more or less as the maritime equivalent of *barbarian*—that is, anyone who was an enemy of the Romans. No matter who or what he actually was, the pirate was reduced to a criminal pure and simple, the very negation of imperial social order.[6]

Pirates did not share this view, as expressed in a pithy and humorous way by an ancient sea robber who had been captured and brought before Alexander the Great, who asked him "what he meant by keeping hostile possession of the sea." The pirate responded with "bold pride": "What thou meanest by seizing the whole earth; but because I do it with a petty ship, I am called a robber, whilst thou who dost it with a great fleet art styled emperor." Augustine, who recorded the story in his *City of God*, considered it "an apt and true reply." It would be repeated down through the centuries. A tradition developed in which smaller pirates were used as the idiom to expose and ridicule big pirates, such as those who ran governments and corporations. The dramatist John Gay used this approach in *The Beggar's Opera* and *Polly* to attack Robert Walpole and his corrupt circle in the late 1720s. Captain Johnson was no stranger to the tactic, as his depiction of the principles of the pirates contrasted sharply with the base and venal ways of the British government. As if to make the point clear for anyone who might have missed it, royal officials and officers cheated naval sailors out of the prize money owed them after their brave and successful attacks against Blackbeard in 1719 and Roberts in 1722![7]

To think of the golden age of piracy is to imagine the gleaming object of desire, the precious metal that promised to reverse the fortunes of those who lived bitter and impoverished lives. Pirates wanted gold, and occasionally they got it. But they did not bury it. When pirates went ashore, "their first care was to find out a Tavern, where they might ease themselves of their Golden Luggage." They did not believe in deferred gratification of any kind. Against what they saw as the forces of death, they wanted a better life, which suggests another meaning of the golden age, evoking the ancient Greek myth of Kronos, the island where all people lived in freedom, equality, harmony, and abundance. Pirates managed to make some part of the myth real, if only for a short time.[8]

Pirates lost the clash with the rulers of their own day, but they have decisively won the debate ever after. They captured the good ship *Popular Imagination*, and three hundred years later they show no sign of surrendering it. They dared to imagine a different life, and they dared to try to live it. They could not resolve the contradictions of their times, and indeed some of them did gruesome things—they tortured, murdered, and committed atrocities. Much of this was a product of war, their declared war against the whole world and their undeclared class war against ship captains, merchants, and royal officials, but a portion of it was the gratuitous ferocity of angry men beyond control.

We are fascinated by the violence, but the blood does hide the gold. We love pirates most of all because they were rebels. They challenged, in one way or another, the conventions of class, race, gender, and nation. They were poor and in low circumstances, but they expressed high ideals. Exploited and often abused by merchant captains, they abolished the wage, established a different discipline, practiced their own kind of democracy and equality, and provided an alternative model for running the deep-sea ship. Shadowed by the grim reaper, they stole his symbolism and laughed in his face. Pirates opposed the high and mighty of their day and by their actions became the villains of all nations. They relished the role, even though "a merry life and a short one" contained a cruel contradiction. The more that pirates built and enjoyed their merry, autonomous existence the more determined the authorities grew to destroy them. These outlaws led audacious, rebellious lives, and we should remember them as long as there are powerful people and oppressive circumstances to be resisted.[9]

NOTES

CHAPTER ONE
A TALE OF TWO TERRORS

1. Abel Boyer, ed., *The Political State of Great Britain*, 60 vols. (London, 1711–40), 28:272–73; Cotton Mather, *The Vial Poured Out upon the Sea: A Remarkable Relation of Certain Pirates* ... (Boston, 1726), 47–48, reprinted in *Pillars of Salt: An Anthology of Early American Criminal Narratives*, ed. Daniel E. Williams (Madison, Wis.: Madison House, 1993), 110–17. See also Captain Charles Johnson, *A General History of the Pyrates*, ed. Manuel Schonhorn (London, 1724, 1728; reprint, Columbia, S.C.: University of South Carolina Press, 1972), 606–13 (hereafter cited as *History of Pyrates*). Throughout the book, italics are in the original unless otherwise noted.

2. Cotton Mather, *The Tryals of Sixteen Persons for Piracy & c.* (Boston, 1726), 14. Mather had written of another crew of pirates who had come to the gallows: "What are these PIRATES now, but so many *Preachers* of those things, which once they could not bear to hear the Servants of GOD *Preach* unto them?" See his *Instructions to the Living, From the Condition of the Dead: A Brief Relation of Remarkables in the Shipwreck of above One Hundred Pirates* (Boston, 1717), 40.

3. Boyer, ed., *Political State*, 33:272–73. Mather also recorded Fly's threat: "He would advise Masters of Vessels to carry it well to their Men, lest they be put upon doing as he had done." Mather, *Vial Poured Out upon the Sea*, 47–48.

4. Mather, *Vial Poured Out upon the Sea*, 112; *Boston News-Letter*, July 7, 1726. Condick, who was considered young, drunk, "stupid and insensible" at the time of his piracy, did indeed get a reprieve. See Benjamin Colman, *It Is a Fearful Thing to Fall into the Hands of the Living God* (Boston, 1726), 37.

5. *History of Pyrates*, 606.

6. Ibid., 606, 608.

7. See the excellent article by Daniel E. Williams, "Puritans and Pirates: A Confrontation between Cotton Mather and William Fly in 1726," *Early American Literature* 22 (1987): 233–51.

8. Colman, *It Is a Fearful Thing*, 39. Jeremiah Bumsted, a "mechanic in moderate circumstances," noted in his diary Fly's refusal to cooperate with the ministers and concluded that he was "an unparraled instance of a hard heart." See "Diary of Jeremiah Bumsted of Boston, 1722–1727," *New England Historical and Genealogical Register* 15 (1861): 309–10.

9. Mather, *Vial Poured Out upon the Sea*, 47, 21; Daniel A. Cohen, *Pillars of Salt, Monuments of Grace: New England Crime Literature and the Origins of American Popular Culture, 1674–1860* (New York: Oxford University Press, 1993).

10. Colman, *It Is a Fearful Thing*. Here I am drawing on comments by Noam Chomsky, "September 11th and Its Aftermath: Where Is the World Heading?" Public Lecture at the Music Academy, Chennai (Madras), India, November 10, 2001; available at http://www.flonnet.com/fl1824/nc.htm.

11. For the idea of the pirate as a modern antihero, see Hans Turley, *Rum, Sodomy, and the Lash: Piracy, Sexuality, and Masculine Identity* (New York: New York University Press, 1999).

12. For a broader view of mobile workers in the seventeenth-, eighteenth-, and early-nineteenth-century Atlantic, see Peter Linebaugh and Marcus Rediker, *The Many-Headed Hydra: Sailors, Slaves, Commoners, and the Hidden History of the Revolutionary Atlantic* (Boston: Beacon Press, 2000).

13. *Boston News-Letter*, May 21, 1716; Spotswood to Council of Trade and Plantations, July 3, 1716, Colonial Office Papers (CO) 5/1364, Public Record Office, London; Examination of John Brown (1717), in *Privateering and Piracy in the Colonial Period: Illustrative Documents*, ed. John Franklin Jameson (New York: Macmillan, 1923), 294.

14. *Boston News-Letter*, April, 29, 1717; "Proceedings of the Court held on the Coast of Africa upon Trying of 100 Pirates taken by his Ma[jes]ties Ship Swallow" (1722), High Court of Admiralty Papers (HCA)1/99, f. 10; *History of Pyrates*, 319; Peter Earle, *The Pirate Wars* (London: Methuen, 2003), 195.

15. *History of Pyrates*, 244, 285–86. See also Robert C. Ritchie, *Captain Kidd and the War against the Pirates* (Cambridge, Mass.: Harvard University Press, 1986), 232–37. Peter Earle has written that "piracy was not an occupation with a very long life expectancy." See his *Pirate Wars*, 206.

16. Cotton Mather, *Useful Remarks: An Essay upon Remarkables in the Way of Wicked Men: A Sermon on the Tragical End, unto which the Way of*

NOTES

Twenty-Six Pirates Brought Them; At New Port on Rhode-Island, July 19, 1723 (New London, Conn., 1723), 31–44, quotation at 33.

17. Archibald Hamilton to Secretary Stanhope, June 12, 1716, CO 137/12, f. 19; *History of Pyrates*, 286, 643, 660; Arthur L. Hayward, ed., *Lives of the Most Remarkable Criminals* (London, 1735; reprint, New York: Dodd, Mead, 1927), 3:603.

18. *History of Pyrates*, 624–59; "The Tryal and Condemnation of Ten Persons for Piracy at New Providence," CO 23/1 (1718), ff. 76, 81, 82; Woodes Rogers to Council of Trade and Plantations, October 31, 1718, CO 23/1, ff. 16–29.

19. R. A. Brock, ed., *The Official Letters of Alexander Spotswood* (Virginia Historical Society, *Collections*, n.s., 2 [Richmond, 1882]), 2:338.

20. *History of Pyrates*, 285–86.

21. *American Weekly Mercury*, March 17, 1720; Brock, ed., *Letters of Spotswood*, 2:338; Mather, *Useful Remarks*, 20. See also Stanley Richards, *Black Bart* (Llandybie, Wales: Christopher Davies, 1966), 104.

22. *Trials of Eight Persons Indited for Piracy* (Boston, 1718), 8–19; "Trial of Thomas Davis," October 28, 1717, in *Privateering and Piracy*, ed. Jameson, 308; *The Tryals of Major Stede Bonnet and Other Pirates* (London, 1719), 45.

23. Governor Hamilton to the Council of Trade and Plantations, October 3, 1720, *Calendar of State Papers, Colonial Series, America and West Indies, 1574–1739*, CD-ROM, consultant editors Karen Ordahl Kupperman, John C. Appleby, and Mandy Banton (London: Routledge, published in association with the Public Record Office, 2000), item 251, vol. 32 (1720–21), 165 (hereafter *CSPC*); H. R. McIlwaine, ed., *Executive Journals of the Council of Colonial Virginia* (Richmond, 1928), 3:542; "News from Barbadoes, Antigua and Jamaica" (1721), *CSPC*, item 463 iii, vol. 32 (1720–21), 295. For a fuller analysis of these acts of revenge, see chapter 5.

24. *History of Pyrates*, 26; Mather, *Useful Remarks*, 22. Captain Charles Johnson was long believed to be Daniel Defoe, as originally suggested by literary critic John Robert Moore in *Defoe in the Pillory and Other Studies* (Bloomington: Indiana University Press, 1939), 129–88, and broadly accepted thereafter. Recently, however, scholars have begun to doubt the attribution. P. N. Furbank and W. R. Owens have challenged Moore; see their *Canonisation of Daniel Defoe* (New Haven: Yale University Press, 1988), 100–121. Having worked on *A General History of the Pyrates* for more than twenty-five years, I have

come to the conclusion that its author had a deeper and more detailed knowledge of things maritime than Defoe could possibly have had. It should also be noted that Johnson is widely regarded as a highly reliable source for factual information (apart from one fictional chapter, on Captain Misson). For comments on his reliability, see Philip Gosse, *The History of Piracy* (New York: Tudor, 1932), 182; Hugh F. Rankin, *The Golden Age of Piracy* (New York: Holt, Rinehart and Winston, 1969), 161; Marcus Rediker, *Between the Devil and the Deep Blue Sea: Merchant Seamen, Pirates, and the Anglo-American Maritime World, 1700–1750* (Cambridge: Cambridge University Press, 1987), 258; B. R. Burg, *Sodomy and the Perception of Evil: English Sea Rovers in the Seventeenth-Century Caribbean* (New York: New York University Press, 1983), 196; and Schonhorn's introduction to *General History of Pyrates*, by Johnson, xxvii–xl.

25. Richards, *Black Bart*, 22.

26. "Anonymous Paper Relating to the Sugar and Tobacco Trade" (1724), CO 388/24, ff. 184–88; Minutes of the Vice-Admiralty Courts of Charleston, South Carolina (1718), Manuscript Division, Library of Congress, f. 424; *History of Pyrates*, 323; *Boston News-Letter*, June 17, 1718.

27. Deposition of Edward North (1718), CO 37/10, f. 37; Deposition of Robert Leonard (1719), CO 152/12, f. 485, CO137/14; Boyer, ed., *Political State*, 21:660.

28. *Boston News-Letter*, August 15, 1720.

29. Ibid., April 16, 1722; *American Weekly Mercury*, December 13, 1720; CO 23/1; H. C. Maxwell Lyte, ed., *Journal of the Commissioners for Trade and Plantations* (London, 1924), 4:321; Richards, *Black Bart*, 57; *American Weekly Mercury*, July 7, 1726; S. Charles Hill, "Episodes of Piracy in Eastern Waters," *Indian Antiquary* 49 (1920): 41; Information of Clement Downing (1722), HCA 1/55, f. 79; Further Information of Clement Downing (1722), HCA 1/55, f. 93; Earle, *Pirate Wars*, 188.

30. It was reported that Captain Green had done nothing to deserve his fate, but Mather noted the claim of Fly and other pirates that the murder and piracy were "Revenge, they said, for *Bad Usage*." See Mather, *Vial Poured Out upon the Sea*, 112. See also my "Seaman as Spirit of Rebellion: Authority, Violence, and Labor Discipline at Sea," in *Between the Devil and the Deep Blue Sea*, chap. 5.

31. Mather, *Vial Poured Out upon the Sea*, 44–45.

1. Virginia Merchants to Lord Dartmouth, June 24, 1713, Colonial
    Office Papers (CO) 389/42, Public Record Office, London; Dummer
    is quoted in Ruth Bourne, *Queen Anne's Navy in the West Indies* (New
    Haven: Yale University Press, 1939), 183.

2. Ralph Davis, *The Rise of the Atlantic Economies* (Ithaca: Cornell Uni-
    versity Press, 1973); Max Savelle, *Empires into Nations: Expansion in
    America, 1713–1824* (Minneapolis: University of Minnesota Press,
    1974), chap. 4. At this time, a factory was a merchant's trading post,
    usually overseas.

3. Marcus Rediker, *Between the Devil and the Deep Blue Sea: Merchant
    Seamen, Pirates, and the Anglo-American Maritime World, 1700–1750*
    (Cambridge: Cambridge University Press, 1987), 32–35; A. H. John,
    "War and the English Economy, 1700–1763," *Economic History Re-
    view*, 2nd ser., 7 (1955): 329–44.

4. J. H. Parry, *Trade and Dominion: The European Overseas Empires in the
    Eighteenth Century* (New York: Praeger, 1971), 93; Ralph Davis, *The
    Rise of the English Shipping Industry in the Seventeenth and Eighteenth
    Centuries* (London: Macmillan, 1962), 15–17; R. G. Davies, *The Royal
    African Company* (New York: Scribner's, 1970), chap. 1; Immanuel
    Wallerstein, *The Modern World System II: Mercantilism and the Con-
    solidation of the European World-Economy, 1600–1750* (New York: Aca-
    demic Press, 1980), 96, 159–61, 249, 269.

5. The theme expropriation is treated in Peter Linebaugh and Marcus
    Rediker, *The Many-Headed Hydra: Sailors, Slaves, Commoners, and the
    Hidden History of the Revolutionary Atlantic* (Boston: Beacon Press,
    2000). For other points in this paragraph, see C. L. R. James, "The
    Atlantic Slave Trade," in *The Future in the Present* (London: Alison
    and Busby, 1980), 235–64; Robin Blackburn, *The Making of New World
    Slavery: From the Baroque to the Modern, 1492–1800* (London: Verso,
    1997), 309; Richard S. Dunn, *Sugar and Slaves: The Rise of the Planter
    Class in the English West Indies, 1624–1713* (Chapel Hill: University of
    North Carolina Press, 1972); and Paul E. Lovejoy, "Volume of the
    Atlantic Slave Trade," *Journal of African History* 23 (1982): 473–501.

6. Christopher Lloyd, *The British Seaman, 1200–1860: A Social Survey*
    (Rutherford, N.J.: Fairleigh Dickinson University Press, 1970), 27,
    287, table 3; *History of Pyrates*, 4; Davis, *English Shipping*, 136–37, 154;

James G. Lydon, *Pirates, Privateers, and Profits* (Upper Saddle River, N.J.: Gregg Press, 1970), 17–20; Hugh F. Rankin, *The Golden Age of Piracy* (New York: Holt, Rinehart and Winston, 1969), 23; Nellis M. Crouse, *The French Struggle for the West Indies* (New York: Columbia University Press, 1943), 310.

7. Savelle, *Empires into Nations*, 122; *History of Pyrates*, 34; Robert C. Ritchie, *Captain Kidd and the War against the Pirates* (Cambridge, Mass.: Harvard University Press, 1986), 236–37; Colin A. Palmer, *Human Cargoes: The British Slave Trade to Spanish America, 1700–1739* (Urbana: University of Illinois Press, 1981).

8. Cornelius van Bynkershoek, *De Domino Maris Dissertatio*, ed. James Brown Scott, trans. Roger Van Deman Magoffin (Amsterdam, 1702; reprint, London: Oxford University Press, 1923), 44, 77.

9. *Powell v. Hardwicke* (1738), High Court of Admiralty Papers (HCA) 24/139, Public Record Office, London; Rediker, *Between the Devil and the Deep Blue Sea*, chaps. 2, 5.

10. Alfred P. Rubin, *The Law of Piracy* (Newport, R.I.: Naval War College Press, 1988), 37, 44, 46, 77, 83, 92; Sir Thomas Parker, ed., *The Laws of Shipping and Insurance, with a Digest of Adjudged Cases* (London, 1775), reprinted in *British Maritime Cases* (Abingdon, Oxfordshire: Professional Books, 1978), 41, 43.

11. Governor Robert Johnson to the Council of Trade and Plantations, June 18, 1718, *Calendar of State Papers, Colonial Series, America and West Indies, 1574–1739*, CD-ROM, consultant editors Karen Ordahl Kupperman, John C. Appleby, and Mandy Banton (London: Routledge, published in association with the Public Record Office, 2000), item 251, vol. 32 (1720–21), 166 (hereafter cited as *CSPC*); Walter Hamilton to the Council of Trade and Plantations, October 3, 1720, *CSPC*, item 556, vol. 30 (1717–18), 266; "A Scheme for Stationing Men of War in the West Indies for better Securing the Trade there from Pirates," 1723, CO 323/8; *Boston News-Letter*, July 7–14, 1726.

12. "An Act for the more Effectual Suppressing of Piracy" (1721), in *Laws of Shipping and Insurance*, ed. Parker, 94–95, 97, 99; *Boston News-Letter*, October 17, 1722; Rubin, *Law of Piracy*, 31.

13. Henry A. Ormerod, *Piracy in the Ancient World* (Liverpool: University of Liverpool Press, 1924; reprint, Baltimore: Johns Hopkins University Press, 1997), 14, 15, 22, 30, 35, 250; Philip Gosse, *The History of Piracy* (New York: Tudor, 1932), 103.

14. Edward Vernon to Josiah Burchett, November 7, 1720, in Edward

Vernon Letter-Book, January–December 1720, Add. MS 40812, British Library, London; *History of Pyrates*, 33–34. For an excellent account of how the naval campaign against the pirates improved over time, through better manning, maintenance of seamen's health, careening, intelligence, knowledge, cruises, and combinations of vessels, see Peter Earle, *The Pirate Wars* (London: Methuen, 2003), 184–88.

15. James Logan, quoted in Shirley Carter Hughson, *The Carolina Pirates and Colonial Commerce, 1670–1740*, Johns Hopkins University Studies in Historical and Political Science, 12 (Baltimore: Johns Hopkins University Press, 1894), 59; Mr. Gale to Colonel Thomas Pitt, Jr., January 29, 1719, CO 23/1, f. 47; *American Weekly Mercury*, December 12, 1720.

16. Other estimates include those by the governor of Bermuda (1717), "at least 1,000," in HCA 1/54, f. 113; Woodes Rogers (1718), "near a thousand," in *History of Pyrates*, 615; Captain Charles Johnson (1720), 1,500, in *History of Pyrates*, 132; and [Anonymous] (1721), 1,500, in *The Political State of Great Britain*, ed. Abel Boyer (London, 1711–40), 21:659.

17. Governor John Hope to Council of Trade and Plantations, August 21, 1724, CO 37/11, f. 145; Representation from Several Merchants Trading to Virginia to Board of Trade, April 15, 1717, CO 5/1318. For estimates of the numbers of men in the Royal Navy, see Lloyd, *British Seaman*, 287.

18. Alexander Spotswood to Council of Trade and Plantations, May 31, 1717, CO 5/1364, f. 483; Governor Pullein to Council of Trade and Plantations, April 22, 1714, CO 37/10, f. 13; Deposition of John Vickers (1716), CO 5/1317.

19. Cotton Mather, *Instructions to the Living, From the Condition of the Dead: A Brief Relation of Remarkables in the Shipwreck of above One Hundred Pirates* (Boston, 1717), 4; meeting of April 1, 1717, in *Journal of the Commissioners for Trade and Plantations*, ed. H. C. Maxwell Lyte (London, 1924), 3:359; *New-England Courant*, March 19, 1722; Deposition of Vickers, CO5/1317; Benjamin Bennett to Council of Trade and Plantations, May 31, 1718, CO 37/10, f. 31, and April 25, 1721, CO 37/10, f. 142; *History of Pyrates*, 7. Kevin Rushby, *Hunting Pirate Heaven: In Search of the Lost Pirate Utopias of the Indian Ocean* (London: Constable, 2001).

20. *History of Pyrates*, 31–34, 131; Leo Francis Stock, ed., *Proceedings and*

Debates of the British Parliaments Respecting North America (Washington, D.C.: Carnegie Institution, 1930), 3:399; Deposition of Adam Baldridge, in *Privateering and Piracy in the Colonial Period: Illustrative Documents*, ed. John Franklin Jameson (New York: Macmillan, 1923), 180–87; R. A. Brock, ed., *The Official Letters of Alexander Spotswood* (Virginia Historical Society, *Collections*, n.s., 2 [Richmond, 1882]), 2:168, 351; William Snelgrave, *A New Account of Some Parts of Guinea and the Slave Trade* (London, 1734; reprint, London: Frank Cass, 1971), 197; Abbe Rochon, "A Voyage to Madagascar and the East Indies," in *A General Collection of the Best and Most Interesting Voyages and Travels*, ed. John Pinkerton (London, 1814), 16:767–71; William Smith, *A New Voyage to Guinea* (London, 1744), 12, 42.

21. *History of Pyrates*, 3; Brock, ed., *Letters of Spotswood*, 2:168, 249.

22. *History of Pyrates*, 74, 264; Stanley Richards, *Black Bart* (Llandybie, Wales: Christopher Davies, 1966), 59; *New-England Courant*, July 26, 1722; Governor Woodes Rogers to the Council of Trade and Plantations, October 31, 1718, *CSPC*, item 737, vol. 30 (1717–18), 372–81; *The Tryals of Major Stede Bonnet and Other Pirates* (London, 1719), 8; Governor Hamilton to the Council of Trade and Plantations, October 3, 1720, *CSPC*, item 251, vol. 32 (1720–21), 165–70; CO 152/14, ff. 43–45. See "Proposals sent by M. de Pas de Feuquières (No. vii) for an Agreement made between the Governor of the French Leeward Islands and Governor Hamilton concerning forces to be sent by the two Nations against the pirates cruising off their coasts etc.," *CSPC*, item 501 ix, x, vol. 32 (1720–21), 320.

23. *History of Pyrates*, 26; Davis, *English Shipping Industry*, 317.

24. George Francis Dow and John Henry Edmonds, *The Pirates of the New England Coast, 1630–1730* (Salem, Mass.: Marine Research Society, 1923), 339; "Account of Jabez Biglow" (1719), Humphrey Morice Papers from the Bank of England, *Slave Trade Journals and Papers* (Marlboro, Wiltshire, England: Adam Mathew Publications, 1998), microfilm; Earle, *Pirate Wars*, 179.

25. William Snelgrave to Humphrey Morice, April 30, 1719, Morice Papers.

26. Captain Mathew Musson to the Council of Trade and Plantations, July 5, 1717, *CSPC*, item 635, vol. 29 (1716–17), 338; General Peter Heywood, Commander in Chief of Jamaica, to the Council of Trade and Plantations, December 3, 1716, *CSPC*, item 411, vol. 29 (1716–17), 212; Davis, *English Shipping Industry*, 31.

27. I gathered the sample of captured vessels over the years, in the course of reading newspapers, merchant and official correspondence, and the many other kinds of documents cited in these endnotes. I also compiled available information: the name of the ship as well as its captain, owner, cargo, value, home port, place of capture, and capturing pirate crew. The sample, drawing largely on English-language sources, does not fully represent the damage done to French, Spanish, Dutch, or Portuguese shipping.

28. *Boston News-Letter*, May 21, 1716; Alexander Spotswood to Council of Trade and Plantations, July 3, 1716, CO 5/1364; Earle, *Pirate Wars*, 166.

29. Examination of John Brown (1717), in *Privateering and Piracy*, ed. Jameson, 294.

30. Earle, *Pirate Wars*, 204.

CHAPTER THREE
WHO WILL GO "A PYRATING"?

1. This miniature biography was cobbled together from four different sources: the account of Kennedy's life that was published after his death, which is reprinted in *Lives of the Most Remarkable Criminals*, ed. Arthur L. Hayward (London, 1735; reprint, New York: Dodd, Mead, 1927); Captain Charles Johnson, *A General History of the Pyrates*, ed. Manuel Schonhorn (1724, 1728; reprint, Columbia, S.C.: University of South Carolina Press, 1972), hereafter cited as *History of Pyrates*; William Snelgrave's account of his encounters with Kennedy during his capture by pirates in April 1719 in his *New Account of Some Parts of Guinea and the Slave Trade* (London, 1734); and legal records gathered in the prosecution of Kennedy and other pirates by the High Court of Admiralty. For points in this paragraph, see Hayward, ed., *Remarkable Criminals*, 34–36; and *History of Pyrates*, 208; Examination of Walter Cannady, High Court of Admiralty Papers (HCA) 1/54, ff. 121–22, Public Record Office, London; Joel H. Baer, "'Captain John Avery' and the Anatomy of a Mutiny," *Eighteenth-Century Life* 18 (1994): 1–26.

2. *History of Pyrates*, 288; Hayward, ed., *Remarkable Criminals*, 36.

3. *History of Pyrates*, 195, 173, 174.

4. Snelgrave, *New Account*, 236.

5. Information of Thomas Grant (1721), HCA 1/54, f. 120.

6. *History of Pyrates*, 206–7; Hayward, ed., *Remarkable Criminals*, 35, 39.

7. *History of Pyrates*, 209; Hayward, ed., *Remarkable Criminals*, 39; Examination of Cannady, HCA 1/54, f. 122.

8. Hayward, ed., *Remarkable Criminals*, 39.

9. Ibid., 37, 35.

10. Ibid., 37.

11. I have, over the years, constructed a database of 778 pirates (774 men and 4 women) from documents of all varieties (as found in these endnotes); I recorded individual pirates by name, dates of activity, age, former occupation, class, family background, and miscellaneous details. Biographical data indicate that 173 of the 178 for whom a labor background is known came from one of these employments; at least 161 had been in the merchant service, and some had served in more than one of these seafaring occupations. See *History of Pyrates*, 116, 196, 215–16; Snelgrave, *New Account*, 203; Deposition of Richard Simes, in *Calendar of State Papers, Colonial Series, America and West Indies, 1574–1739*, CD-ROM, consultant editors Karen Ordahl Kupperman, John C. Appleby, and Mandy Banton (London: Routledge, published in association with the Public Record Office, 2000), item 501 v, vol. 32 (1720–21), 319 (hereafter cited as *CSPC*), and Deposition of John Wickstead, Master of the ship *Prince's*, Gould St. Blowers, second mate, John Crawford, surgeon, and Benjamin Flint, September 18, 1723, *CSPC*, item 754 iv, vol. 33 (1722–23), 365.

12. James Boswell, *The Life of Samuel Johnson* (London, 1791), 86.

13. Jesse Lemisch, "Jack Tar in the Streets: Merchant Seamen in the Politics of Revolutionary America," *William and Mary Quarterly* 25 (1968): 379, 375–76, 406; Richard B. Morris, *Government and Labor in Early America* (New York: Columbia University Press, 1946), 246–47, 257, 262–68; *History of Pyrates*, 244, 359; A. G. Course, *The Merchant Navy: A Social History* (London: F. Muller, 1963), 61; Samuel Cox to the Council of Trade and Plantations, August 23, 1721, *CSPC*, item 621, vol. 32 (1720–21), 392–93; Ralph Davis, *The Rise of the English Shipping Industry in the Seventeenth and Eighteenth Centuries* (London: Macmillan, 1962), 144, 154–55; Nathaniel Uring, *The Voyages and Travels of Captain Nathaniel Uring*, ed. Alfred Dewar (1726; reprint, London: Cassell, 1928), xxviii, 176–78; Arthur Pierce Middleton, *Tobacco Coast: A Maritime History of Chesapeake in the Colonial Era* (Newport News, Va.: Mariners' Museum, 1953), 8, 13, 15, 18, 271, 281; Christopher Lloyd, *The British Seaman, 1200–1860: A Social Survey* (Rutherford, N.J.: Fairleigh Dickinson University Press, 1970), 249,

264; John Atkins, *A Voyage to Guinea, Brasil, and the West-Indies* (London, 1735; reprint, London: Frank Cass, 1970), 261; G. T. Crook, ed., *The Complete Newgate Calendar* (London: Navarre Society, 1926), 3:57–58; S. Charles Hill, "Notes on Piracy in Eastern Waters," *Indian Antiquary* 46 (1927): 130; Hayward, ed., *Remarkable Criminals*, 126; Marcus Rediker, *Between the Devil and the Deep Blue Sea: Merchant Seamen, Pirates, and the Anglo-American Maritime World, 1700–1750* (Cambridge: Cambridge University Press, 1987).

14. Governor Lowther to the Council of Trade and Plantations, July 20, 1717, *CSPC*, item 661, vol. 29 (1716–17), 350–51; Morris, *Government and Labor*, 247; Lemisch, "Jack Tar," 379; Davis, *English Shipping*, 133–37; R. D. Merriman, ed., *Queen Anne's Navy Documents Concerning the Administration of the Navy of Queen Anne, 1702–1714* (London: Navy Records Society, 1961), 170–72, 174, 221–22, 250; Lloyd, *British Seaman*, 44–46, 124–49; Peter Kemp, *The British Sailor: A Social History of the Lower Deck* (London: Dent, 1970), chaps. 4, 5; Arthur N. Gilbert, "Buggery and the British Navy, 1700–1861," *Journal of Social History* 10 (1976): 72–98.

15. Atkins, *Voyage to Guinea*, 139, 187; *The Historical Register, Containing an Impartial Relation of All Transactions . . .* (London, 1722), 7:344.

16. Merriman, *Queen Anne's Navy*, 171; Hayward, ed., *Remarkable Criminals*, 474–77; *History of Pyrates*, 138; Trial of Robert Deal (1721), Colonial Office Papers (CO) 137/14, ff. 22–25, Public Record Office, London. Lloyd, in *British Seaman*, 44, estimates that half of all men pressed between 1600 and 1800 died at sea.

17. Course, *Merchant Navy*, 84; Lloyd, *British Seaman*, 57; "The Memoriall of the Merchants of London Trading to Africa" (1720), Admiralty Papers (ADM) 1/3810, Public Record Office, London; Atkins, *Voyage to Guinea*, 226. For examples of early-eighteenth-century privateering voyages, see Edward Cooke, *A Voyage to the South Sea* (London, 1712), v–vi, 14–16; Woodes Rogers, *A Cruising Voyage round the World*, ed. G. E. Manwaring (1712; reprint, New York: Longmans, Green, 1928), xiv, xxv; George Shelvocke, *A Voyage round the World* (London, 1726), 34–36, 38, 46, 157, 214, 217; William Betagh, *A Voyage round the World* (London, 1728), 4.

18. *History of Pyrates*, 347–48, 373; Trial of John Fillmore and Edward Cheeseman (1724), in *Privateering and Piracy in the Colonial Period: Illustrative Documents*, ed. John Franklin Jameson (New York: Macmillan, 1923), 323–30; Hayward, ed., *Remarkable Criminals*, 474.

19. Jeremiah Dummer to the Council of Trade and Plantations,

February 25, 1720, *CSPC*, item 578, vol. 31 (1719–20), 365; George Henderson, *An Account of the British Settlement of Honduras* (London, 1811), 70; William Dampier, "Mr. Dampier's Voyages to the Bay of Campeachy," in *A Collection of Voyages*, 4th ed. (London, 1729), 89; "A Voyage to Guinea, Antego, Bay of Campeachy, Cuba, Barbadoes, &c., 1714–1723," Add. MS 39,946, British Library; Malachy Postlethwayt, *Universal Dictionary of Trade and Commerce* (London, 1755?). See also Peter Earle, *The Pirate Wars* (London: Methuen, 2003), 161.

20. Colonel Benjamin Bennett to Council of Trade and Plantations, May 31, 1718, and July 30, 1717, CO 37/10, f. 18; *History of Pyrates*, 228; Governor Sir N. Lawes to the Council of Trade and Plantations, September 1, 1718, *CSPC*, item 681, vol. 30 (1717–18), 345.

21. On mutinies in this era, see Rediker, *Between the Devil and the Deep Blue Sea*, appendix E, "Mutiny at Sea, 1700–1750," 308–11.

22. *History of Pyrates*, 115–16; R. A. Brock, ed., *The Official Letters of Alexander Spotswood* (Virginia Historical Society, *Collections*, n.s., 2 [Richmond, 1882]), 2:249; Snelgrave, *New Account*, 203; "Proceedings of the Court held on the Coast of Africa upon Trying of 100 Pirates taken by his Ma[jes]ties Ship Swallow" (1722), HCA 1/99, f. 26.

23. "Proceedings of the Court," HCA 1/99, ff. 138, 81, 24.

24. Trial of Simon Van Vorst and Others (1717), in *Privateering and Piracy*, ed. Jameson, 304, 307, 308; Evidence of Matthew Parry (1724), "Rhode Island of Providence Plantation: Tryals of 10 Persons Brought in by the Judge," HCA 1/99, f. 5; *Trials of Eight Persons Indited for Piracy* (Boston, 1718), 13, 19. For an example of skilled men who were forced, see Deposition of George Barrow, Master of the sloop *Content*, and John Jackson, a passenger, *CSPC*, item 754 iii, vol. 33 (1722–23), 364–65.

25. See n. 11.

26. Only 26 in the sample of 778 are known to have been married. In pirate confessions, regrets were often expressed to parents but seldom to wives or children. See Cotton Mather, *Useful Remarks: An Essay upon Remarkables in the Way of Wicked Men: A Sermon on the Tragical End, unto which the Way of Twenty-Six Pirates Brought Them; At New Port on Rhode-Island, July 19, 1723* (New London, Conn., 1723), 38–42; and *Trials of Eight Persons*, 24, 25. The quotation is in John Barnard's *Ashton's Memorial: An History of the Strange Adventures, and Signal Deliverances of Mr. Philip Ashton* (Boston, 1725), 3.

27. Peter Haywood to Council of Trade and Plantations, December 3,

1716, CO 137/12; Crook, *Complete Newgate Calendar*, 304. See also Lemisch, "Jack Tar," 377, and Davis, *English Shipping*, 114. Biographical data show that 91 of 96 known class backgrounds among pirates were of low status.

28. See n. 11.

29. Walter Hamilton to Council of Trade and Plantations, January 6, 1718, CO 152/12, f. 211; *Boston Gazette*, July 6, 1725; Captain Candler to Josiah Burchett, May 12, 1717, CO 152/12, f. 32; James Vernon to Council of Trade and Plantations, December 21, 1697, *CSPC*, item 115, vol. 16 (1697–98), 70; *Tryals of Thirty-Six Persons for Piracy* (Boston, 1723), 3; Clive Senior, *A Nation of Pirates: English Piracy in Its Heyday* (London: David and Charles Abbott, 1976), 22; Kenneth Kinkor, "From the Seas! Black Men under the Black Flag," *American Prospects* (1995): 27–29.

30. *American Weekly Mercury*, March 17, 1720; *History of Pyrates*, 82.

31. Information of Joseph Smith and Information of John Webley (1721), HCA 1/18, f. 35; Information of William Voisy (1721), HCA 1/55, f. 12. For a trial involving Native American pirates, see *The Trials of Five Persons for Piracy, Felony, and Robbery* (Boston, 1726). The record of relations between pirates and people of African descent is ambiguous, even contradictory. A substantial minority of pirates had worked in the slave trade and had therefore been part of the machinery of enslavement and transportation. Even though many pirates were black, when they took prize vessels, as they did near African and New World ports, slaves were sometimes part of the captured "cargo" and were in turn treated as such—traded or sold as if commodities like any other. Pirate captains known to have traded in slaves included Edward Taylor, Charles Martel, Edward Condent, Christopher Brown, and James Plantain. Pirates also occasionally committed atrocities against the slaves they took.

32. Testimony of Richard Hawkins (1724), in *The Political State of Great Britain*, ed. Abel Boyer (London, 1711–40), 28:153; *Boston News-Letter*, June 17, 1717; *The Tryals of Major Stede Bonnet and Other Pirates* (London, 1719), 46; *History of Pyrates*, 173, 427, 595. See also *Boston News-Letter*, April 29, 1717.

33. *Boston News-Letter*, April 4, 1723.

34. John Gay, *Polly: An Opera* (London, 1729).

35. R. Reynall Bellamy, ed., *Ramblin' Jack: The Journal of Captain John Cremer* (London: J. Cape, 1936), 144; Hugh F. Rankin, *The Golden Age*

of Piracy (New York: Holt, Rinehart and Winston, 1969), 82. See Virginia Council to the Board of Trade, August 11, 1715, CO 5/1317.

36. *History of Pyrates*, 273; Lieutenant Governor Bennett to the Council of Trade and Plantations, May 31, 1718, *CSPC*, item 551, vol. 30 (1717–18), 260.

37. H. Ross, "Some Notes on the Pirates and Slavers around Sierra Leone and the West Coast of Africa, 1680–1723," *Sierra Leone Studies* 11 (1928), 16–53; *History of Pyrates*, 131; L.G. Carr Laughton, "Shantying and Shanties," *Mariner's Mirror* 9 (1923): 48-50; Trial of John McPherson and others, Proceedings of the Court of Admiralty, Philadelphia, 1731; "Proceedings of the Court," HCA 1/99, f. 3; Information of Henry Hull (1729), HCA 1/56, ff. 29–30; Information of William Snelgrave (1721), HCA 1/54, f. 128.

38. Snelgrave, *New Account*, 219–20; *History of Pyrates*, 95.

39. Stephen Smith to the governor of Jamaica, September 23, 1716, CO 137/12, f. 86; Colonel Bennett to the Council of Trade and Plantations, March 29, 1718, CO 27/10, f. 29; Information of Joseph Hollett (1721), HCA 1/55, f. 11; "Proceedings of the Court," HCA 1/99, f. 116.

40. Robert C. Ritchie, *Captain Kidd and the War against the Pirates* (Cambridge, Mass.: Harvard University Press, 1986); Baer, " 'Captain John Avery,' " 1–26; David Cordingly, *Under the Black Flag: The Romance and the Reality of Life among the Pirates* (New York: Random House, 1995); Hans Turley, *Rum, Sodomy, and the Lash: Piracy, Sexuality, and Masculine Identity* (New York: New York University Press, 1999).

41. *Piracy Destroy'd* (London, 1700), 3, 10, 4; Edward Vernon to Josiah Burchett, August 16, 1720, Edward Vernon Letter-Book, January–December 1720, Add. MS 40812, British Library, London.

42. Morris, *Government and Labor*, 252–58.

43. "Proceedings of the Court," HCA 1/99, f. 158; *History of Pyrates*, 656.

44. "Proceedings of the Court held on the Coast of Africa upon Trying of 100 Pirates taken by his Ma[jes]ties Ship Swallow" (1722), HCA 1/99, f. 116; Edward Vernon to Josiah Burchett, August 12, 1721, Vernon Letter-Book, Add. MS 40813, f. 128; Woodes Rogers to Council of Trade and Plantations, May 29, 1719, CO 23/11; Memorial of Samuel Buck (1720), CO 23/1, f. 103. A quantitative measure of the reduced work done by pirates lies in the ton-per-man ratios often used to compute seafaring productivity. For the ports of Jamaica (1729–31), Barbados (1696–98), and Charleston (1735–39) respectively, merchant seamen in vessels of more than 150 tons handled 8.6, 10.7,

and 12.0 tons per man. Pirates, by more general calculations, handled only 3.1 tons per man. See James F. Shepherd and Gary M. Walton, *Shipping, Maritime Trade, and the Economic Development of Colonial North America* (Cambridge: Cambridge University Press, 1972), 201–3.

CHAPTER FOUR
"THE NEW GOVERNMENT OF THE SHIP"

1. Barnaby Slush, *The Navy Royal: or a Sea-Cook Turn'd Projector* (London, 1709), viii.

2. S. Charles Hill, "Episodes of Piracy in Eastern Waters," *Indian Antiquary* 49 (1920): 37; Arthur L. Hayward, ed., *Lives of the Most Remarkable Criminals* (London, 1735; reprint, New York: Dodd, Mead, 1927), 37.

3. William Betagh, *A Voyage round the World* (London, 1728), 148; G. T. Crook, ed., *The Complete Newgate Calendar* (London: Navarre Society, 1926), 3:60.

4. See what must rank as one of the best books written on piracy, Robert C. Ritchie's *Captain Kidd and the War against the Pirates* (Cambridge, Mass.: Harvard University Press, 1987), 147–51. In the eighteenth century piracy was colored less by religious and national antagonism than in the seventeenth century, when hatred for Catholic Spain had energized a great many buccaneers.

5. P. K. Kemp and Christopher Lloyd, *Brethren of the Coast: Buccaneers of the South* (New York: St. Martin's Press, 1960); Carl Bridenbaugh and Roberta Bridenbaugh, *No Peace beyond the Line: The English in the Caribbean, 1624–1690* (New York: Oxford University Press, 1972); C. H. Haring, *The Buccaneers in the West Indies in the XVII Century* (London, 1910; reprint, Hamden, Conn.: Archon Books, 1966), 71, 73; J. S. Bromley, "Outlaws at Sea, 1660–1720: Liberty, Equality, and Fraternity among the Caribbean Freebooters," in *History from Below: Studies in Popular Protest and Popular Ideology in Honour of George Rudé*, ed. Frederick Krantz (Montreal: Concordia University, 1985), 3. For an amplification of some of these points, see Peter Linebaugh and Marcus Rediker, *The Many-Headed Hydra: Sailors, Slaves, Commoners, and the Hidden History of the Revolutionary Atlantic* (Boston: Beacon Press, 2000), chap. 5.

6. See A. L. Morton, *The English Utopia* (London: Lawrence & Wishart, 1952), chap. 1; F. Graus, "Social Utopias in the Middle

Ages," *Past and Present* 38 (1967): 3–19; William McFee, *The Law of the Sea* (Philadelphia: Lippincott, 1951), 50, 54, 59, 72.

7. Kemp and Lloyd, *Brethren of the Coast*, 3; Bridenbaugh and Bridenbaugh, *No Peace beyond the Line*, 62, 176; Alexander Exquemelin, *The Buccaneers of America* (Amsterdam, 1678; reprint, Annapolis: Naval Institute Press, 1993).

8. Richard Price, ed., *Maroon Societies: Rebel Slave Communities in the Americas*, 2nd ed. (Baltimore: Johns Hopkins University Press, 1979). Pirates continued to lead what they called the marooning life into the 1720s. See Examination of Thomas Jones, February 1724, High Court of Admiralty Papers (HCA) 1/55, f. 52, Public Record Office, London.

9. Christopher Hill, "Radical Pirates?" in *The Origins of Anglo-American Radicalism*, ed. Margaret Jacob and James Jacob (London: George Allen & Unwin, 1984), 20; William Dampier, *A New Voyage around the World* (London, 1697), 219–20; Kemp and Lloyd, *Brethren of the Coast*, 17; Bromley, "Outlaws at Sea," 6, 8, 9.

10. "Simsons Voyage," Sloane MSS 86, British Library, London, 43; Bromley, "Outlaws at Sea," 17; Marcus Rediker, "The Common Seaman in the Histories of Capitalism and the Working Class," *International Journal of Maritime History* 1 (1989): 352–53.

11. Captain Charles Johnson, *A General History of the Pyrates*, ed. Manuel Schonhorn (London, 1724, 1728; reprint, Columbia, S.C.: University of South Carolina Press, 1972), 167, 211–13, 298, 307–8, 321 (hereafter cited as *History of Pyrates*); Hayward, ed., *Remarkable Criminals*, 37; Information of Alexander Thompson (1723), HCA 1/55, f. 23; William Snelgrave, *A New Account of Some Parts of Guinea and the Slave Trade* (London, 1734), 220; "Trial of William Phillips and Others" (1724), in *Privateering and Piracy in the Colonial Period: Illustrative Documents*, ed. John Franklin Jameson (New York: Macmillan, 1923), 337; Hugh F. Rankin, *The Golden Age of Piracy* (New York: Holt, Rinehart and Winston, 1969), 31.

12. *History of Pyrates*, 213.

13. Clement Downing, *A Compendious History of the Indian Wars* (1737; reprint, London: Oxford University Press, 1924), 99; *History of Pyrates*, 121, 139, 167–68, 195, 208, 214, 340, 352; Snelgrave, *New Account*, 199; *Trials of Eight Persons Indited for Piracy* (Boston, 1718), 24; Abel Boyer, ed., *The Political State of Great Britain*, 60 vols. (London, 1711–40), 28:152; George Roberts [Daniel Defoe?], *The Four Years Voyages of Captain George Roberts* (London, 1726), 39.

14. "Proceedings of the Court held on the Coast of Africa upon Trying

of 100 Pirates taken by his Ma[jes]ties Ship Swallow," 1722, HCA   { 193 }
1/99, f. 10; Snelgrave, *New Account,* 217; *History of Pyrates,* 213–14;
Downing, *Compendious History,* 99.

15. *History of Pyrates,* 139; Hayward, ed., *Remarkable Criminals,* 37; Boyer,
ed., *Political State,* 28:153; B. R. Burg, "Legitimacy and Authority:
A Case Study of Pirate Commanders in the Seventeenth and Eighteenth Centuries," *American Neptune* 37 (1977): 40–49.

16. Boyer, ed., *Political State,* 28:153; Examination of John Brown (1717),
in *Privateering and Piracy,* ed. Jameson, 294; *History of Pyrates,* 139,
67; George Francis Dow and John Henry Edmonds, *The Pirates of
the New England Coast, 1630–1730* (Salem, Mass.: Marine Research
Society, 1923), 217; *Trials of Eight Persons,* 23; Richard B. Morris, "The
Ghost of Captain Kidd," *New York History* 19 (1938): 282.

17. Snelgrave, *New Account,* 199; Burg, "Legitimacy and Authority," 44–48.

18. Hayward, ed., *Remarkable Criminals,* 37; *History of Pyrates,* 42, 296, 337.

19. *History of Pyrates,* 423, 591; Boyer, ed., *Political State,* 28:151, 153;
Snelgrave, *New Account,* 200, 272; Lloyd Haynes Williams, *Pirates of
Colonial Virginia* (Richmond, Va.: Dietz Press, 1937), 19; *History of
Pyrates,* 138–39, 312. Ralph Davis, in *The Rise of the English Shipping
Industry in the Seventeenth and Eighteenth Centuries* (London: Mac-
millan, 1962), discusses the quite different role of the quartermaster in
the merchant service (113).

20. Roberts, *Four Years Voyages,* 37, 80; Snelgrave, *New Account,* 199–200,
238–39; *History of Pyrates,* 213–25; *Trials of Eight Persons,* 24, 25; *Tryals
of Thirty Six Persons for Piracy* (Boston, 1723), 9; *Boston News-Letter,*
July 15, 1717; Downing, *Compendious History,* 99.

21. *Trials of Eight Persons,* 24; "Proceedings of the Court," HCA 1/99, ff.
35, 40, 90, 163.

22. *Trials of Eight Persons,* 24, 25; "Proceedings of the Court," HCA 1/99,
f. 90; Captain Peter Solgard to Lords of Admiralty, June 12, 1723
Admiralty Papers (ADM) 1/2452, Public Record Office, London;
Information of Thompson, HCA 1/55, f. 23.

23. Boyer, ed., *Political State,* 28:151; Snelgrave, *New Account,* 272; *History
of Pyrates,* 138–39, 312; *The Tryals of Major Stede Bonnet and Other
Pirates* (London, 1719), 37.

24. *History of Pyrates,* 88–89, 117, 145, 167, 222–25, 292, 595; *Trials of Eight
Persons,* 24; Downing, *Compendious History,* 44, 103; HCA 24/132;
Hill, "Episodes of Piracy," 41–42, 59; Roberts, *Four Years Voyages,* 55,
86; Boyer, ed., *Political State,* 28:153. The quotation is from Betagh's
Voyage, 148.

25. "Proceedings of the Court," HCA 1/99, f. 159; Hill, "Episodes of Piracy," 42; *Boston News-Letter*, April 29, 1717; Deposition of John King (1719), HCA 24/132; Boyer, ed., *Political State*, 28:152; "Trial of Thomas Davis" (1717), in *Privateering and Piracy*, ed. Jameson, 307.

26. Information of Henry Treehill (1723), HCA 1/18, f. 38; *History of Pyrates*, 139, 67; "Proceedings of the Court," HCA 1/99, ff. 36, 62; *An Account of the Conduct and Proceedings of the Late John Gow, alias Smith, Captain of the Late Pirates* (London, 1725; reprint, Edinburgh: Gordon Wright Publishing, 1978), introduction; Orme, quoted in *The Pirate Wars*, by Peter Earle (London: Methuen, 2003), 164.

27. *History of Pyrates*, 211–12, 307–8, 342–43; Dow and Edmonds, *Pirates of New England*, 146–47; Hayward, ed., *Remarkable Criminals*, 37; *Tryals of Bonnet*, 22; Morris, "Ghost of Captain Kidd," 283.

28. Philip Gosse, *The History of Piracy* (New York: Tudor, 1932), 103; John Biddulph, *The Pirates of Malabar; and, An Englishwoman ... in India* (London: Smith, Elder, 1907), x, 155; [John Fillmore], "A Narrative of the Singular Sufferings of John Fillmore and Others on Board the Noted Pirate Vessel Commanded by Captain Phillips," Buffalo Historical Society, *Publications* 10 (1907): 32; *History of Pyrates*, 212, 308, 343; Dow and Edmonds, *Pirates of New England*, 147; Pirate Jeremiah Huggins, quoted in "Ghost of Captain Kidd," by Morris, 292; Hill, "Episodes of Piracy," 57.

29. *An Account of ... the Late John Gow*, 3. Immediately after the mutiny, the pirates sought a prize vessel "with Wine, if possible, for that they wanted Extreamly" (13). See also *History of Pyrates*, 307, 319.

30. *History of Pyrates*, 129, 135, 167, 222, 211, 280, 205, 209, 312, 353, 620; "Proceedings of the Court," HCA 1/99, f. 151; *American Weekly Mercury*, March 17, 1720; Snelgrave, *New Account*, 233–38.

31. *History of Pyrates*, 244, 224; Snelgrave, *New Account*, 233; Hill, "Episodes of Piracy," 59; Trial of Simon Van Vorst and Others (1717), in *Privateering and Piracy*, ed. Jameson, 303, 314.

32. *Tryals of Bonnet*, 13; Boyer, ed., *Political State*, 28:153; *History of Pyrates*, 353–54.

33. Colonel Stede Bonnet to Council of Trade and Plantations, July 30, 1717, CO37/10, f. 15; *History of Pyrates*, 243, 279; John Atkins, *A Voyage to Guinea, Brasil, and the West-Indies* (London, 1735; reprint, London: Frank Cass, 1970), 192.

34. *History of Pyrates*, 127, 212, 295, 308, 343; Morris, "Ghost of Captain Kidd," 292.

35. *History of Pyrates*, 74–75.

36. Ibid., 212, 343; B. R. Burg, *Sodomy and the Perception of Evil: English Sea Rovers in the Seventeenth-Century Caribbean* (New York: New York University Press, 1983), 128, 76, 41, xv, 124; Hans Turley, *Rum, Sodomy, and the Lash: Piracy, Sexuality, and Masculine Identity* (New York: New York University Press, 1999), 2, 96; *Tryals of Thirty-Six Persons*, 9; Cotton Mather, *An Essay upon Remarkables in the Way of Wicked Men* (New London, 1723), 32–33.   { 195 }

37. *History of Pyrates*, 307, 212.

38. Ibid., 157–58; Examination of William Terrill (1716), HCA 1/17, 67.

39. *Tryals of Bonnet*, 30; *History of Pyrates*, 211, 212, 343; Biddulph, *Pirates of Malabar*, 163–64; Rankin, *Golden Age*, 37.

40. *History of Pyrates*, 212, 343; Snelgrave, *New Account*, 256; *American Weekly Mercury* (Philadelphia), May 30, 1723. The discussion of discipline takes into account not only the articles themselves but also observations on actual punishments from other sources. See also Stanley Richards, *Black Bart* (Llandybie, Wales: Christopher Davies, 1966), 47; "Proceedings of the Court," HCA 1/99, ff. 45, 50; Boyer, ed., *Political State*, 28:152.

41. Snelgrave, *New Account*, 257; Boyer, ed., *Political State*, 28:153.

42. Trial of Van Vorst, 304; *Trials of Eight Persons*, 19, 21; R. A. Brock, ed., *The Official Letters of Alexander Spotswood* (Virginia Historical Society, *Collections*, n.s., 2 [Richmond, 1882]), 2:249; *History of Pyrates*, 260.

43. *Trials of Eight Persons*, 21; Deposition of Samuel Cooper, 1718, CO 37/10, f. 35; *History of Pyrates*, 116, 196, 216, 228; Boyer, ed., *Political State*, 28, 148; Governor of Bermuda, quoted in *Jolly Roger*, by Patrick Pringle (New York: Norton, 1953), 181; Deposition of Richard Symes, 1721, CO 152/14, f. 33; *American Weekly Mercury*, March 17, 1720; *New-England Courant* (Boston), June 25, 1722.

44. *History of Pyrates*, 167–68.

45. Ibid., 298, 307, 352; Information of Thompson, HCA 1/55, f. 23.

46. Information of John Stephenson (1721), HCA 1/55, f. 5; Snelgrave, *New Account*, 261; Information of Richard Capper (1718), HCA 1/54, f. 90; "Proceedings of the Court," HCA 1/99, ff. 74, 152.

47. "Proceedings of the Court," HCA 1/99, ff. 153, 85, 23; *Trials of Eight Persons*, 8, 24; Examination of Richard Moor (1724), HCA 1/55, f. 96; *History of Pyrates*, 346.

48. Dow and Edmonds, *Pirates of New England*, 278; Lieutenant Governor Benjamin Bennett to Mr. Popple, March 31, 1720, *Calendar of State Papers, Colonial Series, America and West Indies, 1574–1739*, CD-ROM, consultant editors Karen Ordahl Kupperman, John C.

Appleby, and Mandy Banton (London: Routledge, published in association with the Public Record Office, 2000), item 33, vol. 32 (1720–21), 18–19; Hayward, ed., *Remarkable Criminals*, 37; *History of Pyrates*, 225, 313, 226, 342.

49. The total of 3,600 is reached by multiplying the number of ship captains shown in the diagram by the average crew size of 79.5. See *History of Pyrates*, 41–42, 72, 121, 137, 138, 174, 210, 225, 277, 281, 296, 312, 352, 355, 671; *New-England Courant*, June 11, 1722; *American Weekly Mercury*, July 6, 1721, January 5 and September 16, 1725; Pringle, *Jolly Roger*, 181, 190, 244; Biddulph, *Pirates of Malabar*, 135, 187; Snelgrave, *New Account*, 196–97, 199, 272, 280; Shirley Carter Hughson, *The Carolina Pirates and Colonial Commerce, 1670–1740*, Johns Hopkins University Studies in Historical and Political Science 12 (Baltimore: Johns Hopkins University Press, 1894), 70; *Boston News-Letter* August 12–19, 1717, October 13–20 and November 10–17, 1718, February 4–11, 1725, June 30, 1726; Downing, *Compendious History*, 51, 101; Morris, "Ghost of Captain Kidd," 282, 283, 296; *Tryals of Bonnet*, iii, 44–45; Dow and Edmonds, *Pirates of New England*, 117, 135, 201, 283, 287; *Trials of Eight Persons*, 23; Trial of Van Vorst (1717), Case of John Rose Archer and Others (1724), in *Privateering and Piracy*, ed. Jameson, 304, 341; Boyer, ed., *Political State*, 25:198–99; S. Charles Hill, "Notes on Piracy in Eastern Waters," *Indian Antiquary* 52 (1923): 148, 150; Captain Mathew Musson to the Council of Trade and Plantations, July 5, 1717, *CSPC*, item 635, vol. 29 (1716–17), 338; Lieutenant Governor Benjamin Bennett to the Council of Trade and Plantations, June 8, 1719, *CSPC*, item 227, vol. 31 (1719–20), 118; John F. Watson, *Annals of Philadelphia and Pennsylvania* (Philadelphia, 1844), 2:227; *Boston Gazette*, April 27–May 4, 1724.

50. Alexander Spotswood to the Board of Trade, June 16, 1724, Colonial Office (CO) 5/1319, Public Record Office, London.

CHAPTER FIVE
"TO DO JUSTICE TO SAILORS"

1. This and the following three paragraphs are based on Captain Charles Johnson, *A General History of the Pyrates*, ed. Manuel Schonhorn (1724, 1728; reprint, Columbia, S.C.: University of South Carolina Press, 1972), 118–21 (hereafter cited as *History of Pyrates*), especially the "Letter from Captain Mackra, at Bombay," dated November 16, 1720. Other important sources include Clement Downing, *A Com-*

pendious History of the Indian Wars (1737; reprint, London: Oxford University Press, 1924), 44 ; "Narrative of Richard Lazenby of London" (1720), in "Episodes of Piracy in Eastern Waters," by S. Charles Hill, *Indian Antiquary* 49 (1920): 57.

2. Macrae returned to London in 1722 and was immediately rewarded by the East India Company for his courage. He was made deputy governor of the trading post on the Coromandel Coast of India and, soon after, governor of Madras. He returned to Britain with a fortune, which he used to buy several estates in Scotland. See Schonhorn's notes in *History of Pyrates*, 671–72.

3. Testimony of Thomas Checkley (1717), in *Privateering and Piracy in the Colonial Period: Illustrative Documents*, ed. John Franklin Jameson (New York: Macmillan, 1923), 304; *Trials of Eight Persons Indited for Piracy* (Boston, 1718), 11.

4. E. J. Hobsbawm, *Primitive Rebels: Studies in Archaic Forms of Social Movements in the 19th and 20th Centuries* (New York: Praeger, 1959), 5, 17, 18, 27, 28; see also his *Bandits* (New York: Delacorte, 1969), 24–29.

5. Alexander Spotswood to the Board of Trade, June 16, 1724, Colonial Office (CO) 5/1319, Public Record Office, London.

6. *The Tryals of Sixteen Persons for Piracy* (Boston, 1726), 5; *The Tryals of Major Stede Bonnet and Other Pirates* (London, 1719), iii, iv; G. T. Crook, ed., *The Complete Newgate Calendar* (London: Navarre Society, 1926), 3:61; Shirley Carter Hughson, *The Carolina Pirates and Colonial Commerce, 1670–1740*, Johns Hopkins University Studies in Historical and Political Science 12 (Baltimore: Johns Hopkins University Press, 1894), 121; Hugh F. Rankin, *The Golden Age of Piracy* (New York: Holt, Rinehart and Winston, 1969), 28; *History of Pyrates*, 116, 342; Downing, *Compendious History*, 98. An analysis of the names of 44 pirate ships reveals the following patterns: 8 (18.2 percent) made reference to revenge; 7 (15.9 percent) were named *Ranger* or *Rover*, suggesting mobility and perhaps, as discussed later, a watchfulness over the way captains treated their sailors; and 5 (11.4 percent) referred to royalty. It is noteworthy that only 2 names referred to wealth. Other names indicated that places *(Lancaster)*, unidentifiable people *(Mary Anne)*, and animals *(Black Robin)* constituted less significant themes. Two names, *Batchelor's Delight* and *Batchelor's Adventure*, tend to support the probability (see chapter 3) that most pirates were unmarried. See *History of Pyrates*, 220, 313; William P. Palmer, ed., *Calendar of Virginia State Papers* (Richmond, 1875), 1:194.

7. William Betagh, *A Voyage round the World* (London, 1728), 41.

8. Petition of Randolph, Cane, and Halladay (1722), in *Virginia State Papers*, ed. Palmer, 202.

9. "Proceedings of the Court held on the Coast of Africa" (1722), High Court of Admiralty (HCA) 1/99, f. 101; *History of Pyrates*, 338, 582; William Snelgrave, *A New Account of Some Parts of Guinea and the Slave Trade* (London, 1734), 212, 225; George Francis Dow and John Henry Edmonds, *The Pirates of the New England Coast, 1630–1730* (Salem, Mass.: Marine Research Society, 1923), 301; Nathaniel Uring, *The Voyages and Travels of Captain Nathaniel Uring*, ed. Alfred Dewar (1726; reprint, London: Cassell, 1928), xxviii.

10. Abel Boyer, ed., *The Political State of Great Britain* (London, 1711–40), 28:149–50; *History of Pyrates*, 338, 352–53; Dow and Edmonds, *Pirates of New England*, 278; Betagh, *Voyage round the World*, 26. This torture may have exploited the meaning of the verb *to sweat*, which was "to drive hard, to overwork." The construction of a literally vicious circle here seems hardly coincidental. See the *Oxford English Dictionary*, s.v. "sweat"; *Tryals of Sixteen Persons*, 14. Knowledge of this ritualized violence was evidently widespread. In 1722 Bristol merchants informed Parliament that pirates "study how to torture"; see Leo Francis Stock, ed., *Proceedings and Debates of the British Parliaments Respecting North America* (Washington, D.C.: Carnegie Institution, 1930), 3:453.

11. Crook, ed., *Newgate Calendar*, 59; Boyer, ed., *Political State*, 32, 272; *Boston Gazette*, October 24, 1720; Rankin, *Golden Age*, 35, 135, 148; [Cotton Mather], *The Vial Poured Out upon the Sea: A Remarkable Relation of Certain Pirates* (Boston, 1726), 21; John F. Watson, *Annals of Philadelphia and Pennsylvania* (Philadelphia, 1844), 2:227; the quotation is from the *Boston Gazette*, March 21, 1726.

12. Snelgrave, *New Account*, 196, 199. This is a marvelous source written by an intelligent and perceptive man of long experience at sea. The book concerns mainly the slave trade, was addressed to the merchants of London, and apparently was not intended as popular reading.

13. Ibid., 202–8.

14. Ibid., 212, 225. Many perceived piracy as an activity akin to war. See also *History of Pyrates*, 168, 319. Francis R. Stark, in *The Abolition of Privateering and the Declaration of Paris* (New York, 1897), 14, 13, 22, claims that war in the seventeenth and early eighteenth centuries was understood more in terms of "individual enmity" than national struggle. Victors had "absolute right over (1) hostile persons and (2) hostile property." This might partly explain pirates' violence and destructiveness.

15. Snelgrave, *New Account*, 241. For other examples of giving cargo to ship captains and treating them "civilly," see Deposition of Robert Dunn, 1720, CO 152/13, f. 26; Deposition of Richard Symes, 1721, CO 152/14, f. 33; John Biddulph, *The Pirates of Malabar; and, An English-woman ... in India* (London: Smith, Elder, 1907), 139; R. A. Brock, ed., *The Official Letters of Alexander Spotswood* (Virginia Historical Society, *Collections*, n.s., 2 [Richmond, 1882]), 2:339–43; *Boston Gazette*, August 21, 1721; Hill, "Episodes of Piracy," 57; Richard B. Morris, "The Ghost of Captain Kidd," *New York History* 19 (1938): 283; Elizabeth Donnan, ed., *Documents Illustrative of the History of the Slave-Trade to America* (Washington, D.C.: Carnegie Institution, 1935), 4:96; *Tryals of Bonnet*, 13; Boyer, ed., *Political State*, 27:616; Deposition of Henry Bostock, December 9, 1717, *Calendar of State Papers, Colonial Series, America and West Indies, 1574–1739*, CD-ROM, consultant editors Karen Ordahl Kupperman, John C. Appleby, and Mandy Banton (London: Routledge, published in association with the Public Record Office, 2000), item 298 iii, vol. 30 (1717–18), 150–51 (hereafter *CSPC*); *Boston News-Letter*, November 14, 1720; and Spotswood to Craggs, May 20, 1720: "it is a common practice with those Rovers upon the pillageing of a Ship to make presents of other Commodity's to such Masters as they take a fancy to in Lieu of that they have plundered them of" (CO 5/1319).

16. Snelgrave, *New Account*, 241, 242, 243.

17. William Snelgrave to Humphrey Morice, August 1, 1719, Humphrey Morice Papers from the Bank of England, *Slave Trade Journals and Papers* (Marlboro, Wiltshire, England: Adam Mathew Publications, 1998), microfilm; Snelgrave, *New Account*, 275, 276, 284.

18. *History of Pyrates*, 114, 115.

19. Ibid.

20. Stanley Richards, *Black Bart* (Llandybie, Wales: Christopher Davies, 1966), 77, based on "Proceedings of the Court," HCA1/99, f. 101; CO137/14, f. 36.

21. Information of Thomas Grant (1721), HCA 1/54, f. 120; HCA 1/30 (England); Snelgrave, *New Account*, 174. The question of the captain's character helps to explain why pirates destroyed so many ships, as discussed in chapter 2.

22. *History of Pyrates*, 338.

23. *Boston News-Letter*, November 14, 1720; *Boston Gazette*, October 24, 1720; *History of Pyrates*, 607.

24. *History of Pyrates*, 351; Jameson, ed., *Privateering and Piracy*, 341;

Crook, ed., *Newgate Calendar*, 60; Benjamin Colman, *It Is a Fearful Thing to Fall into the Hands of the Living God* (Boston, 1726), 39.

25. Deposition of Samuel Cooper, Mariner, of Bermuda (1718), *CSPC*, item 551 i, vol. 30 (1717–18), 263; Deposition of Edward North (1718), CO37/10, f. 37; *History of Pyrates*, 647; *Tryals of Bonnet*, 13; Snelgrave, *New Account*, 216–17; Peter Earle, *The Pirate Wars* (London: Methuen, 2003), 170.

26. *Tryals of Bonnet*, 8; Deposition of Edward North.

27. Snelgrave, *New Account*, 199; *History of Pyrates*, 138, 174; Morris, "Ghost of Captain Kidd," 282.

28. *Boston News-Letter*, August 15, 1720; *American Weekly Mercury*, September 6, 1722.

29. Mr. Gale to Colonel Thomas Pitt, junr, November 4, 1718, *CSPC*, item 31 i, vol. 31 (1719–20), 10; Board of Trade to J. Methuen, September 3, 1716, CO 23/12; *History of Pyrates*, 315, 582; Downing, *Compendious History*, 98, 104–5; Uring, *Voyages*, 241; George Shelvocke, *A Voyage round the World* (London, 1726), 242; H. R. McIlwaine, ed., *Executive Journals of the Council of Colonial Virginia* (Richmond, 1928), 3:612; Dow and Edmonds, *Pirates of New England*, 341; Deposition of R. Lazenby, in "Episodes of Piracy," by Hill, 60; "Voyage to Guinea, Antego, Bay of Campeachy, Cuba, Barbadoes, &c, 1714–1723," Add. MS 39946, British Library; "Proceedings of the Court," HCA1/99, f. 157; *History of Pyrates*, 640.

30. Trial of Thomas Davis (1717), in *Privateering and Piracy*, ed. Jameson, 308; *Boston News-Letter*, November 4, 1717.

31. *Tryals of Bonnet*, 45.

32. Deposition of Samuel Cooper, Mariner, May, 24, 1718, *CSPC*, item 551 i, vol. 30 (1717–18), 263; *Tryals of Bonnet*, 29, 50; *History of Pyrates*, 195.

33. Governor Hamilton to the Council of Trade and Plantations, October 3, 1720, *CSPC*, item 251, vol. 32 (1720–21), 165; *American Weekly Mercury*, October 27, 1720; *Boston Gazette*, October 24, 1720.

34. Alexander Spotswood to the Council of Trade and Plantations, May 31, 1721, *CSPC*, item 513, vol. 32 (1720–21), 328.

35. Council meeting of May 3, 1721, in *Council of Colonial Virginia*, ed. McIlwaine, 542; abstract of Alexander Spotswood to Board of Trade, June 11, 1722, CO 5/1370; Spotswood to Board of Trade, May 31, 1721, CO 5/1319; Mr. Urmstone to the Secretary, May 10, 1721, Society for the Propagation of the Gospel Archives, Manuscripts A/15, f. 44,

Colonial Virginia Records Project, Virginia State Library, Richmond, Virginia.

36. Dow and Edmonds, *Pirates of New England*, 281–82; *History of Pyrates*, 355; *American Weekly Mercury*, May 21, 1724.

37. Charles Hope to Council of Trade, January 14, 1724, CO 37/11, f. 37.

38. Jameson, *Privateering and Piracy*, 346; Treasury warrant to Captain Knott, August 10, 1722, Treasury Papers (T) 52/32, Public Record Office, London.

39. John Barnard, *Ashton's Memorial: An History of the Strange Adventures, and Signal Deliverances of Mr. Philip Ashton* (Boston, 1725), 2, 4; emphasis added. Perhaps this was what M. A. K. Halliday has called an "anti-language". This is "the acting out of a distinct social structure [in speech]; and this social structure is, in turn, the bearer of an alternative social reality." An "anti-language" exists in "the context of *re*socialization." See his "Anti-Languages," *American Anthropologist* 78 (1976): 572, 575.

40. William Smith, *A New Voyage to Guinea* (London, 1744), 42–43; Snelgrave, *New Account*, 217; Barnard, *Ashton's Memorial*, 7; *History of Pyrates*, 312. See also Morris, "Ghost of Captain Kidd," 286.

41. Anthropologist Raymond Firth argues that flags function as instruments of both power and sentiment, creating solidarity and symbolizing unity. See his *Symbols: Public and Private* (Ithaca, N.Y.: Cornell University Press, 1973), 328, 339; S. Charles Hill, "Notes on Piracy in Eastern Waters," *Indian Antiquary* 52 (1923): 147. For particular pirate crews known to have sailed under the Jolly Roger, see *Boston Gazette*, November 29, 1725 (Captain Lyne); *Boston News-Letter*, September 10, 1716 (Jennings? Leslie?), August 12, 1717 (Napin, Nichols), March 2, 1719 (Thompson), May 28, 1724 (Phillips), and June 5, 1721 (Rackam?); Jameson, ed., *Privateering and Piracy*, 317 (Roberts); *Tryals of Sixteen Persons*, 5 (Fly); Snelgrave, *Account of the Slave Trade*, 199 (Cocklyn, LaBouche, Davis); *Trials of Eight Persons*, 24 (Bellamy); Hughson, *Carolina Pirates*, 113 (Moody); *Tryals of Bonnet*, 44–45 (Bonnet, Teach, Richards); Dow and Edmonds, *Pirates of New England*, 208 (Harris), 213 (Low); Boyer, ed., *Political State*, 28:152 (Spriggs); Biddulph, *Pirates of Malabar*, 135 (Taylor); Donnan, ed., *Documents of the Slave-Trade*, 96 (England); and *History of Pyrates*, 240–41 (Skyrm), 67–68 (Martel), 144 (Vane), 371 (captain unknown), 628 (Macarty, Bunce), 299 (Worley). Royal officials affirmed and

attempted to reroute the power of this symbolism by raising the Jolly Roger on the gallows when hanging pirates. See chapter 8.

42. Boyer, ed., *Political State*, 28:152; Snelgrave, *Account of the Slave Trade*, 236. Pirates also occasionally used red, or "bloody," flags. For a more extended discussion of the Jolly Roger, see chapter 8.

43. Lieutenant Governor Hope to [Lord Carteret?], June 25, 1723, *CSPC*, item 603, vol. 33 (1722–23), 287; Governor John Hope to Council of Trade and Plantations, January 14, 1724, CO 37/11, f. 36.

44. Brock, ed., *Letters of Spotswood*, 2:319, 274; Gale to Pitt, November 4, 1718, CO 23/1, ff. 47–48; *Tryals of Bonnet*, 9.

45. Lieutenant General Mathew to Governor Hamilton, September 29, 1720, CO152/13, f. 23; Governor John Hope to Council of Trade and Plantations, January 14, 1724, CO 37/11, f. 37; Edward Vernon to Josiah Burchett, November 7, 1720, Edward Vernon Letter-Book, Add. MS 40812 (January–December 1720), ff. 96–97.

46. Hughson, *Carolina Pirates*, 112, 100–101; Barnaby Slush, *The Navy Royal: or a Sea-Cook Turn'd Projector* (London, 1709), viii.

47. *History of Pyrates*, 28, 43, 244, 159, 285, 628, 656, 660; Arthur L. Hayward, ed., *Lives of the Most Remarkable Criminals* (London, 1735; reprint, New York: Dodd, Mead, 1927), 39; Rankin, *Golden Age*, 155; [Mather], *Vial Poured Out*, 47; Jameson, ed., *Privateering and Piracy*, 341; extract of letter from Lieutenant General Mathew to Governor Hamilton, September 29, 1720, *CSPC*, item 251 i, vol. 32 (1720–21), 167.

48. Bartholomew Roberts, the Pirate, to Lieutenant General Mathew, *Royall Fortune*, September 27, 1720, *CSPC*, item 251 v, vol. 32 (1720–21), 169.

49. Governor Hamilton to the Council of Trade and Plantations, October 3, 1720, *CSPC*, item 251, vol. 32 (1720–21), 165.

50. Boyer, ed., *Political State*, 28:153. For similar vows and actual attempts, see chapter 8.

CHAPTER SIX
THE WOMEN PIRATES: ANNE BONNY AND MARY READ

1. *Boston News-Letter* December 19, 1720. On the trial, see *The Tryals of Captain John Rackam and Other Pirates* (Jamaica, 1721).

2. Captain Charles Johnson, *A General History of the Pyrates*, ed. Manuel Schonhorn (London, 1724, 1728; reprint, Columbia, S.C.: University of South Carolina Press, 1972), 152 (hereafter cited as *History of Pyrates*).

3. See the important work edited by Jo Stanley, *Bold in Her Breeches: Women Pirates across the Ages* (London: HarperCollins, 1995), and David Cordingly, *Women Sailors and Sailors' Women: An Untold Maritime History* (New York: Random House, 2001).

4. The publishing history of *History of Pyrates* can be followed in *A Bibliography of the Works of Captain Charles Johnson*, by Philip Gosse (London: Dulau, 1927).

5. See "By his Excellency Woodes Rogers, Esq; Governour of New-Providence, &c. A Proclamation," *Boston Gazette*, October 10, 1720; *Tryals of Captain John Rackam*, 16–19; Governor Nicholas Lawes to Council of Trade and Plantations, June 12, 1721, in *Calendar of State Papers, Colonial Series, America and West Indies, 1574–1739*, CD-ROM, consultant editors Karen Ordahl Kupperman, John C. Appleby, and Mandy Banton (London: Routledge, published in association with the Public Record Office, 2000), item 523, vol. 32 (1720–21), 335 (italics in original); *American Weekly Mercury*, January 31, 1721; *Boston Gazette*, February 6, 1721; *Boston News-Letter*, February 13, 1721.

6. It is possible that Captain Johnson used this pamphlet, as he did others, in preparing his text. See Schonhorn's commentary in *History of Pyrates*, 670.

7. *Tryals of Captain John Rackam*, 16.

8. Linda Grant Depauw notes that women frequently worked in artillery units during the American Revolution. See her "Women in Combat: The Revolutionary War Experience," *Armed Forces and Society* 7 (1981): 214–17.

9. *Tryals of Captain John Rackam*, 18.

10. The narratives are in almost all respects plausible. Literary convention of the day played a part in constructing the narratives, to be sure, as in the invocation of the conflict between Mars and Venus in the life of Mary Read.

11. Linda Grant Depauw, *Seafaring Women* (Boston: Houghton Mifflin, 1982), 18, 71. Seafaring was only one of many lines of work formally to exclude women, for the sexual division of labor was clearly established and indeed growing in the eighteenth century, even if not yet as severe in some respects as it would become. Medieval guilds and the apprenticeship system had long before segregated the majority of crafts by sex. See the excellent work by Bridget Hill, *Women, Work, and Sexual Politics in Eighteenth-Century England* (Oxford: Basil Blackwell, 1989), especially her comments at 49, 260.

12. Dianne Dugaw, ed., *The Female Soldier: Or, the Surprising Life and*

Adventures of Hannah Snell (London, 1750; reprint, Los Angeles: Augustan Reprint Society, 1989), v. Linda Grant Depauw has pointed out that during the American Revolution "tens of thousands of women were involved in active combat," a "few hundred" of these— like Deborah Sampson, Sally St. Clair, Margaret Corbin, and a woman known only as "Samuel Gay"—fighting in uniform with the Continental line. See her "Women in Combat," 209.

13. "Female Warriors," originally published in the *British Magazine*, was reprinted as an "unacknowledged essay" in *The Works of Oliver Goldsmith*, ed. Peter Cunningham (New York: Harper and Brothers, 1881), 3:316–19.

14. Historians have only recently begun to study the process by which seafaring became a masculine activity. See Margaret S. Creighton and Lisa Norling, eds., *Iron Men, Wooden Women: Gender and Seafaring in the Atlantic World, 1700–1920* (Baltimore: Johns Hopkins University Press, 1996).

15. Rudolf M. Dekker and Lotte C. van de Pol, *The Tradition of Female Transvestism in Early Modern Europe* (London: Macmillan, 1989), 80, 81; Julia Wheelwright, *Amazons and Military Maids: Women Who Dressed as Men in the Pursuit of Life, Liberty, and Happiness* (London: Pandora, 1989), 51, 53, 78. Maritime employers probably felt about women sailors the way employers of indentured labor felt about the ten thousand or so women who were transported as felons to Britain's American colonies between 1718 and 1775; they considered these women less skilled, less capable of heavy physical labor, and more likely to lose labor time to pregnancy. See A. Roger Ekirch, *Bound for America: The Transportation of British Convicts to the Colonies, 1718–1775* (Oxford: Clarendon Press, 1987), 48–50, 89.

16. Arthur N. Gilbert, "Buggery and the British Navy, 1700–1861," *Journal of Social History* 10 (1976): 87–88.

17. John Flavel, *A Pathetical and Serious Disswassive . . .* (Boston, 1725), 134; Depauw, *Seafaring Women*, 162, 184–85. The women who regularly came aboard were passengers and increasingly the wives of officers, the great majority of whom were separated from the crew by chasms of gender and class. The trend of captains' wives accompanying them to sea reached a peak in the nineteenth century and declined in the twentieth.

18. The fear of female sexuality probably drew on an older superstition about the magical, spiritual, and supernatural powers of women that

arose during the terrifying early days of seafaring. Linda Grant
Depauw maintains that it is a myth and a shoreside invention that
women were regarded as bad luck at sea, having little or nothing to
do with the actual beliefs of seamen. But her argument is contradicted by too much evidence (some of it her own) to be persuasive.
See her *Seafaring Women*, 15–18.

19. Clive Senior, *A Nation of Pirates: English Piracy in Its Heyday* (Lon-
    don: David & Charles Abbott, 1976), 39.

20. *History of Pyrates*, 212, 343; William Snelgrave, *A New Account of Some
    Parts of Guinea and the Slave Trade* (London, 1734; reprint, London:
    Frank Cass, 1971), 256–57.

21. Roberts and his crew may have known—and disapproved—of Bonny
    and Read. Another of their articles of agreement stated: "If any Man
    were found seducing any of the [female] Sex, and carry'd her to Sea,
    disguised, he was to suffer Death." See *History of Pyrates*, 212.

22. *Tryals of Captain John Rackam*, 18.

23. "At a Court held at Williamsburg" (1727), HCA 1/99, ff. 2–8. Harley's
    husband, Thomas, was also involved in the piracy but somehow eluded
    arrest. For information on Thomas and Mary Harley (or Harvey),
    identified as husband and wife, see Peter Wilson Coldham, *English
    Convicts in America*, vol. 1: *Middlesex, 1617–1775* (New Orleans: Poly-
    anthos, 1974), 123. Mary Harley (or Harvey) was transported to the
    colonies in April 1725. Thomas was sentenced in October and trans-
    ported in November of the same year. The leader of the gang, John
    Vidal, requested and was granted the King's mercy, receiving pardon
    for his capital crime in September 1727. See H. R. McIlwaine,
    Executive Journals of the Council of Colonial Virginia (Richmond:
    Virginia State Library, 1930), 4:149, 150.

24. "Proceedings of the Court of Admiralty [in Virginia]" (1729), HCA
    1/99. See also Coldham, *English Convicts in America*, 67 (Crichett)
    and 290 (Williams). No record exists to show whether the hangings
    took place.

25. By limiting the role of women aboard their ships, pirates may have
    made it more difficult to reproduce themselves as a community and
    hence easier for the state to wage its deadly assault on them.

26. Julia Wheelwright writes: "Women who enlisted as soldiers and
    sailors were most often from the labouring classes where they were
    used to hard, physical work. They came from communities where the
    women were confident of their strength as they worked side by side

with men in the fields" or other areas. See her *Amazons and Military Maids*, 42, and Dekker and van de Pol, *Tradition of Female Transvestism*, 2.

27. Based on 119 instances of cross-dressing, which were found in the archives of the Dutch East India Company, Rudolf M. Dekker and Lotte C. van de Pol have concluded: "Throughout the early modern era passing oneself off as a man was a real and viable option for women who had fallen into bad times and were struggling to overcome their difficult circumstances." See their *Tradition of Female Transvestism*, 1–2 (quotation), 11, 13, 42.

28. See Anne Chambers, *Granuaile: The Life and Time of Grace O'Malley, c. 1530–1603* (Dublin: Wolfhound Press, 1983); Sydney is quoted at 85. See also Depauw, *Seafaring Women*, 24–25. Read, who kept an inn at Breda, in turn may have influenced the Netherlands' most famous female cross-dresser, Maria van Antwerpen. See Dekker and van de Pol, *Tradition of Female Transvestism*, 40.

29. James Caulfield, *Portraits, Memoirs, and Characters of Remarkable Persons from the Revolution in 1688 to the End of the Reign of George II* (London: T. H. Whitely, 1820), 2:43–51.

30. Ibid., 4:111, 112.

31. Dugaw, ed., *Female Soldier*, vi, 1, 5, 6, 17, 19, 22–23, 39, 41. Hannah Snell's story was often told in celebration of the British nation, emphasizing the patriotism of her military service. The stories of Bonny and Read admitted no such emphasis, for the inescapable fact remained that they attacked *British* ships and *British* commerce, refusing the logic of nationalism in their depredations.

32. Dianne Dugaw, *Warrior Women and Popular Balladry, 1650–1850* (Cambridge: Cambridge University Press, 1989), 20.

33. Ibid., 1, 48.

34. Ibid., 124, 131, 122 (quotation). Dugaw's conclusion about the positive popular reaction to women warriors appears to be at odds with that of Rudolf M. Dekker and Lotte C. van de Pol, but this may be a matter of a difference in responses in England and the Netherlands. See Dekker and van de Pol, *Tradition of Female Transvestism*, 97–98.

35. Bonny's and Read's cross-dressing and going to sea should be seen in the broader context that Peter Linebaugh suggested: "I think that to the many acts of survival and getting by, we should add the power of seeming to be what you are not as among the characteristics of the thick, scarred, and calloused hide of the English proletariat." See his "All the Atlantic Mountains Shook," *Labour/Le Travail* 10 (1982): 99.

36. In "Women in Combat" (223), Depauw argues that in the eighteenth century "engaging in hand-to-hand combat was not considered un- feminine behavior."

37. *Tryals of Captain John Rackam*, 16, 18.
38. *History of Pyrates*, 151; *Tryals of Captain John Rackam*, 11; Douglas Hay, Peter Linebaugh, and E. P. Thompson, eds., *Albion's Fatal Tree: Crime and Society in Eighteenth-Century England* (New York: Pantheon, 1975); E. P. Thompson, *Whigs and Hunters: The Origin of the Black Act* (New York: Pantheon Books, 1975); Peter Linebaugh, *The London Hanged: Crime and Civil Society in the Eighteenth Century* (Cambridge: Cambridge University Press, 1991).
39. *History of Pyrates*, 597.
40. John Gillis, *For Better, for Worse: British Marriages, 1600 to the Present* (New York: Oxford University Press, 1985), 13, 14, 18, 37, 84, 85, 99 (quotation); anonymous letter from South Carolina, August 1716, Colonial Office Papers (CO) 5/382, f. 47 (quotation), Public Record Office, London. Richard Turnley, who not only refused to witness the wife sale but informed Governor Rogers, became an immediate object of revenge. With "many bitter Oaths and Imprecations," Bonny and Rackam swore that if they had been able to find him (and they went in search of him), they would "have whipp'd him to Death." See *History of Pyrates*, 623, 626. The narrative also suggests that this particular wife sale was initiated not by the husband, as was custom- ary, but by Bonny herself. On wife sales, see E. P. Thompson, *Customs in Common* (London: Merlin Press, 1991) chap. 7; Samuel Pyeatt Menafee, *Wives for Sale* (Oxford: Oxford University Press, 1981); and Hill, *Women, Work, and Sexual Politics*, 216.
41. *History of Pyrates*, 391.
42. See Dugaw, *Warrior Women*, 73, 75, 155, and her essay "Female Sailors Bold: Transvestite Heroines and the Markers of Gender and Class," in *Iron Men, Wooden Women*, ed. Creighton and Norling, 34–54. The warrior woman ballad declined in England just as cross-dressing declined in the Netherlands. See Dekker and van de Pol, *Tradition of Female Transvestism*, 102–3.
43. Wheelwright, *Amazons and Military Maids*, 11, 78, 159; Dugaw, *Warrior Women*, 1, 3–4. On subsequent editions of *History of Pirates*, see Gosse, *A Bibliography of the Works of Captain Charles Johnson*.
44. Natalie Zemon Davis, "Women on Top," in her *Society and Culture in Early Modern France* (Stanford: Stanford University Press, 1975), 131, 144; Wheelwright, *Amazons and Military Maids*, 15, 119 (quotation).

45. Daniel Defoe, *The Fortunes and Misfortunes of the Famous Moll Flanders* (London, 1722; reprint, New York: Penguin, 1978), 28, 33, 228, 208–9.

46. Christopher Hill, A *Tinker and a Poor Man: John Bunyan and His Church, 1628–1688* (New York: Knopf, 1989), 362; Linebaugh, *London Hanged*, 119–20; Dugaw, ed., *Female Soldier*, 40–41.

47. James R. Sutherland, " 'Polly' among the Pirates," *Modern Language Review* 37 (1942): 291–92; Joan Hildreth Owen, "*Polly* and the Choice of Virtue," *Bulletin of the New York Public Library* 77 (1974): 393. Gay's play helps to prove that warrior women were a major "imaginative preoccupation of the early modern era," as suggested by Dugaw in *Warrior Women*, 1; see also her interesting interpretation of *Polly* (191–211).

48. John Gay, *Polly: An Opera, being the Second Part of the Beggar's Opera*, in *John Gay: Dramatic Works*, ed. John Fuller (Oxford: Clarendon Press, 1983), 2:95. The name Morano may refer to the Spanish word *moreno*, meaning brown, or it may refer to *marrano*, the term used to describe Jews who converted to Catholicism rather than leave Spain in 1492. The latter meaning would further play on the theme of disguise.

49. Gay, *Polly*, 2:99, 140.

50. Ibid., 129.

51. On Aeolus, see Rudolf Wittkower, *Allegory and the Migration of Symbols* (New York: Thames and Hudson, 1977), 94, and Michael Grant and John Hazel, *Gods and Mortals in Classical Mythology* (Springfield, Mass.: G. & C. Merriam, 1973), 27–28. It is also possible that the malevolent god Typhon is the source of the winds, which would have made them "the allies of disorder, the powers of chaos." See Yves Bonnefoy, comp., *Mythologies* (Chicago: University of Chicago Press, 1991), 1:510.

52. Maurice Agulhon has noted how allegorical depictions of anarchy included a dagger and a torch, which signified crimes of destruction. See his *Marianne into Battle: Republican Imagery and Symbolism in France, 1789–1880* (Cambridge: Cambridge University Press, 1981), 13. In fashioning this particular image, the unknown artist may have drawn on Pieter Brueghel's eerily powerful painting *Dulle Griet*, which features the wild, disorderly, sword-toting virago named Mad Margot striding fearlessly across the mouth of the gates of hell, impervious to the devils, demons, and creatures all around her. See

Leo van Puyvelde, *Pieter Bruegel's "Dulle Griet"* (London: Percy Lund Humphries, n.d.).

53. The art-historical literature on Delacroix's *Liberty* is enormous. Some of the most important works include Lee Johnson, ed., *The Paintings of Eugene Delacroix: A Critical Catalogue* (Oxford: Clarendon Press, 1981), vol. 1, *1816–1831*, 144–51; George Heard Hamilton, "The Iconographical Origins of Delacroix's 'Liberty Leading the People,'" in *Studies in Art and Literature for Belle Da Costa Greene,* ed. Dorothy Miner (Princeton, N.J.: Princeton University Press, 1954), 55–66; Hélène Adhémar, "La Liberté sur les barricades de Delacroix: Étudiée d'après des documents inédits," *Gazette des Beaux-Arts* 43 (1954): 83–92; N. Hadjinicolaou, "'La Liberté guidant le peuple' de Delacroix devant son premier plan," *Actes de la Recherche en Social Sciences* (June 1979): 3–26; Hélène Toussaint, *La Liberté guidant le peuple de Delacroix* (Paris: Éditions de la Réunion des musées nationaux, 1982); T.J. Clark, *The Absolute Bourgeois: Artists and Politics in France, 1848–1851* (Princeton, N.J.: Princeton University Press, 1973), 17–20, 22, 25–26, 29; Marcia Pointon, "*Liberty on the Barricades*: Women, Politics, and Sexuality in Delacroix," in her *Naked Authority: The Body in Western Painting, 1830–1908* (Cambridge: Cambridge University Press, 1990), 59–82.

54. Marina Warner, *Maidens and Monuments: The Allegory of the Female Form* (London: Weidenfield and Nicolson, 1985), 272.

55. The four winds under the charge of Aeolus were usually depicted as children or beardless men, which might help to explain Delacroix's choice of the youth. See J. S. Cooper, *An Illustrated Encyclopaedia of Traditional Symbols* (New York: Thames and Hudson, 1978), 192.

56. It is curious that art historians have not explored the maritime meanings of the symbolism in the painting, especially in light of Delacroix's proximity to the sea in his youth, where he would have seen bare-breasted women as figureheads on a variety of ships. The artist would also have known that many sailors considered these figures to have protective supernatural powers, in particular the capacity to silence the tempests they faced at sea. See Margaret Baker, *The Folklore of the Sea* (London: David and Charles, 1979), chap. 1; Horace Beck, *Folklore and the Sea* (Middletown, Conn.: Wesleyan University Press, 1973), 15–16.

57. Lynda Nead, *The Female Nude: Art, Obscenity, and Sexuality* (London: Routledge, 1992), 2 (quotation), 9, 47. The distinction between the

naked and the nude was pressed by Kenneth Clark, *The Nude: A Study in Ideal Form* (Princeton, N.J.: Princeton University Press, 1953), 3–29. When, a generation later, the new definition of femininity had taken hold, Eduard Manet would scandalize the art establishment afresh by painting women who were naked rather than nude. See T. J. Clark, "Preliminaries to a Possible Treatment of 'Olympia' in 1865," *Screen* 21 (1980): 18–41.

58. See Warner, *Maidens and Monuments*, chaps. 6, 8, and 12.

59. There is also the story of the "Maid of Saragossa," well known for her courage during the defense of her Spanish home against the French in 1808. For discussion of these sources, see Pointon, *"Liberty on the Barricades,"* 64; Hamilton, "Iconographical Origins," 63–64; Johnson, *Paintings of Delacroix*, 147. The influences discussed here do not displace or diminish the widely acknowledged importance of artists such as Géricault, Gros, and Guérin to Delacroix's painting.

60. The female image of piracy may be seen as the forerunner of a specifically radical image of liberty that emerged during the French Revolution. Lynn Hunt has pointed out that this image—armed, "bare-breasted and fierce of visage," woman as an active agent of change—existed in tension with a conservative image of a woman "seated, stolid, tranquil, and often without lance of liberty cap," woman as a passive reflection of stability. See Lynn Hunt, *Politics, Culture, and Class in the French Revolution* (Berkeley: University of California Press, 1984), 93. On the genesis of liberty as a symbol in France, see Agulhon, *Marianne into Battle*, chap. 1. The radical image would in turn make its way into the socialist tradition. Eric Hobsbawm, "Man and Woman in Socialist Iconography," *History Workshop Journal* 69 (1978): 121–38. See also Maurice Agulhon, "On Political Allegory: A Reply to Eric Hobsbawm," *History Workshop Journal* 8 (1979): 167–73.

61. Gosse, *A Bibliography of the Works of Captain Charles Johnson*.

62. See three articles by George Heard Hamilton: "Eugene Delacroix and Lord Byron," *Gazette des Beaux-Arts* 23 (1943): 99–110; *"Hamlet* or *Childe Harold?* Delacroix and Byron," *Gazette des Beaux-Arts* 26 (1944): 365–86; and "Iconographical Origins," 63, where Hamilton notes that Byron was much on Delacroix's mind during the winter of 1830–31. "The Corsair" can be found in *The Works of Lord Byron*, ed. Ernest Hartley Coleridge (New York: Octagon Books, 1966), 3:227–96.

CHAPTER SEVEN
"TO EXTIRPATE THEM OUT OF THE WORLD"

1. Cotton Mather, *Instructions to the Living, From the Condition of the Dead: A Brief Relation of Remarkables in the Shipwreck of above One Hundred Pirates* (Boston, 1717), 17.

2. *The Tryals of Major Stede Bonnet and Other Pirates* (London, 1719), 2, 8; *Boston News-Letter*, August 15, 1720, July 22 and November 4, 1717; *Boston Gazette*, August 15, April 18, and October 10, 1720, September 6, 1725; *American Weekly* Mercury, September 1, 1720; *Trials of Eight Persons Indited for Piracy* (Boston, 1718), 8; Captain Charles Johnson, *A General History of the Pyrates*, ed. Manuel Schonhorn (1724, 1728: reprint, Columbia, S.C.: University of South Carolina Press, 1972), 228 (hereafter cited as *History of Pyrates*); *New-England Courant*, August 21, 1721.

3. *Boston News-Letter*, April 16, 1722, December 2 and 16, 1717, January 16–24, 1724; *The Trials of Five Persons for Piracy, Felony, and Robbery* (Boston, 1726), 7; *Tryals of Bonnet*, 3, 4; *Trials of Eight Persons*, 6, 7; *American Weekly Mercury*, April 7, 1720; *Boston Gazette*, September 23, 1723; *Tryals of Thirty-Six Persons for Piracy* (Boston, 1723), 3; *History of Pyrates*, 26, 38.

4. *Tryals of Thirty-Six*, 3; *Trials of Eight Persons*, 6; Cotton Mather, *Useful Remarks: An Essay upon Remarkables in the Way of Wicked Men: A Sermon on the Tragical End, unto which the Way of Twenty-Six Pirates Brought Them; At New Port on Rhode-Island, July 19, 1723* (New London, Conn., 1723), 40, 27, 39; *Tryals of Bonnet*, 3, 8, 11; Mather, *Instructions to the Living*, 38; *Boston News-Letter*, July 25–August 1, 1723, April 2–9, 1724; Cotton Mather, *The Vial Poured Out upon the Sea: A Remarkable Relation of Certain Pirates ...* (Boston, 1726), 46; *History of Pyrates*, 287.

5. *Trials of Eight Persons*, 7, 6, 2; *Tryals of Bonnet*, 10, 7, 8; *Boston News-Letter*, March 29, 1714, February 9, 1719, August 15, 1723, September 24, 1724; *Boston Gazette*, October 10. 1720; Benjamin Colman, *It Is a Fearful Thing to Fall into the Hands of the Living God ...* (Boston, 1726), 36; *American Weekly Mercury*, April 7, 1720, August 17, 1721; *Trials of Five Persons*, 11, 16; Mather, *Instructions to the Living*, 5; *History of Pyrates*, 79, 264; *American Weekly Mercury*, June 13, 1723; H. R. McIlwaine, ed., *Executive Journals of the Council of Colonial Virginia* (Richmond, 1928), 3:612.

6. *Trials of Eight*, 6, 2, 7; *Tryals of Thirty-Six*, 3; Arthur L. Hayward, ed., *Lives of the Most Remarkable Criminals* (London, 1735; reprint, New York: Dodd, Mead, 1927), 3:474, 580; Mather, *Vial Poured Out*, 8; *American Weekly Mercury*, April 7, 1720, February 20, 1722; *Boston Gazette*, April 18, 1720, August 19 and September 23, 1723; *Tryals of Bonnet*, 3–10; *Boston News-Letter*, April 13–20, 1719, August 15–22, 1723; *History of Pyrates*, 264; Colman, *It Is a Fearful Thing*, 25; *Tryals of Thirty-Six*, 3; *Trials of Eight*, 2, 6, 7; *American Weekly Mercury*, September 19, 1723; Mather, *Instructions to the Living*, 17 ; *Boston News-Letter*, September 12–19, 1723; *History of Pyrates*, 46, 79, 331.

7. *Tryals of Bonnet*, 8.

8. John Barnard, *Ashton's Memorial: An History of the Strange Adventures, and Signal Deliverances of Mr. Philip Ashton* (Boston, 1725), 62; *Boston News-Letter*, July 15, 1717, April 4, 1723, June 20, 1723; *American Weekly Mercury*, June 20 and September 26, 1723, January 11, 1726, November 29, 1725; *Tryals of Thirty-Six*, 3; Cotton Mather, *Tryals of Sixteen Persons for Piracy, &c.* (Boston, 1726), 14; *Tryals of Bonnet*, iii, 5.

9. Mather, *Useful Remarks*, 10; Barnard, *Ashton's Memorial*, 2, 62, 35, 63, 13; *History of Pyrates*, 210, 216, 219, 224; Mather, *Vial Poured Out*, 34, 20; Mather, *Instructions to the Living*, 60, 38, 49; Hayward, ed., *Remarkable Criminals*, 129, 576; *Boston News-Letter*, August 15, 1722.

10. Barnard, *Ashton's Memorial*, 38, 62, 3, 6, 35, 64; Hayward, ed., *Remarkable Criminals*, 35, 125, 586; *History of Pyrates*, 85, 149, 164, 217; *Boston News-Letter*, August 15, 1722; Colman, *It Is a Fearful Thing*, 35; *American Weekly Mercury*, November 29, 1725; Mather, *Vial Poured Out*, 47.

11. *Trials of Eight*, 6; Barnard, *Ashton's Memorial*, 62, 5, 64; *Tryals of Bonnet*, 3; Mather, *Vial Poured Out*, 8, 45.

12. Mather, *Useful Remarks*, 13, 8, 33; *History of Pyrates*, 129, 135, 209, 312; Barnard, *Ashton's Memorial*, 62; Colman, *It Is a Fearful Thing*, 17; *Boston News-Letter*, December 19, 1720; Hayward, ed., *Remarkable Criminals*, 128; Mather, *Vial Poured Out*, 26; Flavel, *Pathetical and Serious Disswasive ...* (Boston, 1725), 134; Colman, *It Is a Fearful Thing*, 17; Cotton Mather, *The Lord-High-Admiral of all the Seas, Adored* (Boston, 1723), 20.

13. Colman, *It Is a Fearful Thing*, 15; Barnard, *Ashton's Memorial*, 4, ii, 7, 62; *Tryals of Sixteen*, 14; *Trials of Eight*, 8; *American Weekly Mercury*, June 13 and September 26, 1723, January 11, 1726; Hayward, ed., *Remarkable Criminals*, 128; *Boston News-Letter*, August 12, 1717, September 24, 1724, December 23, 1718, July 18, 1723; *Tryals of Thirty-Six*,

3; Mather, *Instructions to the Living*, 19; *Boston Gazette*, March 21, 1726.

14. Mather, *Vial Poured Out*, 9; *Trials of Five Persons*, 5; *Tryals of Sixteen*, 9; Mather, *Lord-High-Admiral*, 20; Barnard, *Ashton's Memorial*, 62, 7; *History of Pyrates*, 312, 332, 24, 6; Colman, *It Is a Fearful Thing*, 36; *Boston News-Letter*, August 15, 1722; Mather, *Useful Remarks*, 42. It is likely that some of these confessions were written by ministers or governmental officials.

15. Mather, *Useful Remarks*, 13; Mather, *Instructions to the Living*, 37; Barnard, *Ashton's Memorial*, 7, 15; Colman, *It Is a Fearful Thing*, 5, 22, 38; Mather, *Useful Remarks*, 15, 26, 37, 39, 41, 42; *Tryals of Sixteen*, 14; Bernard Mandeville, *An Enquiry into the Causes of the Frequent Executions at Tyburn* (1725; reprint, Los Angeles: William Andrews Clark Memorial Library, 1964), 22, 34; Mather, *Instructions to the Living*, 37, 49; *Boston News-Letter*, August 15, 1722, July 25, 1723, May 28, 1724; John Flavel, *Navigation Spiritualized; or, a New Compass for Sea-Men* (Boston, 1726), i, and *Pathetical and Serious Disswasive*, 55, 154; Mather, *Vial Poured Out*, 5, 43, 47, 48; *History of Pyrates*, 246, 312.

16. Mather, *Useful Remarks*, 25, 13, 37; Hayward, ed., *Remarkable Criminals*, 125; Colman, *It Is a Fearful Thing*, 17, 22; Mather, *Instructions to the Living*, 23, 50; *Boston News-Letter*, July 25, 1723; Barnard, *Ashton's Memorial*, 15; Flavel, *Navigation Spiritualized*, i; Flavel, *Pathetical and Serious Disswasives*, 172; Mather, *Vial Poured Out*, 49; See also Arthur N. Gilbert, "Buggery and the British Royal Navy, 1700–1861," *Journal of Social History* 10 (1976): 72–98, and particularly his discussion of homosexuality and order (87–88).

17. Mather, *Useful Remarks*, 13, 15, 23, 24, 31, 36, 37, 40–42; *Tryals of Bonnet*, 11; Colman, *It Is a Fearful Thing*, 36; Mather, *Instructions to the Living*, 16, 38; Barnard, *Ashton's Memorial*, 2, 3, 6, 22, 64; *Boston News-Letter*, July 25, 1723, May 28, 1724; *History of Pyrates*, 264, 350–51, 659–60. *History of Pyrates*, 350–51, 659–60; Mather, *Vial Poured Out*, 48.

18. On maritime labor conditions, see chapters 2 and 3 and A. G. Course, *The Merchant Navy: A Social History* (London: F. Muller, 1963); Ralph Davis, *The Rise of the English Shipping Industry in the Seventeenth and Eighteenth Centuries* (London: Macmillan, 1962); C. D. Merriman, ed., *Queen Anne's Navy Documents Concerning the Administration of the Navy of Queen Anne, 1702–1714* (London: Navy Records Society, 1961); Capt. Alfred Dewar, ed., *The Voyages and Travels of Captain Nathaniel Uring* (1726; reprint, London: Cassell, 1928). Mather, *Vial*

Poured Out, 15; Mather, *Useful Remarks*, 3; *The Mariner's Divine Mate, or, Spiritual Navigation Improved* (Boston, 1715), 34; Mather, *Instructions to the Living*, 42.

19. *Boston News-Letter*, May 27, 1717; Mather, *Lord-High-Admiral*, 9; Flavel, *Navigation Spiritualized*, 11, 14, 1, 63; *Mariner's Divine Mate*, 2, 11; *Trials of Eight Persons*, 6; Mather, *Instructions to the Living*, 4; Mather, *Vial Poured Out*, 33.

20. *Trials of Eight Persons*, 6, 7; "Tryals of the Pirates" (1722), in *History of Pyrates*, 263; Mather, *Lord-High-Admiral*, 4.

21. Mandeville, *An Enquiry into the Causes*, 48.

22. *Tryals of Bonnet*, 11; Colman, *It Is a Fearful Thing*, 9; *Mariner's Divine Mate*, i, 1; Mather, *Lord-High-Admiral*, 6, 22; Barnard, *Ashton's Memorial*, i; Mather, *Useful Remarks*, 4; *Trials of Eight Persons*, 6; *Trials of Thirty-Six*, 3.

23. *American Weekly Mercury*, December 13, 1720; *Tryals of Sixteen*, 14. The rhetorical tactics of exclusion used against pirates (animality, disorder, and so on) are similar to those the English used against Africans, African Americans, and Native Americans in the seventeenth and eighteenth centuries.

24. Deposition of Henry Bostock, 1717, Colonial Office Papers (CO) 152/12, Public Record Office, London; William Snelgrave, *A New Account of Some Parts of Guinea and the Slave Trade* (London, 1734; reprint, London: Frank Cass, 1971), 253; *History of Pyrates*, 217; Alexander Spotswood to Board of Trade, May 31, 1717, CO 5/1318; John Franklin Jameson, ed., *Privateering and Piracy in the Colonial Period: Illustrative Documents* (New York: Macmillan, 1923), 315.

25. Governor Hamilton to Council of Trade, October 3, 1720, *Calendar of State Papers, Colonial Series, America and West Indies, 1574–1739*, CD-ROM, consultant editors Karen Ordahl Kupperman, John C. Appleby, and Mandy Banton (London: Routledge, published in association with the Public Record Office, 2000), item 251, vol. 32 (1720–21), 165 (hereafter cited as *CSPC*). My emphasis on the slave trade is not meant to deny the many other reasons—recently (and insightfully) explicated by Peter Earle—the naval campaign against pirates improved after 1718. See Peter Earle, *The Pirate Wars* (London: Methuen, 2003), 184–88.

26. *Parker v. Boucher* (1719), High Court of Admiralty Papers (HCA) 24/132, Public Record Office, London; *Wise v. Beekman* (1716), HCA 24/131; Willis, quoted in *Pirate Wars*, by Earle, 169. For other instances of conflicts that ended up in court, see *Coleman v. Seamen*

(1718) and *Desbrough v. Christian* (1720), HCA 24/132; *Povey v. Bigelow* (1722), HCA 24/134; and *Wistridge v. Chapman* (1722), HCA 24/135.

27. *History of Pyrates*, 309, 70, 115–16; Information of Alexander Thompson (1723), HCA 1/55, f. 23; see also Petition of John Massey and George Lowther (1721), CO 28/17, f. 199.

28. "Proceedings of the Court held on the Coast of Africa upon Trying of 100 Pirates taken by his Ma[jes]ties Ship Swallow" (1722), HCA 1/99, ff. 4–6; see also John Atkins, *A Voyage to Guinea, Brasil, and the West-Indies* (London, 1735), 91, 186–87; Stanley Richards, *Black Bart* (Llandybie, Wales: Christopher Davies, 1966), 73.

29. Philip D. Curtin, *The Atlantic Slave Trade: A Census* (Madison: University of Wisconsin Press, 1969), 150; *American Weekly Mercury*, March 30, 1721; *History of Pyrates*, 172–73, 195; Proceedings of the Court at Jamaica, January 19, 1720, CO 137/14, ff. 28–30; Petition of John Massey and George Lowther, July 22, 1721, CO 28/17, ff. 197–99.

30. "The Memoriall of the Merchants of London Trading to Africa" (1720), Admiralty Papers (ADM) 1/3810, Public Record Office, London.

31. *Boston Gazette*, June 13, 1720; "Anonymous Paper relating to the Sugar and Tobacco Trade" (1724), CO 388/24, ff. 186–87; Richards, *Black Bart*, 72.

32. "Humphry Morice," in *Dictionary of National Biography*, ed. Sir Leslie Stephen and Sir Sidney Lee (London: Oxford University Press, 1959–60), 13:941; David Eltis, Stephen D. Behrendt, David Richardson, and Herbert S. Klein, *The Transatlantic Slave-Trade: A Data Base on CD-ROM* (Cambridge: Cambridge University Press, 2000); Humphrey Morice to Captain Stephen Bull, December 4, 1718; [an unknown naval officer aboard the *Scarborough*] to Humphrey Morice, September 20, 1724; the Humphrey Morice Papers from the Bank of England, *Slave Trade Journals and Papers* (Marlboro, Wiltshire, England: Adam Mathew Publications, 1998), microfilm.

33. William Snelgrave to Humphrey Morice, April 30, 1719; John Daggs to Humphrey Morice, February 6, 1720; "Account of Jabez Biglow" (1719); all in Morice Papers.

34. "To the Kings most Excellt Majesty the Humble Petition of the Planters Merchts & Traders concernd in the West Indies" (no date, but probably late 1718); "The Memoriall of the Merchants of London Trading to Africa humbly Offered to the Rt. Hon.ble The Lords Commissioners for Executing the Office of Lord High Admirall of

Great Brittaine &c." (no date, but probably February 1720, after the end of the War of the Quadruple Alliance). Morice wrote to Snelgrave on November 24, 1719: "the men of Warr are ready to proceed from here with the first fair wind, as Sir John Jennings told me this day at the House of Commons" (Morice Papers).

35. Richards, *Black Bart*, 63; Leo Francis Stock, ed., *Proceedings and Debates of the British Parliaments Respecting North America* (Washington, D.C.: Carnegie Institution, 1930), 3:453.

36. Atkins, *Voyage*, 98; James A. Rawley, *The Transatlantic Slave Trade: A History* (New York: W. W. Norton, 1981), 155; *Boston Gazette*, August 27, 1722; *New-England Courant*, September 3, 1722; "Proceedings," HCA 1/99, f. 98; Richards, *Black Bart*, 107.

37. Rawley, *Transatlantic Slave Trade*, 162.

38. Ibid., 164, 165; Curtin, *Atlantic Slave Trade*, 150; Eltis et al., *Transatlantic Slave-Trade* (for embarked slaves). Both Douglas C. North and Gary B. Walton emphasize the destruction of piracy as a major cause of the advance in productivity in eighteenth-century shipping. See North, "Sources of Productivity Change in Ocean Shipping, 1600–1850," *Journal of Political Economy* 76 (1968): 953–70, and Walton, "Sources of Productivity Change in Colonial American Shipping," *Economic History Review* 67 (1968): 67–78.

39. *Boston News-Letter*, May 28, 1724, June 7, 1714, July 29, 1717, July 28, 1718, August 18, 1718, April 4, 1723; Mandeville, *An Enquiry into the Causes*, 37; On executions, see Colman, *It Is a Fearful Thing*, 37; Mather, *Useful Remarks*, 42; *Trials of Eight*, 14; *American Weekly Mercury*, March 17, 1720, January 31, March 30, April 27, 1721, June 11, 1724; *Trials of Five Persons*, 34; *Boston Gazette*, June 13, 1720, March 21, 1726; Hayward, ed., *Remarkable Criminals*, 598.

40. Colman, *It Is a Fearful Thing*, 19; Mandeville, *An Enquiry into the Causes*, 18; Mather, *Useful Remarks*, 33; Mather, *Vial Poured Out*, 49; *New-England Courant*, July 22, 1723.

41. *American Weekly Mercury*, March 17, 1720; Hayward, ed., *Remarkable Criminals*, 37, 600, 603; *History of Pyrates*, 144, 185, 264, 186, 660, 286; Mather, *Vial Poured Out*, 47, 16, 20, 44; Colman, *It Is a Fearful Thing*, 37; Mandeville, *An Enquiry into the Causes*, 19, 32; *Boston News-Letter*, July 7, 1726; *Tryals of Bonnet*, 9; Abel Boyer, ed., *The Political State of Great Britain* (London, 1711–40), 32:272; Mather, *Vial Poured Out*, 47; Lorrain, quoted in "In Contrast to History of Pyrates: The Rev. Paul Lorrain, Historian of Crime," by Lincoln B. Faller, *Huntington Library Quarterly* 60 (1976): 69.

42. *Boston News-Letter*, July 7, 1726, May 8, 1721, May 28, 1724; *Tryals of*
Bonnet, 34; Mather, *Vial Poured Out*, 43, 49–50; Mather, *Useful*
Remarks, 20; Colman, *It Is a Fearful Thing*, 39; *American Weekly Mer-*
cury, March 17, 1720; *Boston Gazette*, August 27, 1722, June 1, 1724;
Hayward, ed., *Remarkable Criminals*, 603; *Boston News-Letter*, March
14, 1720, February 20, 1721; *History of Pyrates*, 264; *Trials of Eight*, 14;
Tryals of Thirty-Six, 14; *New-England Courant*, September 2–10, 1722.
Pirates who were executed in a single place were often placed in
chains and strategically spread in several harbors. The best example
of this practice is related in the *Boston Gazette* of August 27, 1722:
chained corpses were placed in five spots.

43. *Trials of Eight*, 6, emphasis added; *Tryals of Thirty-Six*, 3. Mather,
Instructions to the Living, 11, 23; Barnard, *Ashton's Memorial*, 62;
Mather, *Useful Remarks*, 20.

44. Edward Vernon to Nicholas Lawes, October 31, 1720; Edward Vernon
to Josiah Burchett, March 7, 1721; Edward Vernon to Josiah Burchett,
April 18, 1721; all in Edward Vernon's Letter-Book, Add. MS 40813,
British Library, London.

CHAPTER EIGHT
"DEFIANCE OF DEATH ITSELF"

1. *Boston News-Letter*, August 22, 1720.

2. Abel Boyer, ed., *The Political State of Great Britain* (London, 1711–40),
33:149–53.

3. Governor Walter Hamilton to the Council of Trade and Plantations,
October 3, 1720, *Calendar of State Papers, Colonial Series, America and*
West Indies, 1574–1739, CD-ROM, consultant editors Karen Ordahl
Kupperman, John C. Appleby, and Mandy Banton (London: Rout-
ledge, published in association with the Public Record Office, 2000),
item 251, vol. 32 (1720–21), 165 (hereafter cited as *CSPC*); John Barnard, *Ashton's Memorial: An History of the Strange Adventures, and*
Signal Deliverances of Mr. Philip Ashton (Boston, 1725), 239; Arthur L.
Hayward, ed., *Lives of the Most Remarkable Criminals* (London, 1735;
reprint, New York: Dodd, Mead, 1927), 596; *Tryals of Thirty-Six*
Persons for Piracy (Boston, 1723), 9; Captain Charles Johnson, *A Gen-*
eral History of the Pyrates, ed. Manuel Schonhorn (London, 1724, 1728;
reprint, Columbia, S.C.: University of South Carolina Press, 1972),
244 (hereafter cited as *History of Pyrates*).

4. *History of Pyrates*, 241.

5. Alexander Spotswood to Board of Trade, December 22, 1718,

Colonial Office Papers (CO) 5/1318, Public Record Office, London; "Proceedings of the Court held on the Coast of Africa," High Court of Admiralty Papers (HCA) 1/99, f. 158, Public Record Office, London; Stanley Richards, *Black Bart* (Llandybie, Wales: Christopher Davies, 1966), 90; *History of Pyrates*, 83, 245; Solgard, quoted in *The Pirates of the New England Coast, 1630–1730*, by George Francis Dow and John Henry Edmonds (Salem, Mass.: Marine Research Society, 1923), 293; John F. Watson, *Annals of Philadelphia and Pennsylvania* (Philadelphia, 1844),2:227.

6. William Snelgrave, *A New Account of Some Parts of Guinea and the Slave Trade* (London, 1734; reprint, London: Frank Cass, 1971), 210, 270; *Trials of Eight Persons Indited for Piracy* (Boston, 1718), 10; *Tryals of Thirty-Six Persons*, 5.

7. Barnard, *Ashton's Memorial*, 62; Council Journal, May 27, 1719, in *The Colonial Records of North Carolina*, ed. William L. Saunders (Raleigh, N.C.: P.M. Hale, 1886), 2:342; Benjamin Colman, *It Is a Fearful Thing to Fall into the Hands of the Living God* (Boston, 1726), 36; *History of Pyrates*, 312; Snelgrave, *New Account*, 227; [John Fillmore], "A Narrative of the Singular Sufferings of John Fillmore and Others on Board the Noted Pirate Vessel Commanded by Captain Phillips," Buffalo Historical Society, *Publications* 10 (1907): 33.

8. *History of Pyrates*, 246.

9. *The Tryals of Major Stede Bonnet and Other Pirates* (London, 1719), 15; Captain Mathew Musson to the Council of Trade and Plantations, July 5, 1717, *CSPC*, item 635, vol. 29 (1716–17), 338; Proceedings of the Court in Jamaica, January 19, 1720, CO 137/14, f. 28; *History of Pyrates*, 307; Information of Joseph Hollet (1721), HCA 1/55, f. 40.

10. *History of Pyrates*, 292.

11. A thrum cap was made of rough woolen or hempen strands like those used in making a mop. A crow was a grappling hook. A handspike was a wooden pin used to move the windlass or capstan.

12. Governor John Hope to Council of Trade and Plantations, January 14, 1724, CO 37/11, f. 37; Governor John Hart to the Council of Trade and Plantations, March 25, 1724, *CSPC*, item 102, vol. 34 (1724–25), 72.

13. *Tryals of Bonnet*, 15.

14. *History of Pyrates*, 231, 269–71.

15. Quoted in *The Pirate Wars*, by Peter Earle (London: Methuen, 2003), 170.

16. *History of Pyrates*, 308.

17. See, for example, Charles Grey, *Pirates of the Eastern Seas, 1618–1723:*

A Lurid Page of History, ed. George MacMunn (1933; reprint, Port Washington, N.Y.: Kennikat Press, 1971), 16; Patrick Pringle's *Jolly Roger* (New York: Norton, 1953), 104; Richards, *Black Bart* , 17; and Hugh F. Rankin, *The Golden Age of Piracy* (New York: Holt, Rinehart and Winston, 1969), 22-23.

18. J. M. Beattie, *Crime and the Courts in England, 1660–1800* (Princeton, N.J.: Princeton University Press, 1986); A. Roger Ekirch, *Bound for America: The Transportation of British Convicts to the Colonies, 1718–1775* (New York: Oxford University Press, 1987).

19. Governor Hamilton to the Council of Trade and Plantations, October 3, 1720; Cotton Mather, *Useful Remarks: An Essay upon Remarkables in the Way of Wicked Men: A Sermon on the Tragical End, unto which the Way of Twenty-Six Pirates Brought Them; At New Port on Rhode-Island, July 19, 1723* (New London, Conn., 1723), 42; *History of Pyrates*, 35. In accumulating piecemeal evidence about pirates and their fates, I have found that another six hundred, at a minimum, died or were killed.

20. *New-England Courant*, July 22, 1723; *History of Pyrates*, 302.

21. Boyer, ed., *Political State*, 28:152. Pirates also occasionally used red or "bloody" flags.

22. For an overview of English antecedents and New England gravestone art, see Allen I. Ludwig, *Graven Images: New England Stonecarving and Its Symbols, 1650–1815* (Middletown, Conn.: Wesleyan University Press, 1966).

23. Captain Francis Grose, *A Classical Dictionary of the Vulgar Tongue*, ed. Eric Partridge (1785; reprint, New York: Dorset Press, 1992); for "roger" and "to roger," see 289.

24. S. Charles Hill, "Episodes of Piracy in Eastern Waters," *Indian Antiquary* 49 (1920): 37.

25. Snelgrave, *New Account*, 236.

26. *History of Pyrates*, 628, 244. See Robert C. Ritchie, *Captain Kidd and the War against the Pirates* (Cambridge, Mass.: Harvard University Press, 1986), 232–37. When I presented this chapter to the Comparative History Seminar at Cornell University in January 2003, Ray Craib responded to this paragraph by asking whether pirate culture had a touch of Sid Vicious in it. Jeff Cowie wondered whether a better analogy might be Niggaz with Attitude (NWA). Both were right.

27. *History of Pyrates*, 43.

28. Ibid., 245, 240.

1. Hugh Rankin notes that "as more pirates were captured and hanged, the greater cruelty was practiced by those who were still alive." See his *Golden Age of Piracy* (New York: Holt, Rinehart and Winston, 1969), 146.

2. Governor John Hart to the Council of Trade and Plantations, March 25, 1724, *Calendar of State Papers, Colonial Series, America and West Indies, 1574–1739*, CD-ROM, consultant editors Karen Ordahl Kupperman, John C. Appleby, and Mandy Banton (London: Routledge, published in association with the Public Record Office, 2000), item 102, vol. 34 (1724–25), 72. See also Captain Charles Johnson, *A General History of the Pyrates*, ed. Manuel Schonhorn (1724, 1728; reprint, Columbia, S.C.: University of South Carolina Press, 1972), 323–27 (hereafter cited as *History of Pyrates*); Abel Boyer, ed., *The Political State of Great Britain* (London, 1711–40), 27:616, where one of Hart's charges is repeated: Low was "also notorious for his Cruelties even to the British Subjects that fall into his Hands."

3. *Boston News-Letter*, October 1, 1724; George Francis Dow and John Henry Edmonds, *The Pirates of the New England Coast, 1630–1730* (Salem, Mass.: Marine Research Society, 1923), 217; Peter Earle, *The Pirate Wars* (London: Methuen, 2003), 268; Trial of John Fillmore and Edward Cheesman (1724), in *Privateering and Piracy in the Colonial Period: Illustrative Documents*, ed. John Franklin Jameson (New York: Macmillan, 1923), 329. Charles Vane, another violent captain, was also resisted by his own crew and eventually overthrown. Vane once ordered a man hanged until nearly dead, cut down, and beaten, whereupon one of his own crew members intervened and "contradicted it, being (as he said) too great a Cruelty." See Deposition of Nathaniel Catling (1718), Colonial Office Papers (CO) 37/10, f. 41, Public Record Office, London.

4. *History of Pyrates* 588; Cotton Mather, *Instructions to the Living, From the Condition of the Dead: A Brief Relation of Remarkables in the Shipwreck of above One Hundred Pirates* (Boston, 1717), 44.

5. Arthur L. Hayward, ed., *Lives of the Most Remarkable Criminals* (London, 1735; reprint, New York: Dodd, Mead, 1927), 35; *History of Pyrates*, 243; "Proceedings of the Court held on the Coast of Africa," High Court of Admiralty (HCA) 1/99, f. 105; Governor Walter Hamilton to the Council of Trade and Plantations, May 19, 1721, CO

152/14, f. 25; *Boston News-Letter*, March 2 and May 7, 1719; Stanley Richards, *Black Bart* (Llandybie, Wales: Christopher Davies, 1966), 13.

6. Philip de Souza, *Piracy in the Graeco-Roman World* (Cambridge: Cambridge University Press, 1999), 21, 113, 137, 193, 212, 216, 241–42; Henry A. Ormerod, *Piracy in the Ancient World* (Liverpool: University of Liverpool Press, 1924; reprint, Baltimore: Johns Hopkins University Press, 1997), 13–15.

7. Augustine, *De Civitate Dei* (City of God), trans. Marcus Dods (New York: Modern Library, 1993), bk. 4, chap. 4. On prize money, see two letters from Captain George Gordon to Josiah Burchett, September 8 and 14, 1721, Admiralty Papers (ADM) 1/1826, Public Record Office, London; Richards, *Black Bart*, 108. Ironically, after Walpole read about the bilking of the seamen in Johnson's *History of Pyrates*, he intervened personally to pay them. See the *American Weekly Mercury*, July 1, 1725.

8. *American Weekly Mercury*, March 17, 1720; Richards, *Black Bart*, 96. Peter Earle wrote of pirate plunder: "what they chiefly sought aboard a prize were those things which would enable them to maintain their ships and sustain themselves and their way of life, the life itself being as or more important than the dream of returning home rich." See his *Pirate Wars*, 177. On the golden age of Kronos, see Frank E. Manuel and Fritzie P. Manuel, *Utopian Thought in the Western World* (Cambridge, Mass.: Belknap Press of Harvard University Press, 1979), chap. 2.

9. For an account of the ways in which the struggles of sailors and pirates were linked to radical movements around the Atlantic over a longer time, see Peter Linebaugh and Marcus Rediker, *The Many-Headed Hydra: Sailors, Slaves, Commoners, and the Hidden History of the Revolutionary Atlantic* (Boston: Beacon Press, 2000).

ACKNOWLEDGMENTS

I have been working on this book on and off since 1976, when I took up the subject of pirates in a graduate research seminar with Michael Zuckerman at the University of Pennsylvania. The research resulted in a published essay in 1981, and I have been a captive of pirates ever since. Rarely has a week gone by without a journalist, an underwater archaeologist, a novelist, a museum professional, a filmmaker, or a rabid enthusiast contacting me to talk about them. I have come to realize that the cultural appetite for pirates is immense, which in turn encouraged me to write this book, summarizing what I have learned about these outlaws over many years. My first thanks are to Mike for pointing me seaward, toward the dark flag on the horizon, and giving me a push.

Over the years, many people have helped me to think about my subject, most of all, recently, in Australia. I am grateful to Graeme Henderson and the dynamic staff at the Western Australia Maritime Museum in Fremantle; to Paul Hundley and Mary-Louise Williams and the Australian National Maritime Museum in Sydney; to Andrew Fitzmaurice and Shane White in the Department of History, University of Sydney; to Mark Staniforth, Departments of Archaeology and History, Flinders University, Adelaide; and to Cassandra Pybus and Hamish Maxwell-Stewart, Department of History, University of Tasmania. Other useful discussions took place at the Anglo-American Conference titled "The Sea," by the Institute for Historical Research, University of London; the International Congress of Maritime Museums, Willemstad, Curaçao; the "Calibrations" conference, Texas A&M University Center for Humanities Research; the conference titled "Seascapes, Littoral Cultures, and Trans Oceanic Exchanges," organized by the American Historical Association, in Washington, D.C.; the

ACKNOWLEDGMENTS

C. V. Starr Center for the Study of the American Experience, Washington College; the Comparative History Seminar, Cornell University; the Department of History, State University of New York at Buffalo; South Street Seaport Museum, New York; the Mellon Foundation Sawyer Seminar titled "Redress in Social Thought, Law, and Literature," University of California, Irvine; and the United States Merchant Marine Academy. Thanks to all who organized these events and to all who attended and asked their usually passionate questions.

I owe a special debt of gratitude to the students who studied the global history of piracy with me as we sailed around the world on the SS *Universe Explorer*, a floating university, during the spring of 2001. This energetic, motley crew showed up to class with eye patches, hooks, and peg legs, bellowed "aaargh" at every opportunity, collected pirate lore in every port, and hectored me to write this book. They have been a steadfast source of encouragement and a certain proof of the power of the pirate in popular culture, as have my equally enthusiastic and talented (though less rowdy) students at the University of Pittsburgh.

I am keenly conscious of my advantage in writing this book at a time when serious scholarship on pirates is being done more than ever before. I refer to the work of John C. Appleby, J. S. Bromley, B. R. Burg, David Cordingly, Dian Murray, C. R. Pennell, Anne Pérotin-Dumon, Jo Stanley, Janice E. Thomson, and Peter Lamborn Wilson. I thank them all for their valuable work. It has been my special good fortune to work with three of the best scholars of piracy: Joel Baer, Hans Turley, and Robert C. Ritchie. I also had the pleasure of many illuminating conversations about pirates (and other things) with the late Christopher and Bridget Hill, two exceptional historians (and people) who were major influences in my life. I also fondly recall animated discussions with Christopher's college roommate, Norman O. Brown, also recently deceased. I seek to remember him in chapter 8.

My former student Sara Lemmond and my graduate student

{ 223 }

Gabriele Gottlieb provided excellent assistance with research, for which I am most grateful. I owe a special debt of thanks to Frank Shaffer, who has encouraged my work in numerous ways, not least by building a fabulous Web site, which is much better than my ability as an author to draw people to it! It has been an honor—and a profound learning experience—to work with Peter Linebaugh, my coauthor of *The Many-Headed Hydra*, over the years. Finally, warm thanks to my family, Wendy, Zeke, and Eva, who have suffered endless pirate stories with good cheer. Wendy has helped me in more ways than I can count.

My first foray into these seas appeared as "'Under the Banner of King Death': The Social World of Anglo-American Pirates, 1716 to 1726," *William and Mary Quarterly*, ser. 3, 38 (1981): 203–27. I remain grateful after all these years to the superb editor Michael McGiffert, who taught a graduate student much about the art and craft of writing. A revised version of the article appeared in what should be considered a companion volume to the present one, *Between the Devil and the Deep Blue Sea: Merchant Seamen, Pirates, and the Anglo-American Maritime World, 1700–1750* (Cambridge: Cambridge University Press, 1987), on which it was my great good fortune to work with another excellent editor, Frank Smith. I returned to the subject of pirates years later, at the urging of Bob Brugger, Margaret Creighton, and Lisa Norling, when I wrote "Liberty Beneath the Jolly Roger: The Lives of Anne Bonny and Mary Read, Pirates," in *Iron Men, Wooden Women: Gender and Seafaring in the Atlantic World, 1700–1920*, ed. Margaret Creighton and Lisa Norling (Baltimore: Johns Hopkins University Press, 1996). A revised version of this essay appears here, with permission, as chapter 6. Another chapter was presented at a conference in the Netherlands and was published as "Hydrarchy and Libertalia: The Utopian Dimensions of Atlantic Piracy in the Early Eighteenth Century," in *Pirates and Privateers: New Perspectives on the War on Trade in the Eighteenth and Nineteenth Centuries*, ed. David J. Starkey, E. S. Van Eyck van Heslinga, and J. A. de Moor (Exeter, England:

Exeter University Press, 1997). This in turn formed the basis of chapter 5 of *The Many-Headed Hydra: Sailors, Slaves, Commoners, and the Hidden History of the Revolutionary Atlantic* (Boston: Beacon Press; London: Verso, 2000), cowritten with Peter Linebaugh. I am especially grateful to Deborah Chasman, who brought that ship to port and soon after launched this one. Gayatri Patnaik, my new editor at Beacon Press, has been a joy to work with. I have benefited immensely from her intelligence, enthusiasm, and steady good judgment. Thanks to Hyla Willis for drawing the diagram in chapter 4 and to Dalia Geffen for expert copyediting. The book is dedicated to two dear friends and comrades, Michael Jiménez and Steve Sapolsky, who died three weeks apart during an awful summer in 2001. These two were brilliant, compassionate historians, both masters of history from below. All of us are much the poorer for their departure, including the poor, still-forgotten peoples past whose histories they would have brought to life.

{ 225 }

INDEX

INDEX

oaths of honor, 76–77, 79
officers, 47; admirals, 29, 57, 59, 100,
146–47; ill-treatment by, 65; naval,
150, 161; pirate, 42, 155. *See also* captains; captains, merchant; captains,
pirate; mates; quartermasters
officials: colonial, 53, 99; and extermination of piracy, 37, 141; government, 93, 100, 101–2; at hangings,
2, 201–2n41
officials, royal, 54, 85, 86, 99; complaints of, 31–32, 34, 35
Ogle, Challoner, 142–43
O'Malley, Grace, 113
oppression, 17, 85–86, 116, 176
Orme, Humphrey, 69–70, 170

paintings, 123–26, 208n52, 209n56,
210n57, 210n59
pardons, 10, 163, 177n4, 205n23;
ineffectiveness of, 32, 137; offers of,
27, 136–37; requests for, 154, 155
Parry, J. H., 21
passengers, 111, 204n17
Pennsylvania, 29, 32, 99
Phillips, James, 33, 79, 150
Phillips, John, 45, 47, 49, 58, 153;
crew of, 74, 81, 111, 165
Phillips, William, 48, 91, 171
pillage, 71, 199n15. *See also* plunder
piracy: appeal of, 118; causes of, 19, 26,
56, 57–59, 180n30; by mutiny, 46–47,
138; preconditions for, 28–29; stages
of, 35–37
piracy, war against, 99, 127–47, 163,
170, 216n38; end of, 172–73; and
hangings, 127, 130, 132, 143, 144,
145, 146–47; interested parties
in, 128–29, 132, 134; and policies,
136–37; and rhetoric, 127, 130–36,
214n23; and slave trade, 138, 139,
140–41, 142, 143–44, 214n25; and
trials, 129–30, 135, 143

Piracy Destroy'd (pamphlet), 57
pirates, 16, 98, 141, 221n9; from Africa,
52–53, 55; attractions of, 60, 79;
black, 53–56, 120–21, 132, 151; from
Britain, 51–52, 53, 55, 94; conflicts
among, 63, 73, 90; damage done
by, 139–42; from Europe, 52–53, 54,
55, 94; families of, 49–50, 56, 133,
188n26, 205n23; female, 56, 121,
125–26, 203n10; forced, 48–49, 69,
79, 172, 188n24; geographic origins
of, 50–53; image of, 127, 135, 136;
and integration of newcomers,
78–79; numbers of, 29–30, 183n16;
plays by, 155–61; social class of,
50, 189n27; support for, 98–100;
unmarried, 49–50, 197n6; volunteer,
47–48, 67, 77, 78–79, 100. *See also*
Bonny, Anne; buccaneers; crews
and crew members, pirate; executions; hangings; ships, pirate; Read,
Mary; social order of pirates; social
relations of pirates; trials; *names of
individuals*
Plantain, James, 80, 189n31
plantations, 22, 32, 63, 142
Plato, 134–35
plays, 54–55, 120–21, 208n47; by pirates,
155–61
plunder, 14, 44, 79; distribution of, 65,
70, 76; of forts and fortresses, 39,
139; of ships, 7, 9, 21, 33, 199n15,
221n8. *See also* booty; pillage
Plunkett (official), 97
Polly (play), 54–55, 120–21, 175,
208nn47–48
poor people, 38, 125; pirates, 176;
sailors, 6, 28, 50, 57, 92; who
became pirates, 38, 119. *See also*
class, lower; servants
Porter (pirate captain), 80
Portugal, 20, 24, 52, 68, 139; ships of,
88, 171

53186528

DATE DUE
